WAR IN HEAVEN.

A

DISQUISITION, BIBLICAL AND RATIONAL,

CONCERNING

Angels, Devils, and Men,

AND THE

CREATION, FALL, AND REDEMPTION OF THE HUMAN SOUL.

"Many shall run to and fro, and knowledge shall be increased."—DANIEL, 12: 4.

"For there is nothing covered, that shall not be revealed; and hid, that shall not be known."—MATT. 10; 26.

BY JAMES P. SIMMONS,
Lawrenceville, Georgia.

CINCINNATI:
ROBERT CLARKE & Co., PRINTERS.
1871.

PREFACE.

It is considered, by the writer, due alike to the reader and himself that a brief statement of the circumstances under which the peculiar views in the following pages presented were first, by him, conceived.

Having been blest with Christian parents, who required of all their children, as soon as they were able to do so, that each should read a prescribed portion of the Sacred Scriptures on every Sabbath, he acquired, in early life, a habit of frequent and careful reading of that goodBook, and which grew with his growth and strengthened with his strength. At the early age of seventeen, he united with the Church of Christ. When about twenty-one years old, the little society of which he was a member dissolved for want of numbers sufficient to work efficiently, and each member was furnished with a letter of dismission. He had already engaged in the practice of his profession, and within a few years became so completely absorbed in such duties, and in the care of an increasing family, that he found but little time, Sundays only excepted, for theological reading. For some thirteen years he held such Church letter, and was deprived of all those blessed privileges and safeguards which can only be found inside of regular Church membership.

As is usual with young Christians who suffer themselves too much involved in the cares and business of this world, he became far too careless of his dearest interest. His mind was led off and off from the subject of religion; his attention to private devotion and public worship grew less and less, and, as a natural sequence, he began to doubt the truth of first one, then of another, and yet another, and so on, of the fundamental doctrines of our holy religion, until he had neared the awful whirlpool of infidelity.

It may be well, even here, to mention a few of the questions which gave him great trouble. 1. The doctrine of original sin, and the consequent total depravity of man. 2. Of eternal punishment in Hell of all who do not repent and believe the Gospel; and, 3. Of the necessity of Jesus Christ, being himself God, coming into the world and suffering as he did, for our redemption.

These and other kindred truths were not only admitted by all orthodox Christians, but appeared from the most careful reading to be clearly taught by the pen of Inspiration; yet they struck his mind as wonderfully strange, to say the best for them. How it was that the Great

Omniscient, Omnipotent, and All-merciful Creator of the universe—of man and Satan—should create this world, as it was, in all its primeval beauty, and make Adam, and of him Eve, perfect, holy, and pure as they were before their fall, and prepare for them a home—AN EDEN—any tolerable description of which defies all created power—and put them there subject only to the law of their own will, with one single exception only, and that of easy observance; and that He should have permitted Satan, a creature of His own power and fully subject to His control, to beguile, deceive, and utterly ruin that hitherto innocent, confiding, and happy pair, I could not understand. Why it was that we of this remote age, as well as those of all subsequent and future ages of the world, should be held, by a just and merciful God, so far responsible for their sin as to be doomed to that eternal punishment denounced against all, save the elect few, how uprightly, morally, and honestly soever they might live, was, to my mind at least, very mysterious.

After the perfect work of God had been so unaccountably marred by the vile touch of the devil, I could not comprehend why it became necessary that an atonement should be made at such cost.

He could, simply by an act of His will, have pardoned that sin and purified the fountains of life so perfectly, that the whole Adamic race would have been as pure, holy, and good as the angels of heaven, and thereby not only have thwarted the whole scheme of Satan, and achieved a glorious victory over His enemy, but have averted all the ensuing calamities which have befallen this sin-smitten world.

Oppressed with such doubts, I became seriously alarmed about my own spiritual condition, and plied myself with renewed anxiety and zeal to searching the Scriptures in quest of more light. All my labors in that direction, had been for years unsuccessful. My mind was but the more vexed, and my fears the more aroused, until, as intimated above, I was closely verging upon infidelity.

Under these fearful circumstances, I was one Sabbath evening alone in my room, engaged carefully and prayerfully reading the Apocalypse. I read: "And there was war in heaven: Michael and his angels fought against the dragon; and the dragon fought and his angels, and prevailed not; neither was their place found any more in heaven. And the great dragon was cast out, that old serpent, called the Devil, and Satan, which deceiveth the whole world: he was cast out into the earth, and his angels were cast out with him," etc. As I so read, the great truth, which is considered in the following pages, as lightning, flashed upon my mind.

The Apostle Paul, after his memorable trip to Damascus, could have fully appreciated my feelings on that occasion; but I can not describe them. I closed the book, and gave myself up, for once, to *honest* thought. Such an idea had never crossed my mind before, although I had often read that chapter. In quick succession, such questions and answers flitted across my mind, as: Can it be so? Impossible! or everybody would have so understood it long since. But, what else can it mean? I read it over again and again, and then turned rapidly to the several passages noted in the margin, where the same names appeared, or similar language was used. I saw clearly that if the impression then upon my mind as to the meaning of that Scripture was true, all such doubts and difficulties were together and at once removed. In that view, I could readily understand why all these things were so.

The next resolve was to make a thorough examination of that question. For more than three years, all the time I could snatch from my business engagements was employed in that inquiry. The Bible, from first to last, was critically examined, and notes entered in a blank book (which is now before me), of such passages as appeared to bear upon it. Such other helps as came within my reach were also brought into requisition. And the result was, I became *satisfied* that the solemn impression so made upon my mind was but the fearful truth of the case.

My troubled soul was at ease, I then could believe all the important truths taught in the Bible, and give a *reason for my faith*. During all that time I had not communicated to any human being even the fact that I entertained such views. The note book mentioned had been carefully concealed from every eye but my own.

Another subject of doubt soon beset me. That was, as to whether I should give the result of my labors to my fellow-prisoners, or keep them to myself, as theretofore. On that question I have bestowed the most anxious thought for many years. My desire was and is, to do my duty without regard to consequences, as to myself.

In July, 1852, I published an article in a religious paper of this State, headed, "ANGELS, DEVILS, AND MEN," and over the *anonymous* signature, "LAYMAN," in which a number of naked and crude propositions were submitted with references to such passages of Scripture as it was thought might lead to an investigation of the subject. But, beyond a bewildered sort of notice by the editor, I heard no more of it. About the same time I communicated the simple fact that I entertained such opinions to a few friends, but under the most stringent obligations to inform no one else that I had done so. With that, for a great while, I felt disposed to let the matter rest where the Bible leaves it. More serious impressions and anxious thought of late years have, however, satisfied me that I should give the world the humble offering, though poor it may be, of my faith, with the leading reasons for it upon this subject, and which I esteem as second in importance to but one other. Convictions of duty require no less, more I can not do.

A newspaper article having failed to direct public attention to the theory herein presented, I have concluded to pursue a middle ground between that and a full argument, as preferable to either. A careful arrangement and analysis, with a fair construction and application of all the Scriptures, under the surface of which this important truth lies concealed from the careless reader, would necessarily fill a volume of such bulk that it would only be read by comparatively; few while but a brief treatise would be cheap, could be soon read, and yet may prove sufficient to satisfy many, and put others fairly on the way to a more perfect investigation of the subject in its totality.

With these statements in explanation, dear reader, and without other apology, I proceed, invoking the aid of my heavenly Master, to the task which lies before me, and hopefully leave all the issues with Him, who, knowing all the facts, will judge between us righteously.

CONTENTS.

CHAPTER VIII.

CHAPTER IX.

CHAPTER X.

CHAPTER XI.

CHAPTER XII.

CHAPTER XIII.

CHAPTER XIV.

CHAPTER XV.

CHAPTER XVI.

CHAPTER XVII.

CHAPTER XVIII.

CHAPTER XIX.

CHAPTER XX.

CHAPTER XXI.

WAR IN HEAVEN.

CHAPTER I.

Introductory — The Four Different Theories of the Soul — The Fifth Proposed — Caution to the Reader — Motives for this Writing — Causes of Difference of Opinion — King James' Version of the Bible — Copyists — Rules of Construction — Peculiar Style of Sacred Writers — Dangers of being Deceived.

HAVING, in the Preface, explained the fearful circumstances under which the peculiar view of the human soul, which is considered in the following pages, was first conceived and impressed on my own mind, and referred to the Scripture, on reading which that suggestion was first made, I proceed to submit the same to the grave consideration of my fellow-prisoners.

It appears that four different theories as to the human soul, mind, or spirit, have been presented to the world; and the object of this writing is to propound a fifth.

These will be severally noticed in the order in which they are here stated, to-wit:

1. That the soul is but the rational thinking power of man, and although superior to that of other animals, had no previous existence, but is procreated as is the body, and perishes with it.

2. That at the beginning of the world God created the souls of all men, which, however, are not united to the body till the individuals for whom they are destined are begotten or born into the world.

3. That the soul is created at the moment when the body is produced for its habitation.

4. That the soul and body are alike, and together propagated by the parents, neither having had any previous existence.

The theory herein proposed is, that the souls of all men existed before the creation of this world; that they are of the fallen angels, who were engaged in rebellion under Satan in heaven, and were by Michael and his hosts "cast out into the earth;" and that when the body destined for each is prepared, the spirit is sent to occupy it merely as a tenement.

And now, fellow-man, let me beg you not to fly off in a tangent, throw away the book, and pronounce the writer a maniac or a fool. Admit that he is both, if you wish, but remember that although his notion may be new to you, and strike your mind as but the fancy dream of a disordered imagination, the *subject* is one of the first import to yourself. If you are yet in your sins, and my view be correct, your condition is truly a fearful one. You are not only a fallen angel, but you are a *devil*, just from Tartarus, and on but a brief respite. Jesus Christ has called you here, and by his Holy Spirit has met you, and is, while you read, offering you free and full pardon, and inviting you to accept it and return with Him to the blessed realms of glory. And He is at the same time warning you that if you reject the salvation which He has, at the cost of His own blood, purchased and so proffers, you will, ere long, be taken from this, your prison house, and, under strong guard, conducted back to the place of your late confinement, and there kept in safe and close custody, "in chains under darkness," until the great and final Judgment, and that you will then be taken with Satan and all his faithful followers, and safely conducted to the place of eternal punishment (and which is compared to a lake perpetually burning with fire and brimstone), there to remain with him and them forever.

And if you are a Christian, the subject is by no means a trifling one to you. If you have determined to live for Christ, and, if possible, make safe your retreat to heaven, yet the obligations you are under to love and serve Him, depend greatly on the service He has rendered you To redeem a sinner who inherited his soul, body, and sin altogether from his first parents, although he had no control over their conduct, certainly lays him under weighty obligations to the Redeemer; but for the beloved Son of God to leave, for the time, his seat on the right hand of the Father in glory, and voluntarily follow a rebel angel, who had been justly punished for his own sins by himself committed in the effulgent light of heaven, down to the infernal regions and bring him up to earth, and here meet him and offer up his own life as a ransom to the Father for the sins of a devil, certainly brings the spirit so redeemed under obligations, if not more heavy, at least such as are more easily comprehended.

Examine the question, then, my Christian friends, with all the care its magnitude demands; and if you find that you have even received a greater favor from your Lord and Master than you had before suspected, let your energies be in proportion the more aroused, and new zeal awakened within you for the better discharge of all the sacred duties so devolved upon you.

One who received an opinion with the caution, and only after the prolonged, laborious, and careful investigation which the writer gave this (as stated in the Preface), will not expect another of independent thought to accept his theory as true, simply on reading the brief and imperfect statement of it given above. This he does not desire. But I do wish all, who can do so, to read what is herein said about it, and in doing so, turn patiently to the Scriptures referred to, and read not only the texts quoted, but look into the context from which each is taken, and then read the whole of that Book of Books, and see all that is therein said directly, or which bears remotely upon the subject, and thus form an opinion, at least worth having, if not worth giving to others. The *truth* is what we all should most desire to know, and anxiously seek after.

I have read and reasoned in search of the truth in question; and now I wish to induce, if possible, others to do the same. If I am in error, as I may be (for I know myself to be a fallible creature), my earnest desire is to be put right.

And if this hypothesis be correct, I want all to know it, that they may be the more careful to accept of pardon while it may be found.

God knows I feel no interest in the propagation of such error as this, if error it be. My life has not been that of the devoted minister of Jesus Christ, of whom it is written: "How beautiful are the feet of them that preach the Gospel of peace, and bring glad tidings of good things!" And again: "Even so hath the Lord ordained that they which preach the Gospel should live of the Gospel." I have made my living neither off the piety, simplicity, or misfortunes of my fellow-men, but of their wickedness.

For the benefit of such as have never made the sacred writings a study, whether from want of inclination, or of sufficient time from other vocations, by them esteemed of more value, it may be well enough in this place to state some of the chief causes of the vast differences of opinion entertained, even by the most learned and pious men, of the doctrines taught in the Bible. There is good reason to fear that many persons, not worse by nature than others, and who were endowed by the Creator with strong minds, and some of which have also been well cultivated, as to the wisdom of this world, have been deceived by the devil, chiefly by false arguments drawn from the very fact that the most wise and best men could not agree as to what the Scriptures teach, and, being so deceived, have been put off their guard and suffered their frail bark to be driven upon the reef of infidelity, and thus made shipwreck of their immortal souls.

Should this little book, by chance, fall under the eye of one who is now traveling that same highway, suffer me, my dear friend, to whisper a word of caution into your ear, and beseech you to pause and seriously reflect before you further go.

I am not one of those who can ask a man of sense and reason, to blindly accept as true that which is contrary to reason, because *it is said* to be taught in the Bible. On the contrary, as a firm believer in that blessed book, and at least a professed follower of our Lord and Savior Jesus Christ, I am willing—aye, anxious—to submit that book to the touch stone of *reason*. And to accept the proposition that (God being all-wise and the true source of sound reason), if the Bible teaches that which is *unreasonable*, then it is not His Book.

The Scriptures are often mysterious, but that anything taught therein is *unreasonable*, I deny. Thinking, doubting persons have my warmest sympathies. Having traveled that same way to an alarming point, I can feel for my friends who are still exposed to the fatal error of skepticism. I respect—yes, love—a man who dares to think for himself and act upon his judgment. God made us to reflect and act according to reason. But, is it reasonable that we should judge of what the Bible teaches from what others say of it? Would it not better accord with the promptings of that reason which we so much revere, to make for ourselves a most anxious, honest, and critical examination of what it does teach, and let the results of such search govern us in the formation of our opinions? Take up your Bible, and read, review, and compare one passage with another, just as the successful law student studies Blackstone and Chitty. And, my word for it, when you have done so, you will be satisfied, "beyond a reasonable doubt," not only that it is true, but that it has been the most abused, unnecessarily mystified, and least understood of any book that has been read at all, which has ever been written or printed in any age or language.

But to return to a notice of discrepancies between theologians. In the first place, many of the revelations which have been made at different times, from God to man, have been communicated in a mystic form, and for wise purposes, which will be noticed hereinafter. Our Savior taught chiefly by parables. Divine truth He represents as a "pearl of great price," a treasure to be diligently sought for, and when found, not to be cast before swine.

Many teachers of divinity, as we may fairly infer, have not searched for that precious jewel with the necessary diligence, but have contented themselves with the more easy process of adopting the opinions of others, as they found them, ready cut and dried, in the text books of the various Christian denominations to which each belonged.

Another, and to us of the present age of the world, a much greater difficulty, is to be found in the fact, that we have not the Word of God, as it was originally delivered by the mouth of His prophets, or as it was first recorded by inspired penmen; nor have we the sacred words of Jesus Christ, as they fell from His heavenly lips, or as they were written under the guidance of the Holy Spirit. Ours is, of necessity, but a translation of the original Scriptures. All men are imperfect; and, therefore, their best works must be, like themselves, imperfect.

I do not wish to depreciate the value of the Sacred Writings as we have them; they are to us above all estimation of value. Nor do I propose to find fault with those great and good men who have blessed the world with their translations. Furthermore, I have no desire to see any effort made toward displacing the translation made under the direction of King James, in favor of any which have, or can be made. It is true, we have now more men well skilled in the oriental customs and languages than lived in his time; we might, therefore, reasonably expect that a general translation could now be made, which would approximate more nearly a literal rendering of the original than that we now have. Admit all that to be true, yet more would, in all probability, be lost to the cause of Christ by means of the bickerings and ill-tempered discussions, which would inevitably arise between the partisans of the different versions, than would be gained from all the improvements of that sort, which would probably be made.

The most ardent friend to truth may content himself with the way things are now going on in that direction. The labors of that committee have often been, and are constantly being reviewed by men competent to the task; and such errors as are discovered, and considered of sufficient value to require it, are pointed out in marginal notes, commentaries, etc. So that those who feel sufficiently anxious about it, can now get all the light which has been shed upon the subject.

To one who has been a close Bible reader himself, and for the sole purpose of learning his duty there; and who has had neither taste nor occasion to participate in such unprofitable debates, looking upon them as of minor importance at most, and who has stood as a mere "looker-on in Venice," it is easy to see that one prime cause of the differing views of those who conduct them, in various instances, is to be found in imperfections of translation.

A few remarks may suffice to show, however, to any well-balanced mind, that it is utterly impossible for human skill to produce a correct version of the Bible in this age. Suppose an infidel, of sufficient capacity and learning, should undertake the task. He is but a man, subject to the prejudices incident to our fallen nature, and liable to err, as all others. He would go to work under the firm belief that there is neither God nor Devil, Heaven nor Hell; and that the whole Bible is nothing better than the skillful work of bad men, who only sought, by teaching their too simple and confiding fellows such unreasonable and foolish notions, to get the more perfect control of them; and by that means to advance their own selfish and ambitious aspirations. Could a poor, erring man, however honest of purpose he might be, do justice to that or any other writing, of which he entertained so poor an opinion?

Take, then, a Christian man, or a commission of such, and charge him or them with that sacred duty. None but honest men could be trusted in that divine work. If honest and true men, they will act honestly. Will they not? Acting honestly, of course they will give us the best rendering, in our language, they can possibly derive from the original; always being strictly careful to retain the *true sense and actual meaning* of the original as far as possible. Will they not? Of course, they will. Then, what have we gained by another translation? King James' committee did precisely the same thing. They, no doubt, translated the Bible honestly, giving the real meaning just as they had been taught to believe, and did verily believe, was the best interpretation of every passage therein contained. But, of course, they read and rendered in the light of their understanding. As honest and good men, they could not have done otherwise. What then was the result? A version of the Bible just as near correct as was the faith of those who gave it; and containing no more verbal or other errors than they were unable to prevent. Can not this difficulty be obviated, it may be asked, by selecting a commission of theologians differing in faith? Say a Calvanist and an Armenian, a Unitarian and Trinitarian, a Baptist and Pedo-baptist, and, as an umpire, add a Universalian. How would that work? In the first place, it is not at all likely that gentlemen of the requisite qualifications and sufficient high Christian character, of such widely differing views, could be found who would consent to undertake the task, and if they should, we could expect either no translation at all, or as many (at least as to some important passages) as we have members of the committee. They *could not* agree.

Inasmuch, therefore, as our present version has been generally received wherever our language is spoken, and our people have become familiar with, and justly attached to it, the best policy is, most probably, to let it stand as it is, for all future time, with such corrections as have and will be made, as already mentioned.

For myself, I confess to a fondness, approaching veneration, for the antique idiom in which our Scriptures are at present read. That dialect is so far different from the one employed in common conversation and modern writings, as to give them a sort of gravity, dignity, and solemnity of sound, which is well calculated, especially when read from the sacred desk, to elevate the soul with the most humble and holy aspirations to the throne of Him who presides in heaven.

For general use, it answers very well. The large mass of people ever have, and always will look to others, better informed than they, for Scriptural instructions. And those who aspire to teach others can inform themselves sufficiently well with the aid of helps already at hand. The same remark applies to such individuals as have time, and feel sufficient interest to make the effort for themselves.

One of the most embarrassing circumstances connected with our version, and of quite frequent occurrence, arises from erroneous versification and punctuation; and in supplying such words as were thought necessary to make sense in some instances, and in failing to give such as are necessary in others. Competent and careful readers can, however, in most cases, make these corrections for themselves.

A fruitful source of error in all modern copies of the Bible may, with great certainty, be traced to mistakes of copyists. As is generally known, up to about the middle of the fifteenth century the art of printing was unknown, and the Bible, as well as all other books, could only be reproduced in manuscript. This was not only a very tedious and expensive way of procuring books, but, worse than all, to avoid mistakes would have been next to impossible. It is said, by those who should know the facts, that there is at least one passage in the New Testament, and to which some sectarians attach a great deal of importance, which does not appear, save as a marginal note, in older copies now in existence.

These remarks, I repeat, are not made for the purpose of casting suspicion upon, or otherwise underestimating our present version of the Sacred Scriptures, but they are made for the *sole purpose* of putting all on their guard, by notifying them that such errors exist, and thereby hoping to do some good in the way of encouraging a more thorough search and examination, by comparison and otherwise, of the precious truths therein revealed. In fact, I feel that we, of the present age, are under sacred obligations of gratitude to that body of learned and good men whose arduous labor it was, for the service they have rendered, not only to ourselves, but future generations, in furnishing us and them the faithful and valuable translation which they did of Divine Revelation and Law.

There are certain rules which must be observed in the construction of any writing, if we would attain to the true sense and meaning. The Bible consists of two Testaments, the Old and the New. They should be accepted and construed together, as forming but one general scheme, one code of laws, one plan of redemption, one will.

The uninspired mind can do no better than to take rules which have been adopted for the construction of wills by the most distinguished jurists of modern times, as the last result of the experience of all ages, and adopt them, as far as applicable, in constructing the Divine Will. The most important of which are, in substance, the following, to-wit:

1. That the Will should be so construed as to carry into effect the true intent and meaning of the Testator; and, therefore, the construction must also be reasonable, and agreeable to common understanding of the words used.

2. That where the *intention* is clear, too minute a stress be not laid on the strict and precise signification of *words*.

3. That the construction must be made upon the entire Will, and not merely upon disjointed parts of it. And, therefore, that every part of it be (if possible) made to take effect.

4. That if the words will bear two interpretations, one agreeable to the general testamentary scheme, and the other inconsistent with it, that sense is preferred which is most agreeable thereto.

5. That every clause be so construed that all be reconciled and stand together, if that can be done; but if there be two clauses so totally repugnant to each other that they can not stand together, the one first appearing is to be rejected and the last sustained.

6. That words may be supplied in a will, in order to effect the intention, as collected from the context.

7. That when a clause or expression, otherwise senseless or contradictory thereto, can be rendered consistent with the context by being transposed, that will be done.

The reasonableness of these rules is so apparent, that comment is not considered necessary, except as to the fifth one.

Both the Old and New Testaments, being construed together, renders that rule applicable to Biblical construction, because the New modifies, and, in some instances, annuls the Old and enacts different rules. For instance, the law of retaliation as laid down in Exodus 21: "Thou shalt give life for life, eye for eye, tooth for tooth, hand for hand, foot for foot, burning for burning, wound for wound, stripe for stripe," was entirely reversed by our Savior; as in Matthew

5: 38–41: "Ye have heard that it hath been said, An eye for an eye, and a tooth for a tooth; but I say unto you, that ye resist not evil, but whosoever shall smite thee on thy right cheek, turn to him the other also," etc. By that rule, the law, as quoted from Exodus, must be rejected, and that, as found in Matthew, sustained. Considered as but municipal laws, the same rule would apply.

The Bible is wholly unlike any other book in many respects, but perhaps in no other feature more remarkable than for its bold, independent, defiant tone. The whole book, from the first of Genesis to the last of Revelation, appears to have been written in the same confident and fearless style.

The historian seems indifferent as to every consideration, save a strictly faithful narration of the stubborn facts with which he had to deal. The prophet proclaims the divine message, with which he is commissioned, as one feeling that he stands in the presence, and under the immediate protection of that God by whom he is sent.

The apostle cries aloud and spares not; warning all men every-where of sin, righteousness, and the judgment to come; denouncing all manner of vice and immorality in high places, as well as low, and utterly regardless of all personal consequences. Neither scourging, prisons, nor death had the least terror for them. They went forth in all confidence, notwithstanding they were but as lambs among wolves, as the chosen heralds of the Cross, charged with the everlasting Gospel to preach to a wicked and perverse generation.

All revelation is addressed to the understanding; and is intended for the benefit, the reclamation, and eternal salvation of those who receive it in honest hearts, and for the shame, confusion, and final condemnation of such as doubt, cavil, criticise, and condemn those sacred truths as mysterious, incoherent, insufficient, or unreasonable.

Observation clearly teaches that such persons as seek the least after revealed light complain most of the want of it, with the exception of one class, and they are those who read and study the Sacred Writings, but not with honesty of purpose, in search of truth, and for the truth's sake. They are those who pride themselves in their own shame. Infidels already, they boast of their wisdom in being able, by demonstrative evidence, to refute all the childish, feminine, fallacious, and superstitious fancies of the Christian religion. They are of that class of whom it is said: "They received not the love of the truth that they might be saved. And for this cause God shall send them strong delusion, that they should BELIEVE A LIE; that they all might be damned who believed not the truth, but had pleasure in unrighteousness." 2 Thess. 2: 10–12.

They search, not with a desire to be set right, if wrong, but for the sole and wicked purpose of finding fault with the Word of God; for arguments by which they may, as far as possible, support their own cherished dogmas, and so advance the already prosperous cause of their liege lord, the devil!

The sacred writer pauses not to argue with such persons, but passes on, content with denouncing the eternal anathemas of the Almighty against them.

Those who sin against light and knowledge, or who shut their eyes and stop their ears against divine truth, find no consoling promises in God's Book addressed to them, but threats of His wrath and fiery indignation.

They err who believe that Jesus Christ will follow after such persons beyond the limits of the call made in His Gospel. We have no authority for saying that He desires the salvation of such as so sin. He has the power, it is true, to save all men; but we are assured that He will exercise that power only in favor of such as heed His call, as made in His Word, and whispered softly, but often, by the Holy Spirit in their ears, and come to Him freely and voluntarily. He will force no one into His service. Let not Satan deceive you, my erring friend, by pointing you to the oft-repeated and affectionate call made upon you by the Savior to repent, believe, return to Him and be saved, with the delusive hope that He is so over-anxious for your salvation that He will go beyond the prescribed limits to hunt you down in your sins and wickedness, and save you from eternal death.

Believe not that He will violate, in the least particular, His great scheme of redemption in your favor.

As a timely warning, our Savior has said to the learned, the wise, the rich, and the great of this world: "Unto whomsoever much is given, of him shall be much required." Luke 12: 48.

If, then, you are learned, teach the unlearned the way of life. The Sabbath-school offers you a rich field for such work. If wise, give God the fruit of your wisdom by unfolding the hidden riches of His grace to the simple. If wealthy, give of your substance freely to clothe the naked, feed the hungry, and send the Gospel to heathen lands. If noble, throw all the weight of your powerful influence in the scale with the poor, humble Christian.

Such are your high duties and blessed privileges, and if you desire to "lay up for yourselves treasures in heaven," you would do well to "take due notice thereof, and govern yourselves accordingly."

CHAPTER II.

Different Theories of the Soul Considered—Immortality of—Views of the Pre-existiani, of the Creatiani, and Traduciani—Neither Sufficiently Account for the Depravity of Man.

THE first theory, as arranged in the preceding chapter, is: "That the soul is but the thinking power of man, and, although superior to that of other animals, had no previous existence, but is procreated as is the body, and perishes with it."

Whether man is but an animal, or was he endowed with a living soul—an immortal spirit—by the Divine Architect, is a question which has been so fully and so satisfactorily argued by those who have gone before, that the writer feels no disposition to dwell at any considerable length upon it. In fact, reason and revelation concur fully in support of the proposition that the soul of man is immortal. Inasmuch, however, as there are many who deny that the soul survives the body, and, if they are right, the whole foundation on which the theory herein favored stands must fall to the ground, he can not consent entirely to ignore an error that lies immediately in his pathway, and which is so fatal in its consequences. He begs leave, therefore, to present the following extract, which he finds ready prepared, and better than anything original with himself, which he could say in so few words on the subject, and with but few additional remarks to pass on:

"That there is a state of future happiness both reason and Scripture indicate. A general notion of happiness after death has obtained among the wiser sort of heathens, who have only had the light of nature to guide them. If we examine the human mind, it is also evident that there is a natural desire after happiness in all men, and which is equally evident is not attained in this life. It is no less observable that in the present state there is an unequal distribution of things, which makes the providences of God very intricate, and which can not be solved without supposing a future state. That the soul will exist in a future state a good writer says: 'The events of this life to have no reference to another, the whole state of man becomes not only inexplicable, but contradictory and inconsistent. The powers of the inferior animals are perfectly suited to their station. They know nothing higher than their present condition. In gratifying their appetites, they fulfill their destiny and pass away. Man, alone, comes forth to act a part which carries no meaning, and tends to no end. Endowed with capacities which extend far beyond his present sphere, fitted by his rational nature for running the race of immortality, he is stopped short in the very entrance of his course; he squanders his activity on pursuits which he discerns to be vain; he languishes for knowledge which is placed beyond his reach; he thirsts after a happiness which he is doomed never to enjoy; he sees and laments the disasters of his state, and yet, upon this supposition, can find nothing to remedy them. Has the eternal God any pleasure in sporting himself with such a scene of misery and folly as this life (if it had no connection with another) must exhibit to His eye? Did He call into existence this magnificent universe, adorn it with so much beauty and splendor, and surround it with those glorious luminaries which we behold in the heavens, only that some generations of mortal men might arise to behold these wonders and then disappear forever? How unsuitable in this case were the habitation to the wretched inhabitant! How inconsistent the commencement of his being and the mighty preparation of his powers and faculties with his despicable end! How contradictory, in fine, were everything which concerns the state of man to the wisdom and perfection of his Maker."—*Buck.*

The arguments drawn from the concurrent belief of all nations and peoples, and of all ages, that there is a Great Supreme Being who made all things, apply with great force to establish the fact that man is possessed of an immortal soul. The most debased and ignorant savage, whether of the remote ocean isle or the wild and deep forests of America—the most cultivated and renowned statesmen, philosophers, and orators of pagan Greece and Rome, as well as Mohammedans and Christians of our time—all alike believe, or did believe, in the immortality of the soul.

To those who have doubts upon that question, the consoling reflection of Cicero, which follows, is commended. He says: "If I am mistaken in my opinion that the human soul is immortal, I willingly err; nor would I have the pleasant error extorted from me; and if, as some minute philosophers suppose, death should deprive me of my being, I need not fear the raillery of those pretended philosophers when they are no more."

But to the humble, way-worn follower of Jesus Christ, the confident hope, which is so sublimely expressed by Addison, as given below, is far more cheering:

"The soul, secure in her existence, smiles
At the drawn dagger, and defies its point;
The stars shall fade away; the sun himself
Grow dim with age; and nature sink in years;
But thou shalt flourish in immortal youth,
Unhurt amid the war of elements,
The wreck of matter, and the crush of worlds."

Next in order, we will notice the opinion which was held not only by the Platonic school of philosophers, but by many of the early Christian fathers: "That at the beginning of the world God created the souls of all men, which, however, are not united to the body till the individuals for whom they are destined are begotten or born into the world."

As it is absolutely necessary to a satisfactory investigation of the theory of the human soul presented in this work, that the reader should know the opinions which have been held by others in different ages of the world upon that subject, and inasmuch as they have been but little discussed in our age, it is thought best to furnish, in this place, such information as will enable those who have never looked into this question sufficiently to understand what others have believed about it, to enter successfully upon an examination thereof for themselves.

That I be not suspected of having, in any particular, misrepresented the tenets of others as to the origin of the soul, it is preferred to state them in the language of another, and of one who was well versed in such lore, and who could have had no inducement for misrepresentation.

Dr. KNAPP, in his "LECTURES ON CHRISTIAN THEOLOGY," has furnished the most clear, yet succinct statement of all the various hypotheses on that subject with which I have met, and, therefore, his summary of each will be quoted below in its proper place.

Before proceeding to do so, however, it is desired to state, once for all, that this work is intended for the benefit of all classes, and that it may be adapted to the understanding of every one who can read, quotations from ancient and foreign languages, and the use of technical terms, will be avoided as far as practicable, and (except in cases of quotations from others) when introduced, the sound only will be given, and that in Roman or Italic letters; and the meaning will also be supplied in our own vernacular:

"The hypothesis of the *pre-existence of souls.* Those who support this hypothesis, called *Præ-existiana,* affirm that God at the beginning of the world created the souls of all men, which, however, are not united with the body before man is begotten or born into the world. This was the opinion of Pythagoras, Plato and his followers, and of the cabalists among the Jews. Among these, however, there is a difference of opinion—some believing that the soul was originally destined for the body, and unites with it of its own accord; others, with Plato, that it pertained originally to the divine nature, and is incarcerated in the body as a punishment for the sins which it committed in its heavenly state. This hypothesis found advocates in the ancient Christian Church. Some Christians adopted the entire system of the Platonists, and held that the soul was a part of the divine nature, etc. Priscillianus and his followers either held these views or were accused of holding them by Augustine.—*De Hœres, c.* 70. All who professed to believe the pre-existence of the soul can not be proved to have believed that it was a part of the divine nature. This is true of Origen, who agreed with the Platonists in saying, that souls sinned before they were united with a body in which they were imprisoned as a punishment for their sins.—Vide *Huetius*, in his '*Origenianæ*,' 1 *ii. c.* 2, *quæst.* 6. The pre-existence of the soul was early taught by Justin the Martyr.—*Dial. cum Tryphone Jud.* This has been the common opinion of Christian mystics of ancient and modern times. They usually adhere to the Platonic theory and regard the soul as a part of the divine nature, from which it proceeds, and to which it will again return. This doctrine of the pre-existence of the soul is, however, almost entirely abandoned, because it is supposed irreconcilable with the doctrine of original sin, and if the mystics be excepted, it has been left almost without an advocate ever since the time of Augustine."

Upon this hypothesis, it may be remarked that it originated with heathen philosophers, who had not the light of revelation, but were guided alone by the dictates of natural reason. To those who deny that the Holy Spirit enlightens the understanding of such as have not the blessing of the revealed Word of God, the progress made by such men as Pythagoras, Plato, and other heathen philosophers, in finding out the hidden mysteries in relation to the creation of the universe, the cause and purposes of our being here, the immortality of the soul, and of a future state of bliss, of woe, etc., must be wonderful indeed.

From the circumstance that they did make such near approaches to a true understanding, in substance, of the facts as revealed to others on such subjects, we have a potent argument in favor of the hypothesis that the Spirit of God does, in some way, teach all nations. Such similarity of views, as held by heathen and Jew, affords a valuable evidence, also, in favor of the authenticity of the Bible.

All must have understanding enough of the nature and laws of God, a future state, and of their responsibilities to their Creator and duties to their fellow-men, to render them justly responsible for their conduct in this life. Without that, they would not be fit to be judged at the great day and rewarded or punished, as the case of each may require, according to their works, whether they be good or evil. And we are informed by the Sacred Scriptures, that all will be brought before the same bar for judgment and on the same day.

Otherwise, how is it that the heathen and Christian will be alike judged, and at the same time, and each doomed to eternal happiness or misery? All were created by the same omnipotent power. He can instruct the heathen, as well as the Christian, in all his duties. He is said not to be a respecter of persons of men, but a wise and merciful God; of great forbearance and long suffering toward his creatures, willing not the death of any, but that all should return to Him and live. If this be so, is it reasonable that he would bring a vast majority of men into this world in heathen lands and times of darkness, thus denying them all knowledge of himself, of their own condition in this world, and even of the fact that they are to answer for their conduct to any one, or in any way, and then send them to hell forever because they did not observe his laws? If it is unreasonable to believe that such a Creator will so deal with his creatures, then He will not do it: for He is the source, the perfection of reason. We must, then, either believe that the heathen will not be held responsible for their conduct in this world, or that they have knowledge of their accountability. But to return, as it is desired to say more of this in the proper place.

Viewed in this light of human reason, with the aid of such general but vague impressions only as it is believed the Holy Spirit does make on the mind of all men, and in the absence of inspired revelation, this would probably appear to be a reasonable hypothesis, and the most satisfactory to the learned heathen mind of any which was presented. But to us who have the aid of the Bible, as well as philosophical reason, to direct our footsteps in the pathway to truth, objections insuperable will be found, as it is believed, to that theory. For (let it ever be borne in mind), we can not safely adopt any opinion of Biblical truth which does not accord strictly, and alike with the revealed Word and natural reason.

We may err as to the interpretation of Scripture, if we fail to apply the test of reason, and to compare each passage on the same subject with every other one.

Fallible as we all are in this life, we can not safely rely upon our unaided opinion as to the meaning of many passages of Scripture; and much less can we trust our feeble powers of reason to guide us in the way of eternal life. We should, therefore, content ourselves with nothing short of a solution of such difficulty, which will consist with all that is said in the Bible about it, when diligently searched out and carefully compared each with the other, and with the dictates of reason also. When we have arrived at a conclusion as to the truth of a proposition so important as that now under consideration, which will bear all these tests, and shine with the more luster as each is applied, we may confidently rejoice that we have found a jewel of great price.

It will be observed that those who agreed in the main, as to this hypothesis, differed between themselves—some believing that the soul was originally destined for the body and unites with it of its own accord; others, with Plato, that it pertained originally to the divine nature, and is incarcerated in the body as a punishment for the sins which it committed in its heavenly state.

That disagreement was, of itself, sufficient to have cast a thick shade of doubt around the whole edifice. It proves that the foundation on which the building stood was not strong enough to prevent fear for its safety. So it is always with those who are engaged in the advocacy of error. They can not fully agree with each other. And when that is the case, neither should rest satisfied as to the correctness of the common belief on the chief proposition.

We now come to the second theory as held by the Christian Fathers: "That the soul is created at the moment when the body is produced for its habitation." "The hypothesis of the *creation of the soul.* The advocates of this theory, called *Creatiani,* believe that the soul is immediately created by God whenever the body is begotten. A passage in Aristotle (*De Gener.* ii. 3,) was supposed to contain this doctrine; at least, it was so understood by the school-men; and, in truth, Aristotle appears not to be far removed from the opinion ascribed to him. Cyril, of Alexandria, and Theodoret, among the fathers in the Grecian Church, were of this opinion; and Ambrose, Hilarius, and Hieronymus in the Latin Church. The school-men almost universally professed this doctrine, and generally the followers of Pelagius, with whom the school-men, for the most part, agreed in their views with regard to the native character of man; for these views derived a very plausible vindication from the hypothesis that the soul was immediately created by God when it was connected with the body. The argument was this: If God created the souls of men, he must have made them either pure and holy, or impure and sinful. The latter supposition is inconsistent with the holiness of God, and consequently the doctrine of the native depravity of the heart must be rejected. To affirm that God made the heart depraved, would be to avow the blasphemous doctrine that God is the author of sin. The theory of the *Creatiani* was at first favored by Augustine; but he rejected it as soon as he saw how it was employed by the Pelagians. It has continued, however, to the present time to be the common doctrine of the theologians of the Romish Church, who in this follow after the school-men, like them, making little of native depravity and much of the freedom of man in spiritual things. Among the Protestant teachers, Melancthon was inclined to the hypothesis of the *Creatiani;* although after the time of Luther, another hypothesis, which will shortly be noticed, was received with most approbation by Protestants. Still many distinguished Lutheran teachers of the seventeenth century followed Melancthon in his views concerning this doctrine—*e. g.*, G. Calixtus. In the Reformed Church, the hypothesis which we are now considering has had far more advocates than any other, though even they have not agreed in the manner of exhibiting it. Luther would have this subject left without being determined, and many of his contemporaries were of the same opinion."

From the above may be observed a general characteristic which is common even with the wisest and best men. It is that prevailing tendency to warp and bend everything else so as to make it comport with a favorite dogma of our own. The great and good St. Augustine at first favored the theory, that the soul was created at the birth of the body, but his contemporary, the learned Pelagius, the champion of the doctrine of free-will, who agreed with him as to the origin of the soul, was making such strong points upon him, drawn from that source, that it became necessary for him to *change his base*, or abandon his favorite dogma of predestination, which he founded chiefly upon that of total depravity. It was not only true with theologians of that age, that their particular views upon the question of predestination and free-will gave form and tone to all their other religious opinions, but it is equally so at the present time. And, therefore, as soon as Augustine saw that these two doctrines of his could not stand together, he was, no doubt, perfectly satisfied in his own mind that he had been in error as to the origin of the soul. Upon his pet dogma, his mind was fixed; and anything—everything—inconsistent with that had to give way. The same was true with Pelagius; he could not, of course, entertain an opinion on any subject which did not accord with his favorite doctrine of the utmost freedom of the will. That they were both honest in their differing views, there is no reason to doubt, and they may have been both wrong.

> "Each claiming truth,
> And truth disclaming both."—*Cowper.*

The fourth and last noticed old theory of the soul is: "That the soul and body are alike and together propagated by their parents, neither having had any previous existence." Of that, Dr. Knapp says: "The hypothesis of the *propagation of the soul.* According to this theory, the souls of children, as well as their bodies, are propagated from their parents. These two suppositions may be made: Either the souls of children exist in their parents as *real beings* (entia) like the seed in plants, and so have been propagated from Adam through successive generations, which is the opinion of Leibnitz in his '*Theodicée*,' p. i, sec. 91; or they exist in their parents merely *potentially*, and come from them *per propaginem*, or *traducem*. Hence, those who hold this opinion are called *Traduciani*. This opinion agrees with what Epicurus says of human seed, that it is 'σώπατος τὲ καὶ ψυχῆς ἀπόσπασμα.' This hypothesis formerly prevailed in the ancient *Western* Church.

"According to Hieronymus, both Tertullian and Apollinaris were advocates of this opinion, and even '*maxima pars occidentalium*.'—*Vide Epist. ad Marcellin.* Tertullian entered very minutely into the discussion of this subject in his work, '*De Anima*,' c. 25, seq., where he often uses the word *tradux;* but he is very obscure in what he has said. This is the hypothesis to which the opponents of the Pelagians have been most generally inclined (*vide* No. 2), though many who were rigorously orthodox would have nothing definitely settled upon this subject. Even Augustine, who in some passages favored the *Creatiani*, affirmed in his book '*De Origine Animæ*,' *nullum* (sententiam) *temere affirmare oportebit.* Since the Reformation this theory has been more approved than any other, not only by philosophers and naturalists, but also by the Lutheran Church. Luther himself appeared much inclined toward it, although he did not declare himself distinctly in its favor. But in the '*Formula Concordiæ*,' it was distinctly taught that the soul, as well as the body, was propagated by parents in ordinary generation. The reason why this theory is so much preferred by theologians is, that it affords the easiest solution of the doctrine of native depravity. If in the souls of our first progenitors, the souls of all their posterity existed potentially, and the souls of the former were polluted and sinful, those of the latter must be so too. This hypothesis is not, however, free from objections; and it is very difficult to reconcile it with some philosophical opinions which are universally received. We can not, for example, easily conceive how generation and propagation can take place without *extension;* but we can not predicate extension of the soul without making it a material substance. Tertullian and other of the fathers affirm, indeed, that the soul of man, and that spirit in general, is not perfectly pure and simple, but of a refined material nature, of which, consequently, *extension* may be predicated.— *Vide s.* 19, *ad finem*, and *s.* 51, I. *ad finem*. And with these opinions the theory of the propagation of the soul agrees perfectly well, certainly far better than with the opinions which we entertain respecting the nature of spirit, although even with these opinions we can not be sure that a spiritual generation and propagation is impossible; for we do not understand the true nature of spirit, and can not, therefore, determine with certainty what is or is not possible respecting it. There are some psychological phenomena which seem to favor the theory now under consideration; and hence it has always been the favorite theory of psychologists and physicians. The natural disposition of children not unfrequently resembles that of their parents, and the mental excellencies and imperfections of parents are inherited nearly as often by their children as any bodily attributes. Again, the powers of the soul, like those of the body, are at first weak, and attain their full development and perfection only by slow degrees. Many more phenomena of the same sort might be mentioned; but after all that may be said, we must remain in uncertainty with regard to the origin of the human soul. Important objections can be urged against these arguments and any others that might be offered; and if the metaphysical theory of the entire simplicity of the human soul be admitted, the whole subject remains involved in total darkness."

As appears from the preceding quotations from Dr. KNAPP, and from other modern writers also, the doctrine of the preexistence of the soul has been generally abandoned; and the Christian world is now chiefly divided between the two opinions—that the soul of each is created by God when the body is born into the world, or that the soul and body are propagated together by the parents—the Catholic Church holding the former, and the Protestants the latter of these theories.

That they should not have agreed on a question of that sort is natural. And that they may both be wrong is at least possible. Extremes seldom meet, and the truth is often found between them. The centrifugal is stronger than the centripetal force, as between them. I would it were not so.

It is no part of the present undertaking to advocate or oppose the peculiar views entertained by either of the numerous Christian families on any other question than that to which this labor is alone devoted; and, with that understanding, I may be permitted to say that so far as the doctrine of the origin of the soul is concerned, the Catholics have a decided advantage over some of their Protestant brethren.

If the soul is an original and new creature by a perfect Creator, it is not reasonable to suppose that it is doomed by its Creator to eternal punishment before it has committed sin, or that it is not permitted to act as a free agent, and entitled to be judged according to its own works. The doctrine of total depravity is utterly inconsistent with their notion as to the creation of the soul. In fact, the whole fabric of their faith would seem to have been built on that theory. That fact gives them a fair claim to consistency, if nothing more. So much can not be truly said for many Protestants. They are divided upon the questions of election and free-will; yet all, or nearly so, hold that the soul is totally depraved, and that it is propagated from the parents. Should they trouble themselves to examine these questions as closely as did the Christian Fathers, some of them would find that they are involved in sad inconsistencies in that particular.

Dr. KNAPP, no doubt, gives the true reason why there is somuch agreement among Protestants on that subject, when he says (in the last quotation above): "The reason why this theory is so much preferred by theologians is, that it affords the *easiest* solution of the doctrine of native depravity." This is natural. The depravity of man is so clearly taught in the

Bible, and not less so by daily observation, that its truth is beyond the reach of successful denial. That the solution of that problem is more *easy* upon their hypothesis is true. Whether it is *satisfactory* is another and different question.

If we are the product of sinners, we must be full of sin. We are told, however, that like produces its like; and if that be true, the theory of *propagation of the soul* falls far short of affording a satisfactory solution of the doctrine of native depravity. We are informed of but one sin having been committed by our mother Eve, and that was under circumstances of the most trying temptation; and she was certainly deceived, and, by one far wiser than herself, beguiled, and was with great reluctance led into it. And pray, what did she do? Nothing but pluck and eat of a beautiful, fragrant, and sweet fruit from a tree growing in her own garden. That was a violation of God's law, however, and for which she was justly condemned and punished. And that she repented, as in sackcloth and ashes for that, we have every reason to believe, and was pardoned. But we have ten laws to observe, the violation of either one of which is beyond all comparison more sinful than was that which she did; and every one of the ten is violated daily and hourly. She killed nobody, stole nothing, injured none in their rights of person, property, or good name. Her son was a murderer; killed his own brother, for no other reason than that he was a more righteous man than himself.

Adam's sin was possibly worse than that of Eve, but he sinned but in one thing, so far as is recorded, and did that but once. He too, no doubt, repented, and after just punishment was, as is most likely, forgiven.

Cain could, with but poor grace, have excused himself for his crime when God called on him to inquire after his brother, by saying that he inherited his wickedness from his parents, and therefore could not avoid that which he had done. Certain it is that he offered no such excuse.

It may be said that each generation grows worse than the former, but that will not account for the wickedness of Cain above that of his parents; for if we had grown worse and worse in that ratio, our race would, long since, have been extinct. So cruel and bloodthirsty would man have become ere this, that no two could have lived together on the same island or continent, much less in the same house, and have raised a family of children growing up together.

A still more perplexing difficulty arises, however, in the history of the same family in that respect. Abel appears to have been a good man, one who served God acceptably. They were brothers; why so great difference in their dispositions? If they were propagated, soul and body, from the same parents, and associated with no other family, by whose good or bad example they might have been influenced, this will be found a question hard to answer satisfactorily.

Tertullian and others, who, in the early ages of Christianity, held this theory, argued also that the soul possessed a refined material nature, and was, therefore, capable of occupying space, and hence of extension and growth, as other bodies. If that be so, this theory may possibly be true; but on any other hypothesis it is clearly unreasonable.

Modern theologians, however, utterly deny that the soul is material; and insist that it is purely an incorporeal being, or intelligence; thus involving themselves in an absurdity so palpable that no one, so far as I know, has ever undertaken to explain it. That spirit may produce matter is at once philosophical and scriptural, but that matter can produce spirit is inconsistent with both.

These cursory remarks are designed simply as suggestions to the reader of difficulties which surround each of the old theories, and as preparatory for the argument of the main proposition which is submitted in this work. It is, with most of us, more difficult to unlearn that which we have learned amiss, than to comprehend facts, whether of theology or any other science, of which we knew nothing before.

> "O hateful Error, Melancholy's child!
> Why dost thou show to the apt thoughts of men
> The things that are not?"—*Shakspeare.*

He might well have added, *hiding things that are!*

CHAPTER III.

The whole Subject Divided and Arranged under Ten Heads—Atheism Considered—Its Origin—Authenticity of the Old and New Testament—Scriptures—Jesus the Christ.

HAVING, for the present, disposed of the four different theories of the human soul mentioned in the first chapter, as preliminary to that propounded for consideration in this work, let us now, in the fear of God and love of His truth, approach that august subject.

That the reader may be conducted by regular advances to and through the main question, and be thereby the better enabled to give to it a more systematic and satisfactory investigation, the whole is here subdivided for discussion in the order and under the heads following, to-wit:

1. That the heavens and the earth are the workmanship of a Divine Architect, and not the fortuitous productions of accident.

2. That the heavens were created and inhabited by myriads of happy, angelic beings long before this world was made, as recorded by Moses.

3. That all rational creatures were originally made by God "*very good*," and endowed with powers of volition, locomotion, and action, for the glory of God and individual happiness, and were free agents to serve and glorify their Creator or not, just as they chose.

4. That the narrative found in the Apocalypse, although brief, figurative, and mysterious, is nevertheless a faithful and true history of "WAR IN HEAVEN," and of the expulsion of Satan and his deluded followers from the immediate presence of God and His holy angels.

5. That after they were so "*cast out*," a covenant of grace

and mercy was made between the Father and Son, in and by which it was provided that the Son should follow after those lost spirits and offer them, on specified terms, pardon and restoration to that holy and happy estate from which they had fallen.

6. That pursuant to that Divine Covenant, and for the purpose of carrying it into effect, this world was created, or *adapted to its present use*, and God "*made*" man and placed him here for probation.

7. That the body only was then created, "*formed*," and the soul which was "*breathed*" into it was a pre-existent spirit—A FALLEN ANGEL.

8. That the bodies, not the souls, the physical and not the spiritual part of subsequent generations, were created in Adam.

9. That the account given in the Bible of the temptation and fall of man in Eden, although literally true, is also a clear symbolical and allegorical representation of his real temptation and fall by and with Satan in heaven.

10. That this arrangement will be continued until all who were embraced in that Divine antemundane covenant, have, or shall have had, a probationary time here; then will come the final judgment, when all will be restored to their primeval favor with God, or doomed to that final punishment which is due for individual sin by each committed.

Our first proposition then is: "That the heavens and the earth are the workmanship of a Divine Architect, and not the fortuitous productions of accident."

This being merely a preliminary question, yet necessary to the truth of the main proposition before us, and having already attracted the attention and received the careful examination of the best thinkers of all past ages and nations, whether Christian or Pagan, the writer will content himself with giving the extracts which follow from the writings of others, with but few remarks of his own:

"Atheism, in its primary sense, comprehends, or at least goes beyond every heresy in the world; for it professes to acknowledge no religion, true or false. The two leading hypotheses which have prevailed among atheists, respecting this world and its origin, are that of Ocellus Lucanus adopted and improved by Aristotle, that it was eternal; and that of Epicurus, that it was formed by a fortuitous concourse of atoms. 'That the soul is material and mortal, Christianity an imposture, the Scriptures a forgery, the worship of God a superstition, hell a fable, and heaven a dream, our life without providence, and our death without hope, like that of asses and dogs, are part of the glorious gospel of our modern atheists.'

The being of a God may be proved from the marks of design and from the order and beauty visible in the world; from universal consent; from the relation of cause and effect; from internal consciousness; and from the necessity of a final as well as an efficient cause.

Of all the false doctrines and foolish opinions that ever infested the mind of man, nothing can possibly equal that of atheism, which is such a monstrous contradiction of all evidence, of all the powers of understanding, and the dictates of common sense, that it may be well questioned whether any man can really fall into it by a deliberate use of his judgment.

All nature so clearly points out, and so loudly proclaims, a Creator of infinite power, wisdom, and goodness, that whoever hears not its voice, and sees not its proofs, may well be thought willfully deaf and obstinately blind. If it be evident, self-evident, to every man of thought that there can be no effect without a cause, what shall we say of that manifold combination of effects, that series of operations, that system of wonders which fill the universe, which present themselves to all our perceptions, and strike our minds and our senses on every side? Every faculty, every object of every faculty, demonstrates a Deity. The meanest insect we can see, the minutest and most contemptible weed we can tread upon, is really sufficient to confound atheism and baffle all its pretensions. How much more that astonishing variety and multiplicity of God's works with which we are continually surrounded! Let any man survey the face of the earth, or lift up his eyes to the firmament; let him consider the nature and instincts of brute animals, and afterward look into the operation of his own mind, and will he presume to say or suppose that all the objects he meets with are nothing more than the result of unaccountable accident and blind chance? Can he possibly conceive that such wonderful order should spring out of confusion? or that such perfect beauty should be ever formed by the fortuitous operations of unconscious, inactive particles of matter? As well, nay better, and more easily, might he suppose that an earthquake might happen to build towns and cities; or the materials carried down by a flood fit themselves up, without hands, to a regular fleet. For what are towns, cities, or fleets, in comparison of the vast and amazing fabric of the universe! In short, atheism offers such violence to all our faculties that it seems scarce credible it should ever really find any place in the human understanding. Atheism is unreasonable, because it gives no tolerable account of the existence of the world. This is one of the greatest difficulties with which the atheist has to contend. For he must suppose either that the world is eternal, or that it was formed by chance and a fortuitous concourse of the parts of matter. That the world had a beginning is evident from universal tradition and the most ancient history that exists; from there being no memorials of any actions performed previously to the time assigned in that history as the era of the creation; from the origin of learning and arts, and the liability of the parts of matter to decay. That the world was not produced by chance is also evident. Nothing can be more unreasonable than to ascribe to chance an effect which appears with all the characters of a wise design and contrivance. Will chance fit means to ends, even in ten thousand instances, and not fail in a single one? How often might a man, after shaking a set of letters in a bag, throw them on the ground before they would become an exact poem or form a good discourse in prose? In short, the arguments in proof of Deity are so numerous, and at the same time so obvious to a thinking mind, that to waste time in disputing with an atheist is approaching too much toward that irrationality which may be considered as one of the most striking characteristics of the sect."

Dr. Samuel Clarke, in his "*Demonstration of the Being*

of a God," says, that "atheism arises either from stupid ignorance, or from corruption of principles and manners, or from the reasonings of false philosophy;" and he adds, that "the latter, who are the only atheistical persons capable of being reasoned with at all, must, of necessity, own that, supposing it can not be proved to be true, yet it is a thing very desirable, and which any wise man would wish to be true, for the great benefit and happiness of man, that there was a God, an intelligent and wise, a just and good Being, to govern the world. Whatever hypothesis these men can possibly frame, whatever argument they can invent, by which they would exclude God and providence out of the world, that very argument or hypothesis will, of necessity, lead them to this concession. If they argue that our notion of God arises not from nature and reason, but from the art and contrivance of politicians, that argument itself forces them to confess, that it is manifestly for the interest of human society that it should be believed there is a God. If they suppose that the world was made by chance, and is every moment subject to be destroyed by chance again, no man can be so absurd as to contend that it is as comfortable and desirable to live in such an uncertain state of things, and so continually liable to ruin, without any hope of renovation, as in a world that is under the preservation and conduct of a powerful, wise, and good God. If they argue against the being of God, from the faults and defects which they imagine they can find in the frame and constitution of the visible and material world, this supposition obliges them to acknowledge that it would have been better the world had been made by an intelligent and wise Being, who might have prevented all faults and imperfections. If they argue against providence, from the faultiness and inequality which they think they discover in the management of the moral world, this is a plain confession that it is a thing more fit and desirable in itself that the world should be governed by a just and good Being, than by mere chance or unintelligent necessity. Lastly, if they suppose the world to be eternally and necessarily self-existent, and consequently that everything in it is established by a blind and eternal fatality, no rational man can, at the same time, deny but that liberty and choice, or a free power of acting, is a more eligible state than to be determined thus in all our actions, as a stone to move downward by an absolute and inevitable fate. In a word, which way soever they turn themselves, and whatever hypothesis they make concerning the original and frame of things, nothing is so certain and undeniable as that man, considered without the protection and conduct of a Superior Being, is in a far worse case than upon supposition of the being and government of God, and of men's being under his peculiar conduct, protection, and favor."—*Religious Encyclo.*

There are facts connected with the doctrine of atheism, by a careful examination of which we can find its origin with as much ease and certainty, as we can satisfy ourselves that there is a God by observation of things which we see and know to exist.

All history proves that man is, by nature, not only a rational but worshipful creature. No nation of people has ever yet been found who were, or are, so ignorant as not to have some notions of a Great Spirit who made them, who loves justice and mercy, and to whom they are accountable, in some way, for their conduct. Christians understand this universal recognition of a Supreme Being, and of obligation to worship him, as an evidence of the operation of the Holy Spirit on the minds of all men, even in the absence of the revelations contained in the Bible; teaching them such great and leading truths as it is indispensable they should know, to the end that they be justly held accountable for their conduct in this life. Is that opinion well founded? If it is, the Christian religion stands with it; and we may safely look to that Revelation, on which it is based, for evidence that there is a great first Cause, and all doubt of that sort is at once removed. But if that Christian faith is false, the question again presents itself, why this universal agreement of opinion among not only heathen, but savage nations? If not instructed by the Spirit of God, they have not and never have had any common teacher. Those who are found upon small islands, far out in mid-ocean, bound by interminable waters, as they suppose, have never before, at least for many generations, had intercourse with any human being but themselves. Such instances have often occurred. Yet all those people are found to have this all-prevailing opinion of a Great Spirit. They all worship a God of some sort, and in some way. And all do so under the same common impression of dependence upon and duty toward Him who created them, and to whom they are accountable.

It is utterly unreasonable to deny that this universal agreement, on the part of all men, who have not had the light of Revelation on which Christians build their faith, is the effect of some common cause. If that be not the inspiration of God upon the intellect of man, some one more wise than I must answer for it if there be any other hypothesis on which it can be accounted for.

If, then, it be true, that all heathen, pagan, and Christian nations, admit the existence of a Supreme Being, whence arises the doctrine of atheism? This inquiry is fully answered both by sacred and profane history. In the earlier ages of the world, atheism appears to have been unknown. All admitted there was a God, so far as we have any account. Prior to the flood, infidelity had made its appearance, and at that time prevailed to such extent as, together with the wickedness of that generation, to require the destruction of our whole race, save Noah and his family only, for the purpose of carrying out the great plan of redemption for which the world was made, and man brought into his present state of being.

After that time we hear but little more of atheism until Greece began to make those wonderful strides in science and the polite arts for which she was, in her palmiest days, so justly distinguished, and which still does, and must during all time, continue to reflect such eminent honor upon her noble sons.

From Greece, that atheistic philosophy, which proved to be the bane of human reason, was afterward transplanted in Rome, and from there it was brought to France, the most fruitful soil in which that fatal upas was ever planted.

Atheism is, as may be easily shown, the culmination of pride, vanity, ignorance, and wickedness of the unrenewed heart of man. His vaulting pride forbids him to admit the truth of any proposition which he can not fully explain; his vanity will not allow him to confess that there is any great truth in nature which he can not comprehend; his ignorance is so consummate that he can not discover the God of nature in his own works; his wickedness then prompts him, as the only way of escape from his sad dilemma, to deny the very existence of that God whom his conscience warns him he should not only confess but love and worship.

Plato, the most distinguished of all heathen philosophers, who lived some four hundred years before the Christian era, without the aid of other revelation than that of mental impressions which is common to all men, by the power of reasoning upon known facts, approximated nearer the truth, in substance, as to the existence of a God, and his dealings with men, than many of our own age have done, who presume to teach others with the effulgent light of prophecy, the gospel, and revelation all beaming upon them.

The great Jehovah has revealed to the world all the facts which are necessary to a clear and satisfactory understanding of our relations and duties to Him, and of the consequences attendant on our observing or disregarding His law. To that extent we may search and reason at will. But as the surging billows of the vasty deep are restrained within bounds prescribed, so a limit is set to the extent of human knowledge of nature and nature's God, beyond which we may not pass. And every effort to transcend that divine border ever has and must continue to prove abortive, if not disastrous.

He has not authorized, and will not permit, rebellious, sinful man, in our present circumstances, to invade the hallowed precincts of His personal abode, or to know anything more of Himself.

His essence—origin (if that term were applicable to Him), the nature and extent of His other works, as of the creation of worlds and rational or irrational beings there to dwell, must remain, as yet, a sealed book. For this the best and most palpable reasons exist, and of which it is intended to say more in the further progress of this work.

We may reason at will about anything, everything, below that, whether physical or metaphysical. We may go with the botanist, the mineralogist, the geographer, and the naturalist, and see and learn and know all about the vegetable kingdom, the hidden treasures of the earth, her formation and organization, and of her

> Mountains, vales, and little hills,
> Oceans, seas, rivers, and rills;
> Man, beast, bird, and crocodile,
> Insect, fish, and serpent vile.

Our imagination can soar aloft to the sun, moon, and stars; we may, with the aid of science, view the blue canopy of heaven all night, and night after night, if we wish; we may trace the erratic pathway of the wandering comet, search out Orion, Cepheus and his queen; note the evolutions of planets with wonder and delight; and we may gaze upon the beauties and magnificence of Jupiter with his four satellites and gaudy dress. Or, we may go with the theologian and read and reason upon all the great and mysterious truths related in God's holy book; we may admire, yea, adore, the divine author for his power, wisdom, and mercy. All this, and more, we may essay to do, not only with impunity, but with pleasure and profit to ourselves, and with the Divine approval and blessing. But when we presume to enter His celestial courts, and to read hidden things which are recorded there for Him and His alone, we succeed so far only as to receive that humiliation and punishment which our vanity and audacity most justly deserve.

Many persons, no doubt of great learning, but whose *crania* would indicate veneration much less than self-esteem, have vainly attempted to penetrate the secret things of God, and not from admiration of His greatness, or love for His goodness, but simply to gratify an idle and vain curiosity. Such have labored with a determination to know the Deity, or deny His being! and their irreverence has been requited by withholding that divine light which is so freely granted the devout seeker after such knowledge of heaven's laws as is necessary to an enlightened discharge of duty to her

King; and whose puny efforts have resulted in confirmed unbelief and consequent eternal damnation.

It is foreign to the purpose of this writing to argue, at any great length, the question of the authenticity of the Bible; and forbearing to do so, I can not consent, however, to pass in silence a subject of such vital importance, and especially one on the verity of which hinges the truth of every proposition herein favored.

The writer begs leave, therefore, to copy here the following extracts from the *Religious Encyclopedia*, which the indefatigable labors of the editor of that valuable work (and which should have a place in every library) has collected and given at one view. This he does the more cheerfully because the arguments therein found are far more conclusive than any he could flatter himself as being able to produce of his own, within a space anything like so short:

"The sacred penmen, the prophets and apostles, were holy, excellent men, and would not—artless, illiterate men, and, therefore, could not—lay the horrible scheme of deluding mankind. The hope of gain did not influence them, for they were self-denying men, that left all to follow a Master who had not where to lay His head, and whose grand initiating maxim was: 'Except a man forsake all that he hath, he can not be my disciple.' They were so disinterested that they secured nothing on earth but hunger and nakedness, stocks and prisons, racks and tortures, which, indeed, was all they could or did expect in consequence of Christ's express declarations. Neither was a desire of honor the motive of their actions, for their Lord Himself was treated with the utmost contempt, and had more than once assured them that they should certainly share the same fate; besides, they were humble men, not above working as mechanics for a coarse maintenance; and so little desirous of human regard that they exposed to the world the meanness of their birth and occupations, their great ignorance and scandalous falls. Add to this, that they were so many, and lived at such a distance of time and place from each other, that had they been impostors it would have been impracticable for them to contrive and carry on a forgery without being detected. And as they neither could nor would deceive the world, so they neither could nor would be deceived themselves, for they were days, months, and years, eye and ear witnesses of the things which they relate; and, when they had not the fullest evidence of important facts, they insisted on new proof, and even upon sensible demonstrations; as, for instance, Thomas, in the matter of of our Lord's resurrection (John 20: 25); and to leave us no room to question their sincerity, most of them joyfully sealed the truth of their doctrines with their own blood. Did so many and such marks of veracity ever meet in any other authors?

"But even while they lived they confirmed their testimony by a variety of miracles wrought in divers places, and for a number of years—sometimes before thousands of their enemies, as the miracles of Christ and His disciples—sometimes before hundreds of thousands, as those of Moses.

"Reason itself dictates that nothing but the plainest matter of fact could induce so many thousands of prejudiced and persecuting Jews to embrace the humbling, self-denying doctrines of the cross which they so much despised and abhorred. Nothing but the clearest evidence arising from undoubted truth could make multitudes of lawless, luxurious heathens receive, follow, and transmit to posterity the doctrines and writings of the apostles; especially at a time when the vanity of their pretensions to miracles and the gift of tongues could be as easily discovered had they been impostors; and when the profession of Christianity exposed persons of all ranks to the greatest contempt and most imminent danger.

"When the authenticity of the miracles was attested by thousands of living witnesses, religious rites were instituted and performed by hundreds of thousands, agreeable to the Scripture injunctions, in order to perpetuate that authenticity; and these solemn ceremonies have ever since been kept up in all parts of the world: the Passover by the Jews, in remembrance of Moses' miracles in Egypt; and the Eucharist by Christians, as a memorial of Christ's death, and the miracles that accompanied it, some of which are recorded by Phlegon the Trallian, a heathen historian.

"The Scriptures have not only the external sanction of miracles, but the eternal stamp of the omniscient God by a variety of prophecies, some of which have already been most exactly confirmed by the event predicted.

"The scattered, despised people, the Jews, the irreconciliable enemies of the Christians, keep with amazing care the Old Testament, full of the prophetic history of Jesus Christ, and by that means afford the world a striking proof that the New Testament is true; and Christians, in their turn, show that the Old Testament is abundantly confirmed and explained by the New.

"To say nothing of the harmony, venerable antiquity, and wonderful preservation of those books, some of which are by far the most ancient in the world; to pass over the inimitable simplicity and true sublimity of their style; the testimony of the fathers and primitive Christians; they carry with them such characters of truth as command the respect of every unprejudiced reader.

"They open to us the mystery of creation, the nature of God, angels, and men; the immortality of the soul; the end for which we were made; the origin of the moral and natural evil; the vanity of this world, and the glory of the next. There we see inspired shepherds, tradesmen, and fishermen, surpassing as much the greatest philosophers as these did the herd of mankind, both in meekness of wisdom and sublimity of doctrine. There we admire the purest morality in the world, agreeable to the dictates of sound reason, confirmed by the witness which God has placed for himself in our breast, and exemplified in the lives of men of like passions with ourselves. There we discover a vein of ecclesiastical history and theological truth consistently running through a collection of sixty-six different books, written by various authors, in different languages, during the space of above fifteen hundred years. There we find, as in a deep and pure spring, all the genuine drops and streams of spiritual knowledge which can possibly be met with in the largest libraries. There the workings of the human heart are described in a manner that demonstrates the inspiration of the Searcher of Hearts. There we have a particular account of all our spiritual maladies, with their various symptoms, and the method of a certain cure—cure that has been witnessed by multitudes of martyrs and departed saints, and is now enjoyed by thousands of good men who would account it an honor to seal the truth of the Scriptures with their own blood. There you meet with the noblest strains of penitential and joyous devotion, adapted to the dispositions and states of all travelers to Zion. And there you read those awful threatenings and cheering promises which are daily fulfilled in the consciences of men, to the admiration of believers and the astonishment of attentive infidels.

"The wonderful efficacy of the Scriptures is another proof that they are of God. When they are faithfully opened by His ministers, and powerfully applied by His Spirit, they wound and heal; they kill and make alive; they alarm the careless, direct the lost, support the tempted, strengthen the weak, comfort mourners, and nourish pious souls.

"To conclude: It is exceedingly remarkable, that the more humble and holy people are, the more they read, admire, and value the Scriptures; and, on the contrary, the more self-conceited, worldly-minded, and wicked, the more they neglect, despise, and asperse them. As for the objections which are raised against their perspicuity and consistency, those who are both pious and learned, know that they are generally founded on pre-possession and the want of understanding in spiritual things; or, on our ignorance of several customs, idioms, and circumstances, which were perfectly known when those books were written. Frequently, also, the immaterial error arises merely from a wrong punctuation, or a mistake of copyers, printers, or translators, as the daily discoveries of pious critics, and ingenuous confessions of unprejudiced inquirers, abundantly prove."

In addition to the above brief, but cogent, arguments in favor of the authenticity of the Sacred Scriptures, the writer will add but one other:

If Jesus was, and is, the promised Messiah, there can be no doubt remaining of the truth of both the Old and New Testaments. This is too evident to need demonstration. The prophets of old predicted so clearly, and with such coherence, the advent of the Messiah, and the time and circumstances of His coming, that the Jews, as a nation, and many Gentiles also, who had mingled with or been frequently visited by them, were in confident expectation of His appearing about the time Jesus was born in Bethlehem of Judea. This fact is fully authenticated both by sacred and profane history. Many of the best informed Jews believed that He was the Christ. Those who rejected Him, looked for the coming of the true Messiah anxiously and constantly, even while He was here; and they have still been, and yet are, waiting for and expecting His appearance on earth. And, having now been in waiting near nineteen centuries in disappointment, or at least in hope deferred, the reasons for believing that Jesus was the Christ are thereby vastly strengthened, and, as it does seem, should be accepted as conclusive to every unprejudiced mind, whether Gentile or Jew.

CHAPTER IV.

Second Proposition—The Heavens Created and Inhabited before this World—Mosaic History Refers alone to this Creation—Consists with Science—Adam Formed—When Eve was Made—Angels Existed before.

"THAT the heavens were created and inhabited by myriads of happy, angelic beings, long before this world was created, as recorded by Moses," is our next subject for investigation.

This, I know, is in conflict with the commonly received opinion of the creation; but, as is true in relation to many other well-authenticated facts connected with natural science, it is one upon which erroneous views are very generally entertained. To those Bible readers who are content to accept the brief and figurative history of the creation of this world, which is contained in the Mosaic account, as a literal and full exposition of all the mighty works of an eternal, all-wise, and omnipotent Being, such conclusion is quite natural, yet we need not go beyond Divine Revelation to prove conclusively that the account given by Moses related *alone* to the creation of this comparatively small revolving planet on which we live; her appurtenances and inhabitants including man, the crowning work of that week.

Before looking into other sacred authorities for such proof, let us notice the Mosaic account, and see whether it will admit of a construction consistent with this hypothesis.

"In the BEGINNING God CREATED the HEAVEN and the earth."—Gen. 1: 1. The first question arising upon reading this verse is, In what sense is the word "BEGINNING" here used?

Considered alone, it might well be construed as referring to the "*beginning*" of all God's creation, if anything was created before, or, if not, to the creation of this world.

That the history here purported to be given is that of the creation of this world, I think quite clear, for no reference is made to any other creation; hence the most natural inference is that the word "*beginning*" refers to the beginning of the creation then under consideration. It would require a strained construction to say that the idea of any former work of creation is precluded by anything that is said here. And if it should turn out, on looking further into these writings, that other passages are found which can only be reconciled with this by restricting that word, as used here, to the beginning of this creation, we must so construe it, according to the rules referred to in the first chapter, or any other reasonable rule.

For the present, however, it is only assumed that the word *beginning* does not necessarily preclude the idea of a previous creative work. The next inquiry is, How are we to construe the word "*created?*" That is a term of comprehensive import. Its primary meaning as used in our language is: "To produce; to bring into being from nothing; to cause to exist." Among other things it means: "To make or produce, by new combination of matter already created, and by investing these combinations with new forms, constitutions, and qualities; to shape and organize."— *Webster.*

This last appears to be the most common sense in which the word is used by the translators of our Bible. Note, for instance, the following: "For behold I CREATE new heavens and a new earth."—Isa. 65: 17. "*Create* in me a clean heart."—Ps. 51: 10. "We are His workmanship, CREATED in Christ Jesus unto good works."—Eph. 2: 10.

For the purposes of the present argument, it is not material whether the word *created* here is intended to be understood as, "to bring into being from nothing," or a mere alteration, change, or adaptation. For, whether it is accepted in the one sense or the other, it certainly is said that God created this world "in the beginning." But when that was, we are not definitely informed. These remarks are made, however, in passing, and while the text is before me, merely for the purpose of meeting an objection made, by a class of modern deists, to the truth of the Bible, on the ground that certain known facts in science show that the world has been in existence more than six thousand years. I think, myself, it has existed in some form and for some purpose much longer than that; but suppose it has, if the terms used here are perfectly consistent with that idea, as they unquestionably are, no argument can be drawn from that source against the truth of Revelation. It may become necessary to notice this subject again under the sixth head, and therefore we will pass on for the present.

The word "heaven" next strikes our attention. Observe, first, that the singular number is used—*heaven*, and not *heavens*. "The Hebrews acknowledge three heavens: the air, or ærial heaven; the firmament in which the stars are supposed to be planted, and the heaven of heavens, or third heaven, the residence of Jehovah."

We will not suppose, then, that it was intended to be understood as saying that all the *heavens* were then *created*, as that would involve the absurdity of saying, not only that God then made His own celestial abode, but that He made himself also, for He is frequently called "Heaven," as in Job 38: 33: "*Knowest thou the ordinances of Heaven?*"

The definite article is used, "the heaven." From this we infer that the word *heaven* indicates more places or things than one, and that it applies here to a particular place or thing. Then to what place or thing is it more reasonable we should understand it as referring, than to the blue canopy above us, the sky, and the atmosphere surrounding the earth, and which constituted an indispensable part of this creation? If any doubt yet remains on that point, it will be fully removed by reference to the different connections in which the word heaven is elsewhere found; as, for instance, in the twentieth verse of that chapter: "And fowl that may fly above the earth in the open firmament of heaven." No sane man can believe that the word *heaven* there refers to the mystic habitation of Jehovah and His holy angels, but to that air around and above us in which fowls do fly. "God formed every fowl of the AIR."—Gen. 2: 19. "And the fowl of HEAVEN" (were destroyed by the flood).—Gen. 7: 23. "Both the fowl of the HEAVENS and the beasts are fled."—Jer. 9: 10. Read, also, Job 37: 18, "Hast thou with him spread out the sky, *which* is strong, and as a molten lookingglass."

May we not safely assume, then, that the word *heaven*, as here employed, does not necessarily include all that it anywhere and everywhere does?

We will, in this connection, notice the word "firmament," and, for that purpose, quote from the sixth to the ninth verses, inclusive:

"6. And God said, Let there be a firmament in the midst of the waters, and let it divide the waters from the waters.

"7. And God made the firmament, and divided the waters which were *under* the firmament from the waters which *were* above the firmament: and it was so.

"8. And God called the firmament Heaven. And the evening and the morning were the second day.

"9. And God said, Let the waters under the heaven be gathered together unto one place, and let the dry *land* appear: and it was so."

We will observe, 1. That the primary office of this "*firmament*," as appears here, was to "divide the waters from the waters," meaning to separate the waters which were above, and which descend from the clouds in the form of rain, from the waters on the earth.

2. That the name given to that "firmament" was "*Heaven*."

3. That in the next succeeding verse, God, in speaking of it, himself, calls it "Heaven."

The preceding remarks upon the word "*heaven*," therefore, will apply also to the word "*firmament*," as here used by the inspired historian. In fact, a careful reading of the account given us of this creation, must satisfy every one that the several terms *heaven*, *firmament*, *air*, and *sky* are indifferently used, as convertible, and meaning the same thing.

From the fourteenth to the seventeenth verses, we have an account of the creation of the sun, moon, and stars·

"14. And God said, Let there be lights in the firmament of the heaven, to divide the day from the night; and let them be for signs, and for seasons, and for days, and years:

"15. And let them be for lights in the firmament of the heaven to give light upon the earth: and it was so.

"16. And God made two great lights; the greater light to rule the day, and the lesser light to rule the night: *he made* the stars also.

"17. And God set them in the firmament of the heaven to give light upon the earth."

The most natural first impression on the mind, from a casual reading of these verses, would be that they were then made, but a critical examination of them will prove that such conclusion is by no means irresistible, or inconsistent with the idea that the sun and stars existed previously. The moon, being a satellite of the earth, was in all probability, not to say certainly, made whenever she was.

Attention is here called to the fact that no violence is done the context by construing the fourteenth verse as intended simply to state the functions of the "lights in the firmament," as related to this world, which were, "to divide the day from the night," etc., and without any intention to intimate that they were *then*, or *when* they were made. The phraseology of the fifteenth verse favors this view. "And let them be FOR LIGHTS in the firmament of the heaven to give light upon the earth," plainly pointing out a service to be performed by them.

Again, the sixteenth verse repeats the fact of the creation of the sun, moon, and stars, not giving the least clue to the time when it was done, or stating for what purpose they were made, thus greatly favoring such construction. And as this last is in *pari materia* with the two preceding verses, they must all be construed together, and each by the others, to get their true bearing on the whole narrative. The seventeenth and eighteenth contain together but one additional statement of fact, to-wit: "And God set them in the firmament of the heaven;" and repeats in different language, a purpose for placing them there; but do not, in any way, state when it was done, or whether that was *all the object* to be accomplished in their creation. So that, when considered together, it is evident that there was no intention on the part of the writer to say, or desire to be understood as meaning, that they were all *then* for the first time brought into being.

"Thus the heavens and the earth were finished, and all the host of them. And on the seventh day God *ended* his work which he had made, and he rested on the seventh day from all his work which he had made. And God blessed the seventh day and sanctified it; because that in it he had rested from all his work which God created and made."—Gen. 2: 1, 2, 3.

In these three verses, literally construed and without reference to anything which precedes or follows them, we see a contradiction palpable and plain; for God could not have ENDED his work on that day, and at the same time have rested "from all his work."

To end a work is to finish, to complete it, and the finishing a job requires *work* as well as to begin or carry it on to the point of completion. But what sane man with the fear of God before his eyes, would think of offering such violence to His Sacred Word!

The inspired penmen were not careful to avoid the scathing assault of the critic. For such they show no regard. Their sole aim in all cases where mere matters of history were to be written, appears to have been to record in good faith and in a plain way, the facts intrusted to each for preservation, so that they could be transmitted from generation to generation, down the stream of time to the final consummation. And when prophecies of future events were delivered to them for the benefit of their race, their great care seems to have been to report their message as delivered from Heaven, in every instance, just as it was received, leaving every one interested at liberty to search out and apply the interpretation for themselves. It was to the humble, anxious seeker for light, that blessed light which cometh down from heaven, and not to the captious fault-finder, the gainsayer, the reviler of God's messages of love, that those holy men addressed themselves. Such persons are not, however, overlooked or neglected by the divine penmen, but to the contrary, they have their promises of reward according to their works, as well as others.

But to return to the text now under consideration, notwithstanding such apparent discrepancy, and which is purely verbal, the sense is clear to the comprehension of any one of ordinary capacity who really wishes to understand it. The work referred to was the creation of this world, which had been that far accomplished, as designed, and on the seventh day God *having finished*, "ended" that work, rested "from all his work which he HAD made," and no doubt from all that work.

There is not the slighest intimation here that he had created nothing before that week, or that he would make nothing thereafter. All that we have any sufficient reason to believe was intended to be reported here, was the work of the immediately preceding six days. For proof conclusive of the fact that the work of creation did not stop there, it is only necessary to look at the twenty-second verse of this chapter and the twenty-first verse of the third chapter; where it will be seen that the master-piece of architecture, the crowning beauty of all this terrestrial mechanism, was made afterward, and that the necessity for the most trivial articles of all that work, as found of record, had not then arisen.

We will now notice the account of the creation of man, so far as is necessary, to maintain the affirmative of the proposition, that the Mosaic history does not preclude the idea of a previous creation of celestial beings. And for convenience, the several passages referring to it are presented together, and will be so treated:

"And God said: Let us make man in our image, after our likeness: and let them have dominion over the fish of the sea, and over the fowl of the air, and over the cattle, and over all the earth, and over every creeping thing that creepeth upon the earth. So God created man in his *own* image, in the image of God created he him; male and female created he them."—Gen. 1: 26, 27. "Thus the heavens and the earth were finished, and all the host of them." —2: 1. "And the Lord God formed man *of* the dust of the ground, and breathed into his nostrils the breath of life; and man became a living soul."—2: 7.

Had the account of the creation of man stopped with the first statement of it, we would have had no evidence there that he was, in any very distinguishing feature, different from other animals, or that he was endowed with a "living soul;" as the statements there made in relation to his creation are similar to those made of other creatures, except as to his image, and that could readily have been construed as referring to the form and appearance of his body.

But the subject is resumed in the seventh verse of the second chapter, and there we find two additional facts as to the creation of man, and such as are not stated in the history of the creation of any other being. The first is as to the matter of which he is made, "of the dust of the ground;" and (which is to us the most important item of all connected with the whole creation), that the Lord God "*breathed into his nostrils the breath of* LIFE, *and man became a* LIVING SOUL."

That the body of Adam was then made, none doubt, who admit the truth of the Bible; but that the *light*, the LIFE, the LIVING SOUL, which was breathed into that body, was then first brought into existence, is certainly not stated by the sacred historian. And from the bare fact, that a circumstantial account is given of the making of his body, which is but dust, and not a word said about the creation of his soul (of which our Savior asked the potent question: "What shall it profit a man if he shall gain the whole world, and lose his own soul?") such interest is awakened as to the origin, nature, and destiny of the human soul, as to demand the most diligent investigation of that vital question.

But, for the present purpose, it is only sought to show, that the Scripture under review may be true, and yet that the soul of Adam MAY HAVE EXISTED before his body was made.

May not so much be safely assumed without saying more here?

The first verse of the second chapter having been commented on, when speaking of the creation of the sun, moon, and stars, the reader is respectfully referred to the remarks made there as to it. The object for repeating it, as part of the history of the creation of man, was simply to present all that account at one view.

The subject is again, but incidentally only, referred to in the first and second verses of the fifth chapter, thus: "This is the book of the generations of Adam. In THE DAY that God created MAN, in the likeness of God made he him; male and female CREATED he them; and blessed them, and called their name Adam, IN THE DAY WHEN THEY WERE CREATED."

Careful attention is invited to the liberal use of words to express different things, and which appears in all the sacred writings. To read this paragraph alone, every one would agree that God made man and woman at the same time, or at least on the same day; that they were made in the same way, that is, of the same material, and the common name Adam (or man) was applied to, and the blessing pronounced upon them all at once. The contrary of all which is, nevertheless, clearly taught in this very account of the creation.

Man was made on the sixth day. How long it was afterward when Eve was made, no specific account is given; but from what is said about it, some considerable time must have elapsed between the making of the two; it may have been days, weeks, months, or years, so far as anything to the contrary is stated in the Bible.

By reference to the eighth and ninth verses of the second chapter, it will be seen that Adam was not made in the garden of Eden, but somewhere else; and that the garden was afterward planted, and he was "PUT" into it. The trees, herbs, and grass which were first created, were, as it appears, made to spring out of the ground, and miraculously grow up at once into full maturity, bearing fruit and seed, each after its kind, and in perfection; all ready to supply food for beast, fowl, and man. (See chap. 1.) This was necessary for the support of those living creatures which required food to sustain them. It was not so with the production of Eden. We are informed that there: "Out of the ground made the Lord God to grow every tree that is pleasant to the sight, and good for food: the tree of Life also in the midst of the garden, and the tree of Knowledge of good and evil."

The language used here is such as is commonly employed to express the ordinary growth of vegetation. There is no apparent reason why time should not have been allowed for the natural growth of all the trees, shrubs, vines, herbs, etc., in the garden; because food in abundance, doubtless, was already prepared for use outside of it. And it is expressly said: "And the Lord God took the man, and put him into the garden of Eden to dress it and to keep it."—2: 15. This language implies a growth, as in ordinary cases, of the production of the garden, else, why the necessity for its being *dressed* and *kept?*

Adam was alone in the garden also; how long we are not informed. There was a cause for his being there alone, as we must conclude; for we will not admit that God acted in anything without good and sufficient reason. The most natural inference, perhaps, is that by living alone for a time, and having for his associates none but brute beasts, he would the more highly appreciate the value of the companion intended for him. Eve, it seems, was not created until after all the other living creatures had been present before Adam, and each received an appropriate name. All this required time.

"And the Lord God said, *It is* not good that man should be alone; I will make him an help meet for him."—2: 18. This must not be taken to mean that God had just discovered that it "was not good that man should be alone," but that Adam had learned his lonely condition and craved the companionship of a rational being like himself; for that God had intended from the beginning to create Eve also, no one can pretend to doubt. The whole scheme of this creation would have failed of its purpose without her.

Our well-intending, but unfortunately too confiding mother Eve, was, as we have every reason to believe, reserved for the crowning work of this creation. Adam had been made, and had lived outside of that beautiful place. He had afterward been brought into it, and had witnessed the excellencies of that garden above even the virgin perfections of the outside world. Here he had resided in perfect bliss, save that one comfort alone was wanting. When his experience had been sufficient in that manner of life, and his mind was fully prepared to appreciate the blessing, a deep sleep was brought upon him in the garden, and then from his side, near his heart, a rib was taken, and of that to him precious material, and by the immediate hand of his own Maker "an help meet for him" was made. The flesh was closed up and immediately healed by the creative power of God. Adam was then, as we may reasonably infer, gently aroused from his deep sleep, when, to his amazement and delight, before him stood, in the bloom of youth and blushing beauty, Eve—of size and model perfect, her curling tresses waving in the morning breeze, and her sparkling eyes reflecting the wonder of his own.

"Yet was there light around her brow,
A holiness in those dark eyes,
Which show'd, though wand'ring earthward now,
Her spirit's home was in the skies.' —*Moore.*

The ecstatic joy that filled his pure heart (for Adam was then a stranger to sin) may be imagined, but can not be described by any power below that of Him whose loving kindness gave it.

To infer from that passage that Adam and Eve were created on the same day would involve difficulties from which it would be hard to escape. But to construe the expression, "in the day;" which occurs there twice, simply as referring back, in a general way, to the time of their creation, for the purpose of giving their form and common name, and without intending to say that they were both made on the same day, and the sense is plain, and no conflict exists between that and the other statements referred to on the same subject.

We can not be too careful in searching out the true sense and meaning of the sacred writers. This can, in most instances, be done successfully, by comparing the several passages to be found referring to the same thing, with each other. We frequently meet with remarks, which, if taken alone, or construed strictly, would be either untrue or unmeaning. Such, for instance, as the expression by Cain in his alarm: "And it shall come to pass that EVERY ONE THAT FINDETH ME shall slay me."—Gen. 4: 4. "And the Lord said, I will destroy man whom I have created from the face of the earth."—Gen. 6: 7. Noah, although included in the terms of that general denunciation, felt no alarm for himself or family, knowing that he and they were all to be excepted.

Before closing this branch of the subject, let us notice the care with which the jurisdiction and control of Adam was expressed. "And God said, Let us make man in our image, after our likeness; and let them have dominion over the fish of the sea, and over the fowl of the air, and over the cattle, and over all the earth; and over every creeping thing that creepeth upon the earth."—1: 26. The same dominion, but in different form, is repeated in the twenty-eighth verse, and each time the power of Adam was *strictly limited to this earth and things upon it*, by specification of the things over which it was to extend. No general language was used which could be understood as extending it to anything else. Had power been assigned him in words, which would necessarily include all living creatures, a strong inference would have arisen from such expressions that nothing had ever been created previous to that time; and that no living creature was then made but those on this earth, for he certainly could not control such if on another planet, or elsewhere in the heavens above.

With this preliminary review of the Mosaic history of creation, and confidently believing that no one who has, or may examine that history with the care which is due, will fail to be satisfied that nothing is there said which is not consistent with the hypothesis that heaven was created and inhabited by innumerable rational beings before this world was made, I will close this negative inquiry and proceed to the examination of such Scriptures as tend to prove the affirmative of that proposition.

CHAPTER V.

The Same Subject Continued—Nature and Extent of Inspiration—Class from which Inspired Men were chosen—Evidence that Angels Existed before the Creation of the World, Scriptural, Rational—Conclusion.

To a correct understanding of the book of Genesis, it is necessary that we bear in mind the purpose for which it was written. If inferences may be drawn from anything said there, which would conflict with well-authenticated scientific facts, we should not, in hot haste, pronounce the book spurious, but rather pause and inquire with what intent it was written, and what was the object and scope of the writer, etc. And if it is found to have been written for one great purpose only, and that the matter in question was not within the compass of the plan marked out by the writer, we should accept it as what lawyers call a mere *obiter dictum* (a passing remark), and therefore (if not figurative) but casually spoken, or written, and of no force or value.

It requires no argument to show that the writer did not expect that book to be accepted as a work on geology, astronomy, natural history, or any other purely scientific subject; but a succinct account of the creation of man and his early history, and, as connected therewith, of the creation of this world and the creatures found here. Some have wondered why nothing is said there about the creation of angels or devils. This may be sufficiently accounted for on the supposition that the plan of the work did not extend that far, or that the writer knew nothing about it.

Moses may not have been a good geologist or an experienced chemist, yet a man of undoubted veracity and distinguished piety.

Joshua, it is said, commanded the sun to stand "still upon Gibeon, and thou, Moon, in the valley of Ajalon. And the sun stood still, and the moon stayed, until the people had avenged themselves upon their enemies."—Josh. 10: 12, 13.

An astronomer of the present age would not readily believe that account as literally true; but if otherwise inclined to believe the Sacred Writings, he would find it easy to explain that matter to the satisfaction of himself and of all others so disposed.

The mind of Joshua was not then on questions of abstruse science. His ambition was to punish his enemies, the Amorites. His *prayer* was that the sun and moon might stand still—his *desire* was to have more time to pursue and destroy the enemy. God heard his petition, and approving the motive, He granted the request for time, not in the way mentioned, but by producing the effect desired, by suspending the rotation of the earth for the requisite time. Joshua, his army, and the historian probably, all believed that the sun and moon stood still "about a whole day." To them the effect was the same, and their error, as to the manner in which it was accomplished, was immaterial.

God knows all things. Of course, then, no scientific fact, how hidden soever or abstruse to us it may seem, is at all mysterious to Him. Our ignorance of such things He also knows, and the cause of it. He hears our prayers in the true sense and meaning intended, no difference how imperfectly expressed, or in what unscientific language clothed. When he communicates to us, by his prophets or otherwise, he addresses our understanding, and employs such terms as are best adapted to convey to our obtuse intellects the information intended, or produce the desired reflection. Of this the prayer of Joshua, and the conversation with Job (which is found in the thirty-eighth chapter of that book), are striking instances. Job, for instance, no doubt thought that the earth rested on a foundation, supported by corner-stones, as buildings are, and therefore his reflections were properly excited by speaking of things as he understood them to be, and not as they really were.

If Moses intended to say that the matter of which the world was created had no existence before (but I insist that he did not), and if there is conclusive evidence that it did exist before, then a sufficient answer to any objection which may be brought against him on that account, is to say that he was not, and did not pretend to have been inspired of God as to such scientific facts; and that for him, as a mere man, to err was natural; and that in doing so he did that only which most inspired writers who came after him did.

We have abundant reasons for believing that the prayers of the faithful are often answered in the same manner at the present day. The Christian in faith and humility, petitions the throne of grace for that which is most anxiously desired, and which is consistent with the Divine Will. The request is often granted, not in the way expected, but in another not less efficient or satisfactory. God knows our necessities better than we; and to carry into effect any purpose of his, he is at no loss for means.

If every book which contains error, of some sort, is to be rejected as fabulous or false, then we may commit all our libraries to the flames. For I fear not to say, that no book of one hundred pages has ever yet been written and printed (and without having passed through the hands of a hundred and one, or other like large number of translators, copyists, and printers, how faithful soever they may have been) by mortal man, with or without the aid of inspiration, which would not be condemned under that rule.

The prophets, apostles, and teachers of old, who wrote and taught under the direct influence of divine inspiration, made no claim to perfection of wisdom in any matter beyond that mission with which they were each especially charged. That the communications made to them were restricted to the subject matter with which they were commissioned may be proven to the satisfaction of any one, from the Sacred Scriptures alone. Of the many instances in which more information was asked by them than was granted, as stated by themselves, I will refer to the case of Daniel alone. In the twelfth chapter of his Prophecies is to be found a case in point. He says: "I heard but I understood not; then said I, O Lord, what *shall* be the end of these things? And he said: Go thy way, Daniel; for the words are closed up and sealed till the time of the end."

Many of the chosen men of God were of humble birth and but little education. They were best suited to the work assigned them. If the great, learned, and wise men of the world had been selected for those purposes, it would have been said at once, and believed, too, that they were arch-deceivers. They would have been capable of deceiving the great mass of people in many ways, without the aid of special inspiration; and hence their claim to such help could have been with success denied. Not so with the obscure, poor, and illiterate. Their ignorance on most subjects was known, and, therefore, their ability or even desire to deceive was, in proportion, less feared. See 1 Cor. 1: 26, 27, 28. We have no reason to believe that the inspired writers knew any more of things disconnected with the particular facts revealed to them than they knew before their inspiration, or would have otherwise known.

After having proven (or attempted to do so) in the preceding chapter, that there is nothing in the Mosaic account inconsistent with the proposition that the heavens were created and inhabited by holy angels before this world was made and Adam placed here, let us, in the next place, see whether the Scriptures contain affirmative evidence thereof.

In the first chapter of Genesis, twenty-sixth verse, we read: "And God said, Let us make man in our image, after our likeness." The plural number being used here indicates clearly that more than one were present when man was made. I am aware that the generally received opinion is, that the Father and Son are intended as the parties between whom this conversation was had, and some add the third person in the Trinity also. Without stopping to discuss the question, who we are to understand as there, at that time, it is enough for present purposes that there were more than one concerned in the consultation.

If angels did not exist before the creation of the world, how are we to understand the thirty-eighth chapter of Job, and particularly the fourth and seventh verses: "Where wast thou when I laid the foundation of the earth?" "When the morning stars sang together, and all the sons of God shouted for joy?" By the morning stars is evidently intended the holy angels of every degree, of whom it is said: "And all the sons of God shouted for joy." The terms, *morning stars* and *sons of God*, alike referring to those, who, on that glorious morn, sang anthems of praise to God for his goodness and mercies to his fallen creatures, and all, in one happy band, shouted together for joy—that a plan was agreed on and a place of redemption for the lost was found and prepared. Or, was it on some other account that heaven itself was thrown into such ecstacies of joy and gladness? If so, for what was it?

But we are not left to conjecture alone as to the cause of that rejoicing. In the second epistle of Paul to Timothy 1: 9, in speaking of the gifts and power of God, he says: "Who hath saved us and called *us* with an holy calling, not according to our works, but according to his own purpose and grace, WHICH WAS GIVEN US IN CHRIST JESUS BEFORE THE WORLD BEGAN." This is not the time or place for extended comment on this Scripture; but it is thought well enough in passing to drop a hint, at this point, for reflection, as the reader glides along. It is this: To constitute a gift, three things are necessary: first, a party able to give; second, another capable of receiving; and, third, something which may be given by the one party and received by the other *at the time* when the donation is made. If, then, it is true, that God gave to man a holy calling and saving grace, in and through Jesus Christ before the world was made, it follows as another truth, that Christ, man, and saving grace all existed, in some sense, somewhere, and in some condition also, "before the world began."

Well might the sons of God shout for joy on such an

occasion. And that rejoicing has not yet ceased, for "There is joy in the presence of the angels of God over one sinner that repenteth," to the present day.—Luke 15: 10.

"Some have held that the angels were created before the visible world, and that this is the reason why Moses does not mention them. Of this opinion were Origen, Chrysostom, Hieronymus, John of Damascus, and others among the ancients; and among the moderns, Hielmann, Michælis, and others."—*Knapp.*

"Some think that the idea of God's not creating them before this world was made is very contracted. To suppose, say they, that no creatures whatever, neither angels nor other worlds, had been created previous to the creation of our world, is to suppose that a Being of infinite power, wisdom, and goodness, had remained totally inactive from all eternity, and had permitted the infinity of space to continue a perfect vacuum till within the last six thousand years; that such an idea only tends to discredit revelation, instead of serving it."—*Buck.*

If we remember, "that one day is with the Lord as a thousand years, and a thousand years as one day (2 Peter 3: 8), the six thousand years, which have not yet elapsed since the creation of the world, are but as six days with God; and therefore he has remained inactive from all eternity, until the first of, to him, the present week, if nothing was created before this world. In that view the idea that God had created nothing before this world, appears the more unreasonable.

But, again, we find from the time the first revelations were made to man of His works and ways, He has been very active. The whole immensity of the heavens are seen actively and busily at work, and with perfect system and regularity, as but one vast machine. All animal and vegetable life on this earth is busily at work fulfilling each its own destiny. God, by His Holy Spirit, is, without ceasing day or night, constantly engaged in the beneficent work of man's redemption. Strange, indeed, is the thought, then, that he had theretofore remained listless and idle.

There is an important historical fact found in Genesis, which it will be hard to reconcile with the hypothesis that nothing had been created before this world.

The temptation and fall of man, as recorded in the third chapter, is referred to. It is conceded that the "serpent" mentioned there is the same evil spirit which is elsewhere called the Devil and Satan, and who is uniformly represented as the great Apostate; the common enemy of God and man, and the arch-deceiver of our race. He is, as all agree, a created being. As to when he was created, revelation is silent. We are left to inference, scriptural and rational alone, on that question. Guided by these two lights, is it most likely that he was created when the world was, or before? He is said to have once been an angel of light in heaven. "How art thou fallen from heaven, O Lucifer, son of the morning! *how* art thou cut down to the ground, which did weaken the nations." Isa. 14: 12. In Rev. 12: 9, we read; "And the great dragon was cast out, that old serpent, called the Devil and Satan, which deceiveth the whole world; he was cast out into the earth, and his angels were cast out with him."

Our Savior says: "I beheld Satan as lightning fall from heaven." Luke 10: 18.

When he was made or cast out of heaven, or fell to earth, we are not informed. But from the above Scriptures (as well as from many other like passages), we do learn that Satan is not now *what he once was*, or *where he was* first known to have been. That he was at one time in heaven having angels following his lead, and hence that he was an angel of superior order; that he was "cast out into the earth," and that he is the great deceiver of "the whole world," are three facts which can not be successfully denied.

Bear in mind, reader, that the inquiry here is, whether anything was made before this world; and in support of the affirmative it is proposed to prove that Satan and his angels were created prior to that time.

It is further premised, that the Mosaic account only applies to things created *at a certain time* and *place*. The time included is the six days mentioned, and the place was here below. The first reasonable inference to be drawn is, that a full though brief history of all that work was given, in which some notice was taken of all that was then and there created. To infer less would be to charge the writer with dereliction of duty. We are told nothing there of the creation of Satan, or of any other angel, good or evil. Then have we not here, from that fact, strong presumptive evidence that he was not created *then?* The first we hear of him, he was in heaven. We have no evidence in Scripture that he was translated from earth there, as were Enoch and Elijah. The question arises, therefore, if he was created here, how and when did he get up to heaven? If that can not be satisfactorily answered, we have additional reason to believe that he was not created *here* when the world was. If he was not created then or there, it is plain why no account of his creation was given by that historian; and if we accept his history as faithful and true, we are driven to the conclusion that Satan was not made at the time and place of this creation.

It is admitted that he is not self-existent, but a created being. If he was not made *then* and *there*, the inquiry is, *when* and *where* was he created? It must have been either before or after that time, of course. Was it not before? As remarked already, he is not what he once was. He was an angel of heaven, he is now an outcast devil. When he was numbered with the high and holy angels of heaven, he must have been *like* the other celestial beings; and to resemble them it is necessary that he should have been pure, and holy, and good, full of faith, and love, and joy; giving praise to God continually. He is now, if there be anything true in the Bible, just as far removed from what he then was as heaven is from hell.

All that change he has undergone. This required time. What length of days, years, or centuries we can not tell.

If we may form any estimate from what we observe

here, of the changes which are ever progressing around us, we should conclude that a great while has elapsed from his creation as a holy angel, before he was found in Paradise sporting in the form of a serpent (then one of the most beautiful and lovely creatures of that heavenly place, where sin, enmity, or fear had not been known), around and before Eve, and by his wiles and allurements, in all hypocrisy and deceitfulness, seeking not only her overthrow and ruin, but that of Adam and all their posterity, both for time and eternity.

As indicating the utter depravity to which he had arrived, and the black malice by which he was moved on seeing Eve, "thus early, thus alone," walking in the garden, he is fitly represented as soliloquizing thus:

> "Tho'ts, whither have ye led me! with what sweet
> Compulsion thus transported to forget
> What hither brought us! hate, not love, nor hope
> Of Paradise for hell, hope here to taste
> Of pleasure, but all pleasure to destroy,
> Save what is in destroying; other joy
> To me is lost."—*Paradise Lost.*

In reference to the insinuating manner in which he approached his unsuspecting victim, the same author, further on, says:

> "So spake the enemy of mankind, inclos'd
> In serpent, inmate bad, and toward Eve
> Address'd his way, not with indented wave,
> Prone on the ground, as since; but on his rear,
> Circular base of rising folds, that tower'd,
> Fold above fold a surging maze, his head
> Crested aloft, and carbuncle his eyes;
> With burnish'd neck of verdant gold, erect
> Amidst his circling spires, that on the grass
> Floated redundant: pleasing was his shape,
> And lovely: * * * *
> With tract oblique
> At first, as one who sought access, but fear'd
> To interrupt, sidelong he works his way;
> As when a ship by skillful steersman wrought,
> Nigh river's mouth or foreland, where the wind
> Veers oft, as oft so steers, and shifts her sail:

> So varied he, and of his tortuous train
> Curl'd many a wanton wreath in sight of Eve,
> To lure her eye; she busied heard the sound
> Of rustling leaves, but minded not, as us'd
> To such disport before her through the field,
> From every beast, more duteous at her call
> Than at Circean call the herd disguis'd.
> He bolder now, uncall'd before her stood
> But as in gaze admiring; oft he bow'd
> His turret crest, and sleek enamel'd neck,
> Fawning, and lick'd the ground whereon she trod."

If Satan had been made when Adam was, and translated to heaven as his home, is it probable he would have apostatized—been cast out, and so soon found here again, and engaged in such fiendish work on earth? If so, there would seem to be more danger of falling into sin in heaven than on earth, for Adam and Eve had remained pure and spotless, up to that time, as when they were first put here. So to presume would be blasphemy! Would it not, then, be more safe, as well as more consistent with common sense and the Sacred Scriptures to say that Satan was created before Adam? If so, the question recurs, when and where was Satan created? As to the time, revelation gives us no clue, by which we can form any opinion when anything was created except this world and its inhabitants and appurtenances. Our chronology relates to *time* only, as distinguished from *eternity;* and time dates with the creation of the world and of man. Things existing and acts done before that are, uniformly, spoken of by the divine penmen as existing *from all eternity*, or *before the foundation of the world*, or in some other like general terms.

Reasoning from analogy, we would naturally conclude that Satan, his angels, and all other originally angelic beings were created in heaven. They were made to inhabit those celestial realms. Man, beast, fowl, etc., were intended to occupy this world, and they were made here; it is, therefore, most reasonable to suppose that such creatures as were designed to inhabit heaven were created there.

But again. The holy angels who serve about the throne

of God, and are often employed in errands of mercy to man, were created at some time and somewhere. They are by common consent admitted to be of the proper inhabitants of the upper heaven.

We have no authority from Scripture or reason to say that they ever inhabited this earth as their home. No account of their creation is found in Genesis. They were in heaven warring against Satan and his angels, when the latter were expelled from those sacred precincts. The good and evil angels were all there at that time. In the absence of all authority to the contrary, are we not therefore justified in believing that they were all, at some time and for some purpose, created there? And, having no evidence that Satan is older than either class of angels spoken of, why should we say that he existed before they did? If, then, we are satisfied that Satan was created before this world was, why should we doubt that the angels of light, and those of darkness also, were created before the "Lord God formed man of the dust of the ground?"

Before leaving this branch of the subject, it may be well to make a remark or two on the above quotations from Isa. 14: 12, "How art thou fallen from heaven, O Lucifer, son of the morning," etc. The name "*Lucifer*" evidently refers to Satan. We are informed of no other being who could be justly called "son of the morning," and who has "fallen from heaven," and been "cast down to the ground." He is often represented as having been an angel of high order; having his "hosts" following him. The term "morning" is, by many of the inspired writers, used figuratively; as in Ps. 139: 9, "If I take the wings of the morning," etc. Hos. 6: 3, "His (the Lord's) going forth is prepared as the morning." Amos 5: 8, "*Seek him* that maketh the seven stars and Orion, and turneth the shadow of death into the MORNING, and maketh the day dark with night." In the text now under consideration, and in Job 38: 7, the expressions "son of the morning" and "morning stars" are understood as emblematical of the antiquity, excellence, and superiority of those to whom the terms are applied. The morning is the first and most delightful part of the day, so may the *morning*, the first of the day, be considered a fit emblem of the first and most excellent works of creation. In that sense, not only the holy angels, who "shouted for joy" at the creation of the world, may be designated as the "morning stars," but Lucifer, the great fallen, as having been a "son of the morning;" meaning thereby one of the first of created beings, both as regards time of creation and exaltation of rank.

These epithets would but poorly fit one of the depraved, fallen, and lost sons of Adam. They can, with propriety, be applied to none but those of an older and better race than we now appear. If so, then there must have been such beings, else all such references are but idle prate—words without meaning. Who will so receive them?

Reader, have you carefully examined the Scriptures bearing upon this subject? Have you reflected on it seriously, and in the light of natural reason? You have, say you.

Will you now, after such investigation, deny that the heavens were created and inhabited by angelic beings before this world was made? If you will, I must consider you as the party named in Hosea 4: 17, and obey that command.

CHAPTER VI.

Third Proposition—All Created Holy—Free-will—Predestination—Christians Persecuting each other—Charity Commended—Temper of Disputants Moderating.

OUR third proposition is, "That all rational creatures were originally created by God 'very good,' and endowed with powers of volition, locomotion, and action, for the glory of God and individual happiness, and were free agents to serve and glorify their Creator, or not, just as they chose."

The Bible informs us that God created all things in heaven and on earth. "And God saw everything that he had made; and behold, *it was* very good."—Gen. 1: 31.

It has already been insisted that the Mosaic history of creation applies only to this world, and persons and things here. This was, however, the last creation—of rational creatures at least—of which the Scriptures anywhere give an account, and must be understood as applicable to all things by him created up to that time.

We find ourselves here surrounded, nevertheless, by good and evil, and of which the evil quality appears largely to preponderate. Admitting the truth of the Sacred Word, this state of facts furnishes a problem for solution which deserves and has demanded the attention of the most profound philosophers and learned theologians of all Christian ages and countries.

God is said to possess the powers of omniscience, omnipotence, and omnipresence, without stint or limit, and to be full of love and mercy to his creatures.

That he has all these attributes, in perfection, no one will doubt who will search the Scriptures or observe his works and ways, and who believes there is a God. The heathen, who know nothing of the Bible, believe this as firmly as those who have it.

If, then, He is good, and made all things like Himself, good, and has all these qualities in perfection, it does become an interesting question, how came so much evil in the world?

Notwithstanding the general agreement of men as to the attributes of Deity, the difficulty of reconciling the apparent inconsistencies which strike the mind at the threshold of this subject has, no doubt, been a prominent cause of the infidelity that exists in the world. The chief inducement to write this chapter is to remove this source of doubt and consequent eternal death, as far as possible, by accounting for such seeming inconsistencies, and showing that they exist in appearance only.

That there is a God who made and overrules all things has been already argued. That He possesses all the attributes here assigned Him is so manifest, and has been so clearly proven by others, that it is assumed as true without stopping here to produce evidence as to either. It is not thought necessary to say a great deal about the perfection of His works. That a builder, who is himself perfect, should put up a deficient edifice is not to be expected.

No legitimate inference can be drawn against the belief that all rational creatures were originally made perfectly pure and free from sin and all its baleful consequences, if we admit that they were all left free agents.

Deviating here from the regular line of argument, as suggested by the shape in which the present proposition is stated, let us notice, first, the question of free agency.

It is not desired to take sides for or against either of the parties who have, with so much learning and ability, and, I regret to say in many instances, with much more acrimony than Christian charity, from the time of Pelagius and St. Augustine to the present day, debated this vexed question. That so much bitterness of feeling should have been indulged is, and has long been to my mind, a thing mysterious and wonderful. Why one holding the doctrine of either the one or the other of these parties, who otherwise had every appearance of a pious and faithful Christian, should have been not only denied church communion, but thought a fit subject for the most vindictive persecution, by those of the other party, can not be accounted for without admitting together the total depravity of our nature, and that Satan, the common enemy of all, had spies in the camps of each party and cunningly contrived to direct the batteries of both.

"And the serpent cast out of his mouth water as a flood, after the woman, that he might cause her to be carried away of the flood."—Rev. 12: 15. Will not this do for an interpretation of that Scripture: By the "serpent," we are to understand Satan as intended; by the "woman," the whole Christian Church as one family; and by the "water as a flood," the bickerings, strifes, persecutions, and wars which the devil has from time to time fomented between them, and cast out of his mouth, as a flood, "after the woman, that he might cause her to be carried away of the flood," that is, destroyed by persecuting each other?

The maxim of Mr. Jefferson, that "error ceases to be dangerous when reason is left free to combat it," had not obtained with Christians of that age. The learned and pious Mr. Henry, of the eighteenth century, in his Commentaries on Rev. 12, says: "The Church of God is in more danger from heretics than from persecution; and herecies are as certainly from the devil as open force and violence." While I can not concur with that able and highly esteemed theologian in that particular, I must not express my own opinion of that matter too freely, for fear some might think it would amount, in substance, to charging many great lights of the church, both ancient and modern, with having been and now being in the service of the devil. That they intended well, I do not question; but that they had more zeal than knowledge, is the most charitable conclusion at which we can fairly arrive.

Inasmuch as some yet entertain the same sort of prejudices against those who differ from them, on this and similar subjects, that gave rise to such persecutions among the earlier Christians, before the civil laws put a stop to them, or, as it is expressed in the next verse, before the powers of this world came to the rescue of the church, "and the earth opened her mouth, and swallowed up the flood," it is affectionately suggested to all professed Christians who are unwilling to recognize as brethren those who entertain views of that sort, however different from their own they may be, yet who profess to be on the Lord's side, and whose walk and conversation testify for them that they love Jesus Christ and his people, that they carefully examine the ground occupied by themselves.

To the warfare in which Christians are engaged there are but two parties. We are either in the service of Christ or of Satan. There is no middle ground here. If we would be in the service of the blessed Redeemer, we must be faithful in the observance of his laws. We must love one another. Read 1 Cor. 13: *charity* means *love*. Where love abounds as required there, no room is left in the Christian's soul for envy, hatred, or malice. If your brother believes that man is a free agent, and may serve God or the devil as he chooses, and you *know* that he is wrong, and that the destiny of all men was fixed and settled by a divine covenant before they were made, have charity for your poor, deluded fellow-man! Do not cast him off simply because you are more wise than he, but talk to him, labor with him, and if you can not bring him over to your faith, believe that he is honest of purpose, but too stupid to receive instruction on such *plain* and *simple* matters of Bible truth; and love him none the less. This is your duty, as St. Paul teaches in that chapter. We should ever bear in mind that we are all fallible. Even in our most firmly established opinions it is *possible* that the best informed of us may be in error. This is a fact taught in the Bible so plainly, and by daily observation so fully, that none deny it. This should induce all to exercise charity toward those of differing views from their own, and at the same time drive ultra dogmatism from their own bosoms.

All men are deeply interested in every important theological question. The simple fact that others having the same interest in them which we have, and as good or better opportunities for a correct understanding of them than ours, should induce us to pause before we undertake to say, "*I know I am right.*" That is a *dangerous* expression to use as to controverted points between Christians.

It is right, however, "That ye should earnestly contend for the faith which was once delivered unto the saints."—Jude 3. This is not the thing complained of. We may contend earnestly, but not violently; affectionately, yet with none the less, but far more success.

To approach a brother in that affectionately kind manner which so well becomes a follower of the meek and lowly Jesus, and talk with him in love of the matter of his supposed error, is a far more befitting and successful way to bring him to the truth than to prefer charges against him for heresy, and have him expelled from the communion of the church, and driven out to buffet the jeers of a wicked and gainsaying world. And if we consider our own fallible condition, it will be found a great deal the more safe way for ourselves, as it may turn out that the brother was right, and the difference between us was the result of our own mistake.

With these preliminary remarks, this delicate question is approached not, I repeat, to side with either party, but to establish such facts as lie in the pathway to the main theory propounded for consideration in this work.

If Satan and his followers were not, to some extent, free agents, neither he nor they could justly have been held responsible for anything they did or said. If he and they were, in all things, absolutely controlled by an overruling Providence, and acted in obedience to that irresistible power which directed them, as the strong arm of the engine impels the driving wheel, that which they did can not truly be said to have been their work.

It is a legal maxim that what a man does by another he does by himself. For the act done, the principal is held accountable, and not the agent. This we can understand and approve as right. The reason which brings us to that conclusion is the gift of God. Shall we so abuse His gift as to impute injustice to Him, when there is no necessity, real or imaginary, for so doing? The most bloody penal code in existence will not hold a man answerable for an act done under compulsion. The party who procured and caused the act to be done is the one held to account for it. To compel an inferior to do an unlawful act, and then inflict the penalties of a violated law upon him for having done it, is equivalent to a superior punishing an inferior who has done no wrong, but, as it would seem, purely for the pleasure of witnessing the pains of the innocent. Is that what is charged by rebellious, sinful, yet dependent man against Him who made us, and to whose tender mercies it is that we owe every breath we draw? None may answer, yes! but it is virtually what by far too many have done, unwittingly however, as I charitably hope and believe.

It may be remarked as one of the most singular features of the unnatural, unaccountable, and wicked war which has been so long and vindictively waged by different factions of the so-called Christian Church against each other, that those who held and advocated doctrines which involved their Creator in such inconsistencies, professed to be, and doubtless esteemed themselves as being, the most zealous and only reliable supporters of the dignity, justice, and mercy of God. Strange as it may look, such is, nevertheless, the fact! They went upon the fancy idea, that if a creature may act freely and for himself, and in so doing should escape the torments of hell, he would be entitled to some credit therefor, and hence God would be deprived of a part of the glory which is justly His due.

And again, that if the salvation of the creature depends to any extent upon his works, the result must remain uncertain up to the time of his death, and to admit that would be to deny the foreknowledge of God; because a thing can not be foreknown the result of which is involved in uncertainty. With such it was a favorite maxim that, "What is to be, will be."

There is certainly nothing more true than that.

Let us briefly examine the views upon which such strange inconsistencies arose. Is it true, that if the salvation of a sinner in any way depends upon himself, that the glory due to God is any less than it would have been if his salvation had been fixed by a decree of heaven, and therefore certain before he was born?

To answer that question satisfactorily, we must go back and see what was the state and condition of the sinner before he fell; and consider, also, whether God would be the more glorified by making his creatures all free, or by holding them under bonds to serve Him.

The question of free will is only noticed here in so far as it is connected with and bears upon the great truths discussed.

If it is true that the soul of man was an angel of light before the fall, and that from having associated with the prince and people of darkness since, he has degenerated and been reduced to his present depraved condition, then the wisdom of God would be best sustained, and consequently his glory too, upon the hypothesis that he had left the questions of repentance and salvation, in part at least, with each to settle for himself.

They certainly were free to act for themselves before they fell; because there was no devil to tempt them before Satan fell himself, so far as we are informed or have any sort of ground to believe. He was an angel of high degree; once as pure and holy as those he left behind him—as the Scriptures authorize us to believe. Yet he was a creature of God, and as perfectly subject to His control and disposal as is man in his present state. If God had so willed, He could have controlled his conduct and enforced the most abject obedience by Satan. Or, after he became rebellious, God could have controlled each and all of his followers, and restrained them from following after his baleful example to their own overthrow. A denial of that power to God would indeed be in derogation of His just claim to sovereignty. He did not control Satan or any of his angels, but permitted him and them to act for themselves, as free agents, in that awful affair.

They having voluntarily abandoned the service of the Creator for that of a creature, and God having allowed them to act for themselves on that occasion, it is most reasonable to suppose that He will not coerce obedience from any of them now, and save them from the just reward of their own folly and wickedness.

Were He to do otherwise, and restore any without sufficient evidence of voluntary contrition and repentance on their part, the probabilities are that should they be left free again, the same thing would be repeated. In that event, a defect in His providence would be manifest, even to the limited capacities of men, and which would certainly reflect less glory on God than would the success of His schemes.

And to put any one in a situation calculated to excite a hope of pardon for past transgression, and restoration to the Divine favor, without really offering any opportunity for repentance or salvation, would be to trifle with the feelings of a creature in his distresses. Few men would confess a willingness so to act themselves, and surely the number can not be greater of those who would assume to charge the beneficent Creator of the universe with such cruelty, even to a devil. It then would seem the most likely, that God allows His rational creatures the privilege, in some degree, of acting for themselves, and that He will hold them to answer for their conduct.

Would it not redound more to the glory of God that His creatures be granted perfect freedom of will to serve Him or not, as they please? Or the question may be better stated thus: Is the voluntary homage of the free, or the servile obeisance of the slave, most acceptable to the sovereign?

"The love of liberty with life is given,
And life itself th inferior gift of Heaven."

There is nothing more true than this. The love of liberty is an all-pervading instinct of nature, and is not peculiar to man, but common with all animated beings. Whence this universal agreement?

A characteristic so striking and uniform can only be traced to a common origin; to God the maker of all. If He has inspired all living creatures with the love of liberty, is it not proof conclusive that He loves it himself? Liberty being more agreeable to the Divine Nature than slavery, and having full power over all His creatures, is it reasonable that He would surround himself, in heaven, with a band of slaves, rather than a universe of spirits, like Himself, free?

That Satan and his comrades are in bondage now, we have abundant scriptural evidence. They are represented as held in "chains under darkness unto the judgment of the great day."—2 Pet. 2: 4; Jude 6. We are often spoken of as the servants of the devil. The glorious mission of Christ was to make us free. "Wherefore thou art no more a servant, but a son."—Gal. 4: 1 to 7. "And ye shall know the truth and the truth shall make you free." "If the son, therefore, shall make you free, ye shall be free indeed."—John 8: 32, 36.

We observe here the condition of the sinner is represented as one of servitude; no such terms being applied to the holy angels of heaven, the presumption thence arises, that they are not slaves but free. The redeemed of earth are to be "free indeed." As they are to become as the angels of heaven, we infer again that the angels are free.

But again. Slavery is the opposite of liberty. Sinners who are in servitude are subject to all sorts of sorrows, pain, and misery; which is just the reverse of the estate of holy angels in heaven, and of that which is reserved for the people of God. May we not, therefore, presume, that as the latter are to be free, the former are free also? It can not be necessary to run these analogies, or press such inferences further. The subject is inexhaustible, and such conclusions are not to be resisted.

With a few words, therefore, as to the meaning of the term "servant," and we will pass on.

Service is of two sorts, voluntary and constrained. Those of each class who serve, are designated by the sacred writers indifferently as "*servants.*" The followers of Jesus Christ are always by them treated as of the former, and the adherents of Satan as of the latter class of servants.

No inference can, in this view, be drawn from the fact that the righteous are sometimes called the servants of God, or of Christ, that they are not free, who are expressly declared to be so.

The discussion of free will as opposed to predestination illustrates, fearfully, the natural proneness of man to run into extremes. The absurdities into which the one party has been driven can alone be equaled by those of the other. And, as is usual in such cases, the truth can only be found between them. The one ascribes everything to a stern, unyielding fate, and the other to the result of free will.

If anything is taught in the Bible so clearly as to bar and foreclose all doubt, it is the doctrine of the foreknowledge of God. That is one of the chief attributes of Deity, and necessary to the government of His creatures. Without prescience of the effect of every cause, and of the conduct of all rational beings, His laws would be found but little better than those of men; and, like ours, they would have to be changed about as often as the moon.

To those who admit the Bible to be true, there can be no necessity to offer argument to sustain the foreknowledge of God. Such Scriptures as the following, and which abound in that inspired Book, to all that class, must be proof sufficient on this point: "Him, being delivered by the determinate counsel and foreknowledge of God, ye have taken, and by wicked hands have crucified and slain."—Acts 2: 23. "Known unto God are all his works from the beginning of the world."—Acts 15: 18. "Elect according to the foreknowledge of God the Father." —1 Pet. 1: 2. Regardless of all reason, and such scriptural evidence, some ultra advocates of the free-will dogma have been driven to deny that God did foreknow all things.

Such is often the consequence of suffering ourselves to become over-anxious to support a pet idea.

The immediate cause of such zealots falling into an error so absurd, in most, if not in all cases, is and has been their inability to reconcile the foreknowledge of the Creator with the free agency and consequent accountability of the creature.

All who think to any profit know that there are many things which it is much easier to comprehend and understand fully, to our own satisfaction, than it is to explain them to, and engraft them upon, the minds of others. This is a problem of that sort. Whether the difficulty, in this instance, lies more with the incompetency of the teacher or pupil, all are left to form their own judgment.

It is said, "there are none so blind as those who will not see." Were it not uncharitable, apparent facts and circumstances would justify the dark suspicion that the obtuseness of some persons in this particular is less real than affected. There is danger of doing injustice to some, however, in so accounting for that in all cases, which does sometimes, to say the least we can for it, appear very strange indeed. The eyes of erring man are subject to become so far blinded, and their judgment so perverted by prejudice, arising from the influence of preconceived opinions, bias, growing out of overestimating the value of some favorite and conflicting notion, allowing themselves to be carried too far by the fervor of debate, etc., that well-intending persons, of strong mind and great learning are, on that account, many times, as we can not doubt, unwittingly led far away from the plain and simple paths of Gospel truth, and lost in the mazes of mysticism, ultraism, and other like baleful isms.

Any protracted discussion of this question, which is only preliminary to that propounded for examination in this work, is forbidden by the limits prescribed. A few suggestions, in the way of directing the inquiring mind to a pleasant and fruitful field for thought, in reference to it, may not, nevertheless, prove amiss.

That there are passages of scripture, which, if considered alone, teach the doctrine of fatality, and others, viewed in the same way, prove that of ultra free agency, in some degree, will not be denied. If there be any conflict here (but really there is none), it must be reconciled, or our faith falls to the ground. To do that, they must be compared and construed together. In doing so, if a hypothesis be discovered on which such apparent discrepancy is removed, that is to be accepted as the correct one, if found reasonable in itself.

We should always bear in mind this scripture: "My thoughts *are* not your thoughts, neither *are* your ways my ways, saith the LORD. For *as* the heavens are higher than the earth, so are my ways higher than your ways, and my thoughts than your thoughts."—Isa. 55: 8, 9.

So viewing the wisdom and power of God, as contrasted with our imperfections as to both, I must confess that I see no difficulty in understanding how it is, that God foreknew all things from the beginning, and yet that man is a free agent to a degree sufficient to render him justly accountable for his own conduct.

In the redemption of man, God works by means. He may *know* what effect the means employed will have in each case, without exercising any extraordinary power to *produce the result*, foreknown, *in either*. If all He permits to be done is chargeable to Himself, as He has power to prevent it, He is responsible for all the sins committed both in heaven and on earth. But, on the contrary, if His rational creatures are allowed to exercise their own pleasure as to the discharge or omission of every duty arising in all the relations of their being, it is easy to understand how Satan may have sinned in heaven, and man on earth, and why God, foreknowing they would do so, did not prevent it, is not Himself responsible for it, and should hold each to a strict and just account for his own evil doings.

It is gratifying to witness the fact that, in the present age, ultraism on this, and other religious questions, is on the wane.

Few divines, who have any claim to learning, now hold the extreme views above mentioned, on either side. The foreknowledge of God and the freedom of will, so far as to constitute man an accountable being, are both pretty generally acknowledged on all sides. The margin left for debate is narrowing down to insignificance, and the tone of disputants much less acrid than heretofore.

CHAPTER VII.

War in Heaven—Dr. A. Clark's Analysis of the Apocalypse—How the Emblems have been Construed—Satan—The Bible—Anti-Christ—Rev. 12 : 7 to 17, Quoted—Three Questions Asked and Considered—Identity of Michael and Christ—Of the Dragon with Satan—Dr. Gill and Mr. Henry as to Michael—An Adventure—Literal Construction—Great Men Deceive Themselves—The Dragon and his Angels—Dark Questions put.

OUR fourth proposition is: "That the narrative found in the Apocalypse, although brief, figurative and mysterious, is, nevertheless, a faithful and true history of 'War in Heaven,' and of the expulsion of Satan and his deluded followers from the immediate presence of God and his holy angels."

Revelation has been considered in all Christian ages the most mysterious book contained in the Bible. Although it has been the subject of the most frequent comment of any portion of the Sacred Writings, no two of the vast number of those who have attempted to expound it, have yet agreed as to the interpretation of many of its hidden secrets.

Dr. Adam Clark, in his preface to the valuable notes he has made on it, says: "Among the interpreters of the *Apocalypse*, both in ancient and modern times, we find a vast diversity of opinions; but they may be reduced to four principal hypotheses or modes of interpretation:

"1. The Apocalypse contains a prophetical description of the destruction of Jerusalem, of the Jewish war, and the civil wars of the Romans.

"2. It contains predictions of the persecutions of the Christians under the heathen emperor's of Rome, and of the happy days of the church under Christian emperors from Constantine downward.

"3. It contains prophecies concerning the tyrannical and oppressive conduct of the Roman pontiffs, the true Anti-Christ, and foretells the final destruction of popery.

"4. It is a prophetic declaration of the cisms and heresies of Martin Luther, those called Reformers and their successors, and the final destruction of the Protestant religion."

From the above analysis of Dr. Clark it is observable that, notwithstanding the "vast diversity of opinions," which have, in every age, obtained as to the solution of some questions which have arisen between commentators of the same age, those of each period have uniformly so interpreted the Apocalyptic prophecies as to direct them against those who were, at the time, considered their most dangerous enemies.

Thus, in the age immediately succeeding that of St. John, the Christians generally, whether originally Jews or Gentiles, looked upon the infidel Jews as their common and most to be dreaded enemies; and they construed them as applying to the Jews and Jerusalem. The heathen emperors of Rome became the next persecutors of the Church, and they were accepted as the parties intended.

The Roman pontiffs next became the terror of dissenting Christians, and they found a ready solution of the whole mystery in applying it to them, and the Catholic Church generally. And, in turn, the Catholics appear quite as well satisfied that Luther and his Protestant followers are the great Anti-Christ predicted.

And so stands the controversy between these two great and opposing families of Christians at the present time.

In the preface referred to, Dr. Clark further says: "My readers will naturally expect that I should either give a decided preference to some one of the opinions stated above, or produce one of my own; I can do neither, nor can I pretend to explain the book; I do not understand it, and in the things that concern so sublime and awful a subject, I dare not, as my predecessors, indulge in *conjectures*," etc. He, therefore, contented himself with adding a few philological and critical notes, etc.

No further evidence is considered necessary to establish

the fact that this Book has not been fully understood, and that it is still open for investigation and explication.

Inasmuch as the writer, like most persons, is always fond of being able to show that he is in the way of high precedent, he will, in what he has to say of this sublime and mysterious Book, follow the example of all those referred to above. And as he thinks the *devil*, is the worst enemy we have to fear, he will construe that which he considers the most important revelation therein made, one only excepted, as referring to him. The most important fact from heaven revealed to men is the precious truth that Jesus Christ is still our friend, and has voluntarily undertaken the redemption of all who will repent of their sins, and accept salvation on the liberal terms proposed. Next in value stands that knowledge of ourselves, by which we may learn, and knowing, fairly appreciate the real magnitude and nature of our crimes and guilt, the awful danger to which we stand exposed, and the unsuspected worth of that salvation which has been so dearly bought, is now so freely proffered, and yet by many is so triflingly esteemed.

The first conception, in my mind, of that great and fearful truth (as is explained in the preface), was made while reading Rev. 12, all of which chapter refers, in one way or other, to the same subject, and which, beginning with verse 7, reads as follows, to-wit:

"7. And there was war in heaven: Michael and his angels fought against the dragon; and the dragon fought and his angels,

"8. And prevailed not; neither was their place found any more in heaven.

"9. And the great dragon was cast out, that old serpent, called the devil, and Satan, which deceiveth the whole world: he was cast out into the earth, and his angels were cast out with him.

"10. And I heard a loud voice saying in heaven, Now is come salvation, and strength, and the kingdom of our God, and the power of his Christ: for the accuser of our brethren is cast down, which accused them before our God day and night.

"11. And they overcame him by the blood of the Lamb, and by the word of their testimony; and they loved not their lives unto the death.

"12. Therefore rejoice, *ye* heavens, and ye that dwell in them. Woe to the inhabiters of the earth, and of the sea! for the devil is come down unto you, having great wrath, because he knoweth that he hath but a short time.

"13. And when the dragon saw that he was cast unto the earth he persecuted the woman which brought forth the man *child*.

"14. And to the woman were given two wings of a great eagle, that she might fly into the wilderness, into her place, where she is nourished for a time and times, and half a time, from the face of the serpent.

"15. And the serpent cast out of his mouth water as a flood after the woman, that he might cause her to be carried away of the flood.

"16. And the earth helped the woman, and the earth opened her mouth, and swallowed up the flood which the dragon cast out of his mouth.

"17. And the dragon was wroth with the woman, and went to make war with the remnant of her seed, which keep the commandments of God, and have the testimony of Jesus Christ."

The first inquiry which naturally arises here is, What are we to understand of that "War in Heaven?" Who are intended by "Michael and his angels?" Who by the expression, "the dragon" and "his angels?" All these questions meet us right at the threshold, and at every effort to comprehend the meaning of the remarkable Scripture here quoted.

If we can first identify, satisfactorily, the parties engaged in that "WAR," we shall have made some progress toward ascertaining what sort of war it was; whether it was real, or existed only in the imagination of St. John; and, if such war was indeed waged, we will have a starting point from which to investigate the cause and character of it, when and where it was carried on, and how and in what it resulted.

In this connection I proceed to the introduction of evidence to prove that Jesus Christ and his angels, and Satan and his, were the opposing parties so engaged.

We first meet with the name, "*Michael*," in the prophecy of Daniel. After the angel who visited the prophet had informed him that his prayers had been heard from the time they were offered up, and that he (the angel) had been promptly dispatched to his comfort, the angel said to him: "But the prince of the kingdom of Persia withstood me one and twenty days: but, lo, Michael, one of the chief princes (or as others render it, "THE FIRST PRINCE") came to help me."—Dan. 10: 13.

Let it be borne in mind, that the first we hear of *Michael*, by that name, he was actively engaged on the side of God's chosen people, and in opposing the evil machinations of "the prince of the kingdom of Persia," by which description Satan is unquestionably meant.

In the twenty-first verse we read: "But I will shew thee that which is noted in the scripture of truth: and *there is* none that holdeth with me in these things, but Michael, your prince." Note the phraseology, "MICHAEL, YOUR PRINCE:" not, as before, "one of the chief princes," or, generally, a prince, or a chief prince, but he is here, with emphasis, denominated "*your prince.*"

The word rendered "holdeth," in the twenty-first verse, is by others understood as meaning, "strengtheneth himself." The latter is, no doubt, the better translation; for to *hold* with another may mean no more than to agree with him in opinion, but if one is said to *strengthen himself* with another, it must be understood to mean that one is co-operating with, and giving aid and assistance to the other. The inference then is clear, that the angel speaking to Daniel informed him that *Michael was his prince*, and, at the same time, that he was acting under the sole authority of that prince. Daniel was thereby fully informed that Michael was his and his people's prince—that he was "the first," or chief prince and power under God the Father, and that he (the angel) was commissioned and supported in his mission by a power no less than that. In all which the person, power, and office of Christ were fitly represented.

In the first verse of the last chapter of Daniel the name *Michael* occurs again. "1. And at that time shall Michael stand up, the great prince which standeth for the children of thy people: and there shall be a time of trouble, such as never was since there was a nation *even* to that same time; and at that time thy people shall be delivered, every one that shall be found written in the book. 2. And many of them that sleep in the dust of the earth shall awake, some to everlasting life, and some to shame *and* everlasting contempt. 3. And they that be wise shall shine as the brightness of the firmament; and they that turn many to righteousness as the stars for ever and ever. 4. But thou, O Daniel, shut up the words, and seal the book, *even* to the time of the end: many shall run to and fro, and knowledge shall be increased."

I present the whole paragraph, including the first four verses, so that the reader can see it all at one view, and for the purpose of calling attention to the fact that the great and final judgment is, unquestionably, alluded to by the prophet. This prophecy has been considered as referring to the destruction of Jerusalem. That it does is most likely; but many of the prophecies apply to two or more events, as all admit, and, therefore, it is not necessary to join issue with those who so construe it, to prove that it points, also, to the last judgment; for it may include both together.

Several expressions there employed are such as are elsewhere found, used in connection with the final judgment, and which apply well to it, but are wholly inapplicable to the events connected with the destruction of that devoted city. The phrase, "found written in the book," and the whole of the second and third verses, are of this sort; and the whole paragraph is strictly applicable to the great and final consummation of all temporal things.

If I am right in this, all that is said of *Michael* in this place corresponds perfectly with what is said of Jesus Christ in the New Testament Scriptures in connection with that event.

From these Scriptures a cogent argument may be drawn in favor of the identity of Michael with the Messiah.

The Jewish Rabbins, as it is said, understood the "*Michael*" of Daniel the "Angel of the Lord," who often visited the patriarchs, and the "*Messiah*" which was promised, as all referring to the same being. "And the angel of the LORD called unto him out of heaven, and said, Abraham, Abraham."—Gen. 22: 11. This was to prevent the patriarch from slaying his son Isaac for sacrifice.

In Zech. 3: 1, Joshua the high priest is represented as "standing before the angel of the LORD, and Satan standing at his right hand to resist him." Here again the angel of the Lord (or Michael) and Satan appear as adversaries.

Stephen the martyr, in his defense, speaking of Jesus Christ, said: "This is he, that was in the church in the wilderness with the angel which spake to him (Moses) in the Mount Sinai, and *with* our fathers: who received the lively oracles to give unto us."—Acts 7: 38. Thus testifying, conclusively, that Christ was the same who was called the "angel of the Lord," in the patriarchal age.

Dr. Gill, in his Commentaries on Jude 9, says: "*Yet Michael the archangel.*" By whom is meant, not a created angel, but an increated one, the Lord Jesus Christ, as appears from his name, *Michael*, which signifies *who is as God;* and who is as God or like unto him, but the Son of God, who is equal with God? and from his character as the archangel, or prince of angels, for Christ is the head of all principality and power; and from what is elsewhere said of Michael, as that he is the great Prince, and on the side of the people of God, and to have angels under him and at his command.—Dan. 10: 21, and 12: 1; Rev. 12: 7.

So Philo the Jew calls the most ancient Word, "first born of God, the archangel."

On Rev. 12: 7, the same distinguished author, after repeating very much the same, as to Michael, that he had said when on Jude 9, and reviewing several Rabbinical writers on the subject, proceeds thus: "Lord Napier thinks that the Holy Ghost is designed, who is equally and truly God, as the Father and the Son, and who in the hearts of the saints opposes Satan and his temptations; but it seems best to interpret it of Jesus Christ, who is equal with God, is one with the Father, and in whom the fullness of the Godhead dwells bodily; he is the archangel, the first of the chief princes, the head of all principality and power, who is on the side of the Lord's people, pleads their cause, defends their persons, and saves them."

See further Dr. A. Clark's Commentaries on Jude 9, and Religious Encyclopedia, Title "Angel" and "Angel of the Lord."

Matthew Henry, in his Commentaries on Genesis, says that "the original word which is translated 'LORD,' and printed in small capital letters in our Bible, is *Jehovah*, and that 'Jehovah' is the great and incommunicable name of God, which denotes His having His being of Himself." He also says that the word "Elohim," means "*a God of power,*" and "*Jehovah Elohim*" means "*a God of power and perfection.*"

We should, therefore, understand the term "angel of the LORD," wherever so found, as meaning the *angel of Jehovah*, or of God the Father. If the translators of our Bible had preserved the distinction between the words *Jehovah* and *Elohim*, by transferring the first as it is here, and as they often did into our copy, and translating the latter "God," as they did in most cases, if not in every instance, it would probably have been better; as leaving it easier for us to determine whether the Father or Son was intended. To read the term "angel of the Lord," *angel of Jehovah*, as it would then have stood, and to admit Jesus Christ as indicated both by the name of *Michael* and term *angel of Jehovah*, it will be found that what is said of the being referred to under both appellations consists with the idea that the same is intended, and agrees perfectly with what is said of the Messiah, however denominated elsewhere in both the Old and New Testaments.

By reference to Rev. 19, it will be seen that he who sat on the white horse and was called the "*Word of God*," was Christ himself beyond doubt, and of him it is said: "And he *was* clothed with a vesture dipped in blood: and his name is called The Word of God. And the armies *which were* in heaven followed him upon white horses, clothed in fine linen, white and clean."

Thus we find that in the twelfth chapter of that book, the leader of the hosts of heaven is called "*Michael*," and in the nineteenth he is called the "*Word of God*." What better evidence, as to the identity of the two, could be desired?

This argument could be protracted indefinitely; but it is hoped that what has been said, with the authorities which may be found from the references already made, will prove sufficient to satisfy all who have capacity to understand, and industry enough to read the evidence furnished them, that the "*Michael*" of the text now under consideration is identical with Jesus Christ.

The second division of the question now before us (who are intended by Michael and his angels?) is easy to answer after having shown who was intended by Michael. For, if by Michael, Christ is to be understood as the leader of the hosts on one side, "his angels" are those which follow him (Jesus Christ), the angels of God—those who "shouted for joy," when the plan for the redemption of man was perfected. The Scriptures referred to already are deemed proof sufficient of this fact, but as it is desired to establish each proposition by proof so plain that "he that runs may read," the writer begs leave to re-introduce Dr. Gill as a witness. He is a good witness, as far as he testifies for me, because he is either disinterested, or if he has any bias it is against me, as he is one of those who construe this war which is said to have been waged in heaven figuratively, and as applicable to the Christian warfare going on in this world, and considers the Catholic Church and its great head, the chief offenders and parties denounced.

After arguing in this place, that Jesus Christ is intended by Michael, he says: "And by *his angels* may be meant either the good angels, literally understood, who are his creatures, his ministers, and whom he employs under him, in protecting his people, and in destroying his enemies." And then goes on to say: "The ministers of the Gospel, the Christian emperors, Constantine and others, may be intended." The latter supposition being by him conceived probable, on his hypothesis that the Roman empire was the seat of the war. For the purposes of the present argument, however, his testimony is as valuable one way as the other, for whether the one or the other class of angels is intended, he insists that the angels of Jesus Christ are those who were so engaged under *Michael.* If, then, that rebellion occurred before the creation of the world, of course, the holy angels of heaven are they that were so employed in the service of Michael, or Messiah, or by whatever name he may be called; and it is utterly inconsistent with other facts plainly taught in the Bible that it should have occurred since.

We are next to inquire who are meant by the expression, "and the dragon fought and his angels."

Those who have gone out of the Bible in quest of some explication of what they esteem a great mystery, that the word "dragon" should have been used here, have, as frequently happens with those who travel narrow paths of dark nights, brought themselves to grief. One of whom, in his midnight rambles in search of something that would fill his strained imagination of the sort of beast it was, had the ill luck, as Don Quixotte would say, of "an adventure" with a *myth!* There it was—of vast length, proportions full, in circle coiled about, his color red, his crest erect, with heads just seven, a hideous crown on each—horns ten, oft counted proved the same, nor more or less—of frightful pitch and point—all which he saw, or thought he did, in forest deep, one murky night; and knew it was the same. Intent his watch to keep, his game not lose ere morn, and, if he could, himself to save from harm. Still as the monster lay, stood he, nor foot dared move or noise make, save that of thumping heart, till daylight broke his spell; when lo! it proved, as he confessed himself, "an entirely fabulous beast of antiquity," having no existence whatever, but in fancy's wide domain.

Hoping to fare better, I will be careful and not stray off so far, and try to keep that narrow way along which the light of Revelation shines.

By reading the ninth verse I find something more than a myth, and which explains the matter much more to my liking; it is this: "And the great dragon was cast out, that old serpent, called the Devil, and Satan, which deceiveth the whole world: he was cast out into the earth, and his angels were cast out with him."

Here we learn all about the "dragon." We find him called by three other names, with each of which it has been our sad misfortune to have become quite familiar. He is so well described, also, by his evil practices, as "the deceiver of the whole world," and as the same who having "prevailed not" in the fight, "was cast out into the earth, and his angels were cast out with him," that the wonder is why any one should have failed to see at once what was intended by the *dragon;* and that the word *dragon* was used as emblematical of a personage no less than his Satanic Majesty.

This is but one of many instances in which great and good men from following previously conceived opinions, rather than an impartial desire to know the truth, have wasted their learning, talents, and time in vain search for evidence, both in the Word of Truth and out of it, by which to sustain some pet dogma of their own, when, of which there may not be, and, as is often the case, there is not "*the least track, trace, or remembrance*" of any such thing to be found in that holy Book.

On no better hypothesis can we account for many of the egregious errors which have, and do prevail in the Christian world.

For some doctrines and practices now accepted and pursued by Christians as wise as any and as good as the best of us, and who are esteemed as orthodox, there is not the slightest precept or example recorded in the Gospel, or fairly to be inferred from anything which our blessed

Redeemer, his apostles, or any of his immediate disciples, said or did; and which tenets and practices if tried by the test of reason would be adjudged equally unfounded. It is not my present task to designate what these fallacies are, or who it is that so teach and practice. It may not injure any of us to inquire, Is it I?

Should any kind reader, of his abundant charity, feel disposed to except to the bit of humor indulged in this connection above, I have a twofold excuse to offer. First, it is said:

> "A little nonsense now and then,
> Is relished by the wisest men."

The other is, that when we observe the blind prejudice, by which great minds are sometimes led, and see the palpable fallacies and wonderful fancies into which they fall, it is so hard to withhold the cutting blade of ridicule, or sharp point of sarcasm, that we may pardon a harmless and affectionate touch of burlesque, even if indulged at our own expense.

So much is bearable. But no countenance should be given to anything like bitterness of feeling in the discussion of theological questions, whether it appears in the way of sarcasm, ridicule, burlesque, or otherwise, except it be in extreme cases, and then used strictly in self-defense. Some think it right "to fight the devil with fire," and, if fight he will, and with a weapon not less hot, we have no choice but run or meet him with his own.

But, begging pardon for having digressed so far, I return to inquire, what we are to understand as intended by "*his angels.*"

The text says: "And the dragon fought and his angels."

On this last division of the question, I can conceive of no line of argument which could be pursued, of no authority which could be read, if written expressly to suit this occasion and in the plainest style known to rhetoric, which would render an answer more clear, full, or satisfactory than does the Inspired Word now under examination. The plain, natural, and, as I entertain no doubt, the true meaning, as to who or what his angels were, is the literal one which first strikes the mind of every one on reading it. The very way in which the terms, "dragon," "serpent," "devil," and "Satan," are used in the ninth verse, is proof sufficient to any one except those who are "so blind they will not see," that these names all apply to the same being, and that the party so indicated is the deceiver of the whole world, who was once in heaven and warring there, and who "was cast out into the earth," and is known here by various names, but by no other so common as the *Devil* and *Satan*. This being so, it is no less plain who his angels were. They were those who followed his lead in that celestial war, and who likewise, failing of success, were cast out with him into this world.

These Scripture truths suffice to identify those poor, misguided, deceived, lost, and ruined creatures of a God, who is full of compassion for all His penitent, tho' erring souls, as they who were once holy, happy, and free angels of light, rejoicing about the throne of heaven. And who, for and on account of having participated in that diabolical rebellion, were justly driven away—far, far away—from the pure and lovely place where the God of, peace and love abides; and who are now here with us on earth, and known as demons, devils, and spirits damned.

It appears to be pretty generally conceded that *pride* and consequent *envy* were the sins into which Satan fell; and that opinion is well sustained by the Sacred Scriptures. I will, therefore, not stop to argue this point, but content myself with assigning that as the prime cause of all our misfortunes. As to their present condition and future prospects, the relations existing between us and them in this world, and why we, who were created pure and good, were placed here with and subject to be contaminated by the vile touch of Satan and his followers, who had already proven him and themselves unfit associates for such confiding innocents as, before the fall, our first parents were, etc., many questions present themselves to every thinking mind, and which are worthy the most serious consideration;

but this is not the time or place to argue them. Of such are they which follow:

If they for punishment were sent, which never was to cease,
Why keep them here, midway so long? For they must go at last.
What kith, or kin, are they of ours? and why together bound?
There's room enough in hell and earth for each a home to find.

Why Michael them expel from heaven, Messiah save us here?
As they and we one Christ will judge, and that at the same bar.
When God man made why put he not them on yonder fair moon,
Or other orb, a safe retreat, where Satan could not come?

Why leave them here, to sin exposed, if sin they ne'er had known;
Where Satan, far more arch than we, at will with us could roam?
Why not give us the seats they left unoccupied in heav'n,
And leave him here with them alone who out with him were driven?

Or, if for hell we were create, in fire to ever burn,
Why not us salamanders make and put us near the sun,
On Mercury's more fitting disk, when our career began?
Then we had been, by heat, prepared a happy race to run.

And, last of all, but not the least of these dark questions put,
Why they and we, so much unlike, to the same hell commit?
Were we and they one and the same, these things would all be plain,
And if you knew that to be true, would you not loud exclaim:
"O carry me back, O carry me back,
To" (*heaven's happy*) "shores!"

CHAPTER VIII.

Same Subject Continued--This Scripture to be Literally Construed—Mysterious and Figurative, yet True—So Construed Consists with other Scriptures—Satan known by various Titles—Of Fallen Angels—Tartarus, What and Where—Hades—Hell—Nature of that War—General View of Rev. 12—Double Interpretation of Emblems—Persecution—Now restrained by Law and how at present carried on.

If the evidence offered in the preceding chapter be considered as sufficient to establish the identity of the parties engaged in that celestial warfare, as insisted there, it will be found an easy task to satisfy the reader that the narrative under consideration is a faithful and true history of "*War in Heaven*" (Rev. 12: 7 to 17), and that, although brief, figurative, and mysterious, we are to accept it in its most literal sense.

That it is brief, if literally true, will be conceded by all. Why an event fraught with such momentous consequences should have been related in so few words is, at first view, hard to comprehend; but if we reflect carefully, and compare the manner in which this revelation is made with the mode adopted to communicate other facts of the first magnitude, those connected with the great and final judgment for instance, we will find that we are as fully informed of the particulars of that "War in Heaven," as we are of those which relate to the judgment; and many other things of vast interest to us in our present critical condition.

It is also involved in great mystery, but not more so than are many other of the most precious truths related in the Bible, and which are accredited as true by all Christians.

The language and terms employed are eminently figurative, not more so, however, than we often find used by our Savior himself, when with us in person, in his favorite and sublime method of teaching by parables.

We must not, therefore, discredit this part of God's revelation to men for any of these, or similar reasons, and refuse it credence in its most literal interpretation, if we find it, in that sense, consistent with both natural reason and everything else which is clearly taught in the Sacred Scriptures.

Is this wonderful chapter, when literally construed, consistent with the other Scriptures?

Let us examine this question by comparing this with a few other facts which are elsewhere plainly taught in the Bible. In this investigation we must constantly bear in mind, that by "*Michael*," Jesus Christ is intended, and by the "*dragon*" Satan is represented; and that Satan and his angels were "cast out into the earth."

What do we next hear of them? In the form of a serpent figuring before Eve in Eden, Satan first makes his appearance to our race. From then till now he has been, by one name or other, the acknowledged leader, chief head and prince of devils. In Eph. 2: 2, he is called "the prince of the power of the air." He is often called "the prince of this world," as in John 12: 31. He is the same that was sometimes called by the Jews, "*Beelzebub*," but by the Savior, Satan. (See Mark 3: 22 to 26.) Of that great apostate much is said by the New Testament writers; and if we make the search to which the subject is entitled, we may learn a great deal about "his angels," that were "cast out with him," from the same Scriptures.

St. Jude says: "And the angels which kept not their first estate, but left their own habitation, he hath reserved in everlasting chains under darkness unto the judgment of the great day."—V. 6.

In his second general epistle, 2: 4, the apostle Peter, speaking of the certainty and severity of the punishment of the wicked, says of them: "For if God spared not the angels that sinned, but cast *them* down to HELL, and delivered *them* into chains of darkness, to be reserved unto judgment." Speaking of the final judgment the Savior said: "Then shall he say also unto them on the left hand, Depart from me, ye cursed, into everlasting fire, prepared for the devil and his angels."—Mat. 25: 41.

The word translated *hell* in the above quotation from Peter, is neither of the Greek words *gehenna* nor *hades*, which are usually translated *hell*, but a name, and should have been rendered *Tartarus*. Why it was translated *hell*, I can not conceive. The word *Tartarus*, it is said, occurs nowhere else in the New Testament; but it is one which was often used by the old Greek and Latin poets.

Dr. A. Clark says: "The ancient Greeks appear to have received by tradition an account of the punishment of the 'fallen angels,' and of bad men after death."

Tartarus is the name of the place or condition to which they supposed such *fallen angels* and the souls of bad men were sent or held. They do not appear to have had any clear or distinct idea as to where that place was; but they all seem to agree that it was somewhere on, in, or under this earth. Hesiod speaks of it as "Black *Tartarus*, within earth's spacious womb." Of Homer's description of it Pope says:

"No sun e'er gilds the gloomy horrors there;
No cheerful gales refresh the lazy air;
But murky *Tartarus* attends around."

The explanation of the fable of *Tartarus* by the Abbe Banier will reflect much light upon the question, as to the true sense and meaning of the word Tartarus as there used by St. Peter. He says: "The Greeks regarded the places situated to the east of them as higher than those which lay to the west; and hence they placed heaven in the former and hell in the latter."

According to his notion, the earliest Greeks placed their hell either in Spain, the residence of Pluto, or in Italy, countries situate to the west of them, and at that time but little known."—See *Watson*, *A. Clark*, *Lempriere*, and *Bickersteth.*

Without such explanation, as all must see, Peter is made to differ sadly with what is said in Revelation and by Jude, as to the place where and condition in which the *fallen angels* were at first sent, and are now retained; and to appear as inconsistent or unmeaning, in what he says of them himself.

In Rev. 12, they are represented as simply having been cast out "into the earth," without then saying anything more of them. Jude adds, that they are "reserved in everlasting chains under darkness unto the judgment of the great day;" and Peter is made to say that they were cast "*down to hell*" at once, as the language used fully implies, and then further to add, "and delivered them into chains of darkness, to be reserved unto the judgment."

If they were committed to hell then, for what good reason could they have been "*reserved unto the judgment?*" We must do that divinely inspired and faithful apostle more justice than to charge him with such error of faith or ignorance of the proper use of terms. The word "*Tartarus*" was in common use, and its meaning well understood in his time, as all classical readers well know. It is but fair, therefore, to presume that he employed that term in its usual sense; and by *Tartarus* he intended the same place or condition usually called *hades.* And that our translators misconceived his meaning as to where the fallen angels were sent, and hence, most innocently, made him say they were sent directly to *hell:* the place prepared for the final reception and eternal punishment of "*the devil and his angels;*" whoever at the time of the judgment for which they are reserved, may be found to be "*his angels,*" whether they or we, or both, or only part of each be so adjudged.

If those who translated our Bible had ever conceived the idea that any mercy whatever was to be shown those rebellious spirits, they would not have done Peter's letter the violence they so did. But they would have understood why it was that although it is so often repeated in the New Testament writings, in one form of words or other, that there is a place called *hell*, prepared for the ultimate reception and punishment of the devil and all other sinful and impenitent spirits of this world, yet neither St. John, Jude, Peter, nor any other sacred writer has, anywhere, said that the *fallen angels* were sent there. It is not only true that none of them have so said, but that they all agree that they were sent down into this world, and that they are *reserved* for the final judgment, at which we will be held to account for all our evil doings, although judged in great mercy.

The same Jehovah made them that made us. He left us all free to observe his laws and stand, or violate them and fall.

They sinned and fell, and so did we. Are we by nature better than they who were once angels of light? We hope for mercy, yet deny it them! So write and speak our great divines, since inspiration ceased; yet not a word so cold to them has ever prophet spoke. Reader, is this true? But more of that anon.

Let it be borne in mind that the point now under consideration is, whether the account of "War in Heaven" is to be literally construed. It was to aid us in this investigation that the preceding quotations from Jude, Peter, and Matthew were made. Giving to them a literal interpretation, and substituting *Tartarus*, in Peter, for *hell*, and reading them in connection with the brief history of that war, we will find the following a fair summary of the whole, to-wit: That there was, at some time, a great rebellion in heaven; that the opposing leaders in the war, which grew out of it, were Michael and Satan, the former of which headed the faithful, and the latter the rebellious hosts; that Satan, having failed of success, was, with all his followers, cast out of heaven, and down to this world; that he and they were not then sentenced to the punishment due for their disobedient and rebellious conduct, but were confined here safely to await a general and final judgment, which is yet to come; and that then Satan and all his angels, including wicked men, with those who were cast out of heaven with him, will be adjudged and required to depart "into everlasting fire, prepared for the devil and his angels."

When that war was, where that place is, or when it was "*prepared*," we are not fully informed, it is true; but the truth of the leading facts above mentioned, no one can deny who admits that the Bible is true.

If such "*War in Heaven*" had no real existence, and what is said of it in the Apocalypse was intended only as a figurative prophecy of the contentions which should arise in the Christian Church in this world, or between Christians and pagans, and that the Roman empire is the "*heaven*" referred to, as has generally been held by Christian writers, it would be found difficult to account for many other facts which all admit the Scriptures do teach. Take the three passages, for instance, copied above from Jude 6, Peter, and Matthew. What could Jude have meant by "the angels which kept not their first estate, but left their own habitation, he hath reserved in everlasting chains under darkness unto the judgment of the great day?" To what angels could he have had reference, but those who were cast out with Satan? To what judgment were they "*reserved*," if not for that appointed for Satan and his angels? To what other "*angels that sinned*" had Peter reference? If there were others, when and in what did they sin? Why are they held up for the same judgment that awaits us? From what Jude and Peter say about it, there is no evidence that the dragon, serpent, devil, or Satan were in any way complicated in their sins; if not committed at the time of that rebellion, then why are they subject to be cast into that "everlasting fire prepared for the devil and his angels?" And again, all Christians believe there are fallen angels, lost spirits, and devils. When did they fall? What sin did they commit? Why have we no account of their fall in the Bible? And what scriptural evidence have we of the nature of their sin, or of the complicity of Satan with them, if it is not that found in Revelation? If there really are wicked spirits—fallen angels—devils confined in this world with us (as all admit there are), it is, at least, desirable that we should know it; then are we to believe that such is the case, and that no revelation has been given us directly concerning them? when at the same time we find recorded in God's Book, a plain, simple, and, in substance, sufficient narrative of all the material facts connected with their rebellion and fall, if we could be permitted to accept it as literally true. And must we reject that as but little better than an idle fable, a mere allegory, and believe, nevertheless, that the very facts there related are in substance true?

To some minds it may be thought reasonable to do so, but I freely confess that I can not understand that sort of philosophy. I think it more reasonable to receive what the angel revealed to St. John as true, in letter and spirit, and am sure that it better accords with other parts of the Sacred Scriptures so to construe this. I feel more safe when I find my faith consistent with both reason and revelation, than I should in laboring to prop up a rickety old dogma which does not consist with either.

While I insist on a natural and literal construction of this Scripture, I do not wish to be understood as saying that it is free from figurative form of expression. It is, on the contrary, highly figurative. What I wish to say is, that although figurative, it is not the less true. What is said of Satan, for instance, when spoken of as "a great red dragon," is entitled to as much credit as if expressed in any other manner of speech, *provided* he is the party intended by the emblem.

The expression, "*And there was war in heaven*," must be understood as, in some degree, figurative. The term, "*war*," was used to convey to us an idea of the character of the accusations, strifes, and rebellion which occurred there, and which resulted in the expulsion of those who originated and participated in them. We are not required to believe that such bloody conflict was witnessed in heaven as those at Thermopylæ, Waterloo, or Gettysburg.

That was one of those events of which we must be content with such information as God has been pleased to give us; and inasmuch as we are interested in it, we should feel grateful for the knowledge we have, and believe that just as much has been revealed as it is best that we, in our present condition, should know of that first, great, and awfully calamitous warfare.

Having, in the preceding chapter, endeavored to prove the identity of the two chiefs and leaders in that heavenly contest, with those who head the two great armies in the Christian warfare which is now progressing in this world, and to show who are intended as the "*angels*" of both Michael and Satan; and having insisted in the preceding pages of this chapter on a fair, natural, and, in the main, literal reading of the Apocalyptic account of the "WAR IN HEAVEN," it is desired now to give but a brief, bird's-eye view of the other most remarkable features of that mysterious chapter, and with that close what I have to say under this head.

1. "And there appeared a great wonder (*or sign*) in heaven; a woman clothed with the sun, and the moon under her feet, and upon her head a crown of twelve stars."

By the woman we may understand the Christian Church as represented. She was "clothed with the sun, and the moon under her feet." As the moon is the lesser light and the sun the greater, so may the moon here represent the Jewish dispensation of rites and ceremonies, on which the Church of God stood, and the sun, the more bright and glorious light of the Gospel with which the (woman) Church was then being and thereafter to be clad.

The "crown of twelve stars" is a beautiful emblem of the Gospel dispensation, with Christ, as the crown, sitting on her head, and his twelve apostles as the first and brightest stars of that royal diadem.

2. "And she being with child cried, travailing in birth, and pained to be delivered."

This verse, most likely, refers to the period of, and that immediately preceding, the birth of Christ, and, if so, the "*woman*" in the emblem represents, not only the Church, but the virgin Mother of Christ, her great head. This view may be thought a novel one; but that is not material, if it is well founded. There is nothing unreasonable, or contrary to what is said by the prophet in it.

By reference to the seventeenth chapter of the same book, it will be found that the angel gave to John two interpretations of the "seven heads and ten horns" of the "scarlet colored beast," on which the woman sat, which are as distinct from each other as those proposed in this case. This is suggested not because it is the only, or a rare instance of such double meaning of the same emblem, but because it was given in a kindred illustration and is found near at hand. The prophecies abound with instances of two or more meanings intended by the same words or figures.

In the fifth verse, we are informed that she was delivered of "a man child," who was to rule all nations, etc., and that "her child was caught up unto God, and *to* his throne." In the view suggested no doubt is left as to who the "*man child*" was. All that is said of him applies to Michael, as the Messiah, and to no other.

3. "And there appeared another wonder (or sign) in heaven; and behold a great red dragon, having seven heads and ten horns, and seven crowns upon his heads.

4. "And his tail drew the third part of the stars of heaven, and did cast them to the earth: and the dragon stood before the woman which was ready to be delivered, for to devour her child as soon as it was born.

5. "And she brought forth a man child, who was to rule all nations with a rod of iron: and her child was caught up unto God, and *to* his throne.

6. "And the woman fled into the wilderness, where she hath a place prepared of God, that they should feed her there a thousand two hundred *and* threescore days."

The "*dragon*" with his "seven heads" and "ten horns" is evidently an emblem of the devil. In addition to what I have already said about that, I will invite a careful reading of what is said of that monster. He stood before the woman anxious to destroy her child; that "child" being our Savior, Satan, of all others, would have been the most solicitous for his destruction. From the seventh and following verses (copied in the preceding chapter), we learn that he is the same demon who had previously fought against Michael in heaven, and been by him driven out into the earth, and that he was actually called, and known by the several names, "*the dragon*," "*the serpent*," "*the devil*," and "*Satan*." He is also said to have been overcome "*by the blood of the Lamb*;" and is represented all through, not only this chapter, but the whole book, and by the different names, "*dragon*," "*Satan*," etc., as the enemy and persecutor of Christ and his Church.

His seven heads, ten horns, and seven crowns were most likely indicative of so many and different instruments of his opposition to Jesus Christ and the Christian Church; and may also have referred to the seven hills on which Rome was built—the ten horns to the ten provinces into which heathen Rome was divided, etc., as has been generally understood.

"And his tail drew the third part of the stars of heaven, and did cast them to the earth." If these words followed immediately after the close of the ninth verse, it would be easy to form an opinion of their meaning, whether true or false. By the "stars of heaven" the angels of God are, in most, if not in all instances, to be understood. It may be properly applied as if found there. The prophets have not generally spoken of events in the same order in which they are to occur. In this Book, as well as older ones, a different order is pursued. Remarks are made which apply to the final judgment, as is generally conceded, before others which have reference to the destruction of the city of Jerusalem. But as this inquiry, although an interesting one, has no necessary bearing upon the subject of this work, I will pass on.

All the other verses down to the tenth have been noticed already. 10. "And I heard a loud voice saying in heaven, Now is come salvation, and strength, and the kingdom of our God, and the power of his Christ: for the accuser of our brethren is cast down, which accused them before our God day and night."

This was a triumphant song of rejoicing at the success

of Michael and the faithful angels in driving away Satan and his envious and malicious followers, who brought false accusations before God against them continually. Peace was again restored in heaven.

11. "And they overcame him by the blood of the Lamb, and by the word of their testimony; and they loved not their lives unto the death." That is, *they* who were driven out with *Satan*, overcame *him* by the virtue which was given in the intercession, crucifixion, and resurrection of Jesus Christ; and by their persistent "*testimony*" to their faith in him, even in the most cruel and bloody persecutions which Satan could excite against them. Well may it be said that they loved not the miserable lives which they lived in this world of devils "*unto the death.*"

In the twelfth verse, the heavens and they that dwell in them are again invited to rejoice at this second victory of Christ over his and our enemy. A glorious victory, was it not! And there is yet rejoicing in heaven over every sinner that repents and turns to Christ.

When the devil was cast down to earth, great sympathy and anxiety are expressed for the inhabitants of the "earth and of the sea." This was in anticipation of the fiendish hinderances Satan would throw in the way of those who might repent and seek pardon for their sins; and of the evils which the fall of man would bring upon all animate creatures in this world. And, as considered in reference to the time when this revelation was made, it applied to the then existing state of things here. For that, there was certainly sufficient cause, as the results have proved.

This verse furnishes another striking instance of an event of later occurrence being mentioned after one of a much earlier period. It is certain that Satan was in this world, actively engaged in his work of deception and death, long before the crucifixion, or the persecutions of the Church afterward.

13. The persecution of the "woman which brought forth the man child," by the dragon, of course refers to the persecutions of the Church by the instigation of the devil, if

the views previously expressed, as to the "*dragon,*" and the "*woman,*" be correct.

14. This is most likely an allegorical expression, and by the wings given the woman, on which she might fly into the wilderness, etc., it was probably intended to represent the safe conduct, which God would, by His providence, furnish His people, that they might escape from the torments of the persecutions at Rome, and, it may be, from other populous cities also, into the more sparsely settled and remote districts of country, where they would be "*nourished*" by the same divine Providence, "*from the face of the serpent*"—that is, from the presence and power of the cruel emperors, and others who were used by Satan as his ministers.

15. As was casually mentioned in a former chapter of this work, by the water which the serpent cast out of his mouth after the woman, we are to understand the persecutions of Christians by each other, which arose soon after they were delivered by Constantine and others from the power of paganism. This has been the most efficient means that Satan has yet found by which to obstruct and hinder the onward march of the Christian Church to that perfect triumph which still awaits her. Had Christians loved each other, and exercised that charity which the Apostle Paul *tried* to teach them, one toward another, the work of Christianizing the world would, long ages ere this, have been completed. But O! how sadly different has been, and is now, the manner of Christians. How many sects have we to-day, and who, in many, very many instances, are not only cold and indifferent to each other, but even misrepresent, traduce, envy, and (as I fear sometimes) hate one another! It is painful to admit the existence of such feeling between those who profess to be the followers of the meek and lowly Jesus in this late age of the Church; but it is a truth well known, and is often adverted to by the more consistent adherents of Satan, to the great detriment of the Church of Christ. This pen would have been the last to record such disreputable fact, were it not well known to, and so used by the enemy already; and it is now

done with the humble hope that some good may come of it in modifying the evil complained of, if nothing more.

16. "And the earth helped the woman," etc. By the "*earth*" here we are to understand the powers of earth, or the political government which "*helped the woman*"—the Church. God in His wisdom and tender mercies saw fit to interpose the strong arm of civil power to put a stop to the fiendish barbarities which were being so unmercifully, so frequently, and upon such vast numbers, inflicted in the most civilized and populous nations and countries.

But for such *help*, He only knows what would have been the consequences, or the present condition of the Church.

Is the spirit of persecution yet dead? I will not attempt to answer this question, but must say, I have no desire to see a practical test applied by the repeal of all laws preventing its exercise.

17. When the devil saw himself so completely overreached and disarmed by the laws of so many and such powerful people, preventing his favorite amusements, he "was wroth with the woman, and went to make war with the remnant of her seed, which keep the commandments of God, and have the testimony of Jesus Christ." Finding himself so crippled, and his plans so perfectly thwarted in the rich fields wherein he had reaped such abundant harvests, he went out into the rural districts, mountain fastnesses, and less civilized countries, whither they had fled for safety, there to persecute, by whatever means he could find, the few scattered and defenseless Christians inhabiting such localities.

This chapter, as it will be observed, covers the whole period from the rebellion of Satan and his hosts in heaven, and their descent to this world, to *the present time*, and closes, leaving the state of the Church just as it is to-day. It may now be considered, therefore, as a *revelation* of things that are past, as distinguished from a prophecy of things to come.

The same subjects, it is true, are referred to, and in various ways, both in the chapters which precede and follow after the twelfth, but it is rather singular that (in a writing which covers so many subjects, and in which revelation and prophecy are so mingled together, and each is so mixed up as to render it next to impossible for us, in some instances, even to classify them satisfactorily, to say nothing of the difficulty of correctly applying the latter) one chapter is found to consist of revelation only, or prophecy fulfilled, and that concerning but one train of events.

This is truly a wonderful Book; one out of which he that "is instructed unto the kingdom of heaven, bringeth forth out of his treasure *things* new and old."—Matt. 13: 52.

"The mandrakes give a smell, and at our gates are all manner of pleasant *fruits*, new and old, which I have laid up for thee, O my beloved."—Cant. 7: 13.

CHAPTER IX.

Subject Stated—Covenant of Redemption—Made after the Fall of Angels—Why after that—For whom Made—For the Lost or New Creatures?—Proof of such Covenant—Vicarious—Christ Representing Man—Terms Liberal and Prudential—Will be Approved by the Lost—Made before this World—Hermas Clear—Sustained by Paul and others—Devils knew Christ—Kingdom Prepared for the Faithful, and When—Part of the Covenant Scheme—The Mission of Messiah—A Question Propounded.

WE have now reached our fifth proposition, which is: "That after they were so '*cast out*,' a covenant of grace and mercy was made between the Father and the Son, in and by which it was provided that the Son should follow after those lost spirits, and offer them, on specified terms, pardon and restoration to that holy estate from which they had fallen."

If such covenant was made at all, we must believe it was done after the fall of those for whose benefit it was designed; for previous to that time they had no need of such special and extraordinary grace. And it will not do to say it was made before their apostasy and in anticipation of it, as that would involve the Deity in the imperfection of entering upon a work which was then wholly unnecessary, and which never would have been required, if He had seen fit to interfere in the matter *at that time.* For it would have been quite as easy for Him to have prevented their fall, before they had gone so far in sin and rebellion (for which purpose a simple act of His will would have been sufficient) as to have suffered them to go on and on, in their downward tendencies, until they had worked out their own damnation and eternal ruin, without the costly redemption which was, in pursuance of that divine covenant, afterward purchased for them. We had as well say that such covenant was made before the creation of the angels who fell, as that it was made before their fall, for if their redemption was provided for before its necessity arose, and if that is the plan on which the great Architect of the universe works, we can see no good reason why all his work was not finished when it first began. The God revealed in the Bible has all power and wisdom, including prescience and perfection in all His attributes. He could, therefore, have made all His rational creatures so perfect that they never would have violated His laws. Could He not? But He did not so make them. This *we know*, if He made us; for we are but poor erring creatures, as the same holy Book teaches and our own observation proves.

Foreknowing that they would apostatize as they were, and not having made them more perfect, so as to prevent it, if He intended to permit them to fall away, as they did, and then to redeem them as He (to some extent and on some terms) has done, why could He not have done all that He intended ever to do for their redemption, and for any and all other purposes, at the same time? Had that been His plan, He could have done all His work "in the beginning," and had one eternal Sabbath of rest from all His works, running through that vast eternity spoken of by all the sacred writers, but of which our limited capacity can form no just conception. But did He do so? All nature, with one euphonious voice, cries aloud, No! and Inspiration, from Genesis to Revelation, echoes back the sound, No! no! Our blessed Savior says: "My Father worketh hitherto, and I work."—John 5: 17. As, then, the great Creator is still at work, and as He is *a perfect workman*, we will presume that He progresses regularly and systematically with all His work, never failing to do any thing at the right time, and doing nothing out of its regular order, and that He sits happily in quiet and ease, on His high throne in heaven, observing with His "all-seeing eye," every motion of the vast machinery which He has set at work; and through His own chosen and effective agents and instrumentalities, directs all things continually, as the perfection of His wisdom and plenitude of His power may, from time to time, and at all times require and enable Him to do; and never failing to carry into effect all, or any, of His divine schemes.

If He so progresses with perfect system and success, we may not suppose that He went so far ahead of the designs which He had marked out for Himself, as to redeem those which were not lost. But some one may inquire what evidence have we that any redemption has been prepared for those fallen angels? To such a question my answer would be, if that had not been done, and we were newly created beings, the argument applies to us with redoubled force. For if the Bible be true, and our souls are procreated as are our bodies, as is generally believed, a divine covenant was made for our redemption, thousands of years before we had any sort of real being whatever. Or, if the souls of all men were created when Adam was, as some think, or, if they are created each a new creature, when the body is prepared for occupation, as others say, in either view, that divine intermundane covenant was entered into for our restoration, not only before our fall, but really before we were created at all; and when it would have been just as easy for our Creator to have made us above temptation, as to have made us fallible, and then to have put us directly under the influence of the devil.

Some may think that such are the facts of the case, and yet believe that the work was well done; "*very good*," but I must confess my own inability so to understand it. This may be one of the results of my great stupidity; but if so, the Bible is so written as to be well calculated to mislead and deceive all persons of such humble capacity. That is hard to believe, however; for we are taught in that good Book, that it is the province of Satan *to deceive*, and of God *to instruct*.

Then, was there any such covenant? Let us see what the Scriptures say about that: "Behold, I will send my messenger, and he shall prepare the way before me: and the Lord, whom ye seek, shall suddenly come to his temple, even the messenger of the COVENANT, whom ye delight in: behold, he shall come, saith the Lord of hosts."—Mal. 3:1. The messenger mentioned first in this verse is evidently John the Baptist, but that, by him who is introduced as "the Lord whom ye seek," and described as "THE MESSENGER OF THE COVENANT," Jesus Christ is intended, is equally clear. In Heb. 12: 24, he is called the "Mediator of the new covenant," by which the covenant of grace was intended as distinguished from the covenant of works. God said to Noah: "But with thee I will establish my covenant." —Gen. 6: 18. To Abraham, He said: "And I will establish my covenant between me and thee and thy seed after thee, in their generations for an everlasting covenant, to be a God unto thee, and to thy seed after thee."—Gen. 17: 7, Again, in the nineteenth verse of the same chapter: "Sarah thy wife shall bear thee a son indeed; and thou shalt call his name Isaac: and I will establish my covenant with him for an everlasting covenant, *and* with his seed after him." As all Bible readers know, page after page could be filled with such Scriptures, were it deemed necessary; but the above must suffice for the present.

What are we to understand by "*covenant*" in these and other like passages? With us, it means a contract or agreement, and can only be made between two or more parties, and must relate to some particular thing or things. The word is used in a different sense in the Bible. Our covenant, to be valid, must be made with the assent of all the parties affected by it, and must be mutually binding on all, or else it is void as to each.

Observe the phraseology in which that divine covenant is always expressed. Nothing like the mutual stipulations which are uniformly contained in covenants between men are to be found in them. The language is: "Behold, I will send MY messenger;" "With thee will I establish MY COVENANT;" "I WILL establish MY COVENANT between me and thee, and thy seed after thee;" "I will establish MY COVENANT with him (Isaac) for an everlasting covenant," etc., etc. These are not the reciprocal promises and obligations which are expressed in covenants between equals, and bind both parties to the same extent. It is true that conditions are in some places expressed and in others implied, on compliance with which, on the part of man, the promised blessings depend; yet unlike a breach of our contracts with each other, the consequence of non-performance by one party does not operate as a release of the other; but by failure to comply with the terms expressed, man incurs a penalty, and the possibility of non-performance by the other party, so far from being provided for, is not so much as intimated.

As communicated to man, it is called a "*covenant*" indeed, and we must admit that it was properly so called. It is not, however, spoken of as *our covenant*, *our contract*, *our agreement*, but as "MY COVENANT." Then, if it belongs to one party exclusively, why is it denominated "*a covenant?*" My answer is, because it was, and is *a covenant*. Not a contract originally entered into between the great Jehovah, as one of the contracting parties, and poor, fallen, sinning man, in person, as the other; but a "*covenant of grace and mercy*," made between God the Father as the party offended, and God the Son (the beloved of the Father), acting as the friend and agent of man, and who voluntarily took upon himself the responsibilities and painful office of Mediator between God and man, and Redeemer of those who were already lost. Hence it was that when either the Father, by his angels, or the Son, spoke to man of the beneficent arrangement which had been made for his benefit, it was called "*my covenant*." Either could properly so claim it. "I and my Father are one," says the Savior. It was the compact of each and of both, at the same time, and either could well claim it as "*my covenant*."

Without stopping to discuss all, or any, of the metaphysical and mysterious questions which have so much perplexed the Christian world, as to the unity or several existence of the Father and Son, we can readily understand why they are said to be *one*, so far as our redemption is concerned, and it is only in that regard that we are at present interested in the question of their unity. In virtue of the covenant stipulations now under consideration, they have jointly undertaken the recovery of such of our race as may deserve such divine favor when most mercifully bestowed.

In this heavenly work they co-operate with each other. The object is one, the work is joint, their interest is common, and therefore it is as natural and proper to consider and speak of them as ONE, as it is so to esteem and call a man and his wife *one*. And certainly, in this view, there was no impropriety in the Son speaking of himself and the Father as *one*, as that was the uniform way in which parties so related were spoken of, when he was here in person. Witness Math. 19: 6, "Wherefore they are no more twain, but ONE flesh." And John 1: 1, "In the beginning was the word, and the word was with God and the word was God."

Everybody knows, who knows anything, that St. Matthew did not wish to be understood as saying that a man and a woman, on the celebration of matrimonial bans between them, became absolutely merged so as to constitute but one individual being in every sense; and as thereafter constituting but one individual person, and capable of having but one soul. Nor did St. John undertake to say that the WORD, who was with God "*in the beginning*," and God the Father, were so completely *one* and indivisible as that the one could not invoke the blessings of the other, or that they could not covenant together. So to construe Matthew would be to render that remark of his simply ridiculous; and to accept that passage from John in such a sense, would put him in direct conflict with our Savior himself, and every gospel writer who has recorded anything on that subject. It may be well enough to say here, that the Savior, in speaking of the unity of himself and the Father, uses the plural verb each time: "I and my Father ARE one"—John 10: 30; and 17: 11, "That they may be one as WE ARE." Just as a man may say of his wife, or a merchant of his partner in trade.

The argument that the covenant was vicarious; and not made directly between God and man, as well as the atonement which was afterward made in compliance with it, may be strengthened by reference to the fact that the covenant relations, as communicated to Abraham (and quoted above), did not cease with him, but were to extend down to Isaac, a son afterward to be born; and through him to "his seed after him." Abraham had no right to bind, not only his son, who was yet unborn, but all *his seed* from age to age, and of every age after him, to the performance of any sort o: stipulations on his and their part, which he (Abraham) could have made for them.

In Malachi, Jesus Christ is predicted as "the messenger of the covenant." The terms *messenger* and angel are not unfrequently employed by the sacred writers as convertible and meaning the same thing. We had best, therefore, consider the term *messenger* there as meaning *angel* of the covenant.

Then, what are we to understand as meant by the coming of the angel of the covenant? Admitting that Jesus Christ was a party to that compact, and that he is intended as the "*messenger of the covenant,*" as well as by "the Lord whom ye seek," we will meet with but little difficulty in answering that question. The Messiah had been prophesied of for many long ages before the time of Malachi, and thousands of pious Jews were then confidently expecting and anxiously awaiting his advent, hoping soon to realize their deliverance from all their enemies, and the establishment of a kingdom which should stand forever. This prophecy was by them understood as an assurance from Heaven that the Lord would "suddenly come to his temple," and that all the happy consequences which they had been taught to believe would flow from his appearing with them, would soon be witnessed.

In such fond hopes and expectations they were only, of necessity, disappointed as to the nature of the kingdom he was to set up, and the enemies from whom they were to be delivered. He came as predicted; his messenger having prepared "*the way before*" him, and established his heavenly kingdom, which will endure forever. By the coming of the angel of the covenant, therefore, was meant the advent of the promised Messiah, who should fulfill all the beneficent promises which had been made from God to them from the earliest ages of the world. And Christ being that Messiah, Angel of the Lord, Prince of Peace, the Word of God, and by whatever title called, the one on whom all those prophecies centered, and one of the parties to the covenant, also, was very appropriately designated "*the messenger of the covenant.*"

Notwithstanding that covenant was so made between the Father and the Son, the latter acting as the friend and agent of man, it became at once and still is a compact between God the Father and men his creatures; binding, however, on such of us only as see fit to ratify and accept the same on the terms therein stipulated. As the Savior acted voluntarily and on his own responsibility in the matter, not having been previously commissioned by us, and thereby authorized to bind us without further assent on our part, and the Father also knowing that fact, neither would, of course, desire to hold us bound by that agreement contrary to our wishes. The obligations by it imposed being therefore provisional, and subject to be disclaimed by any who may choose so to do, no one can be prejudiced thereby. And hence, at the great and final judgment, the good faith and benevolent intentions of our blessed Redeemer will be so manifest, and the tender care which he so wisely observed, so to provide as that none could possibly be injured by his intervention, will be so apparent to all that none will feel the least disposition to complain of him, for having interceded for us as he did. On the contrary, those who may persistently reject the overtures of salvation so made them, throughout this life, and whose wretched lot it may become, on that awful day, to hear the irrevocable sentence pronounced against them, "Depart from me, ye cursed, into everlasting fire prepared for the devil and his angels," will feel constrained to bow down and confess their ingratitude to a friend so great and good as the ever blessed Jesus will have proved himself to be. All such, although overwhelmed with a sense of their own folly and madness in so doing, and in present view of the dreadful future on which they are about to enter, will, nevertheless, if for the first time, fully and freely offer their unfeigned and grateful acknowledgments to that Mediator who has, at such cost to himself, purchased for them that great salvation which they have, or may have, so wickedly refused.

And they will go down to their final abode praising God, and cursing their own folly and wickedness, and that arch *deceiver*, who led them into their original sin, and by flattering but false promises kept them aloof from their best, their only friend, who had the power to deliver them from the eternal pangs of that death which never dies.

To the support of this theory, it is not only necessary that there should have been such covenant, but that it should have been made before the creation of man, as recorded in Genesis.

I have a witness at hand, by whom I can prove the latter branch of the proposition conclusively; but the difficulty is, that his reliability has been questioned. He has been sustained, however, by such great and good men as Irenæus, Origen, Archbishop Wake, and others, and therefore I feel authorized to put him on the stand, and submit his testimony for what it is worth.

Hermas, in his second vision, saw an "*old woman*," "*walking and* reading in a certain book," which she gave him. Referring to it, he further on says: "Moreover, brethren, it was revealed to me, as I was sleeping, by a very goodly young man, saying unto me, What thinkest thou of that old woman from whom thou receivedst the book? Who is she? I answered, a Sibyl. Thou art mistaken, said he. She is not, I replied. Who is she, then, sir? He answered me, '*It is the Church of God.*' And I said unto him, Why does *she* appear old? She is, therefore, said he, an old woman, because she *was the first of all the creation, and the world was made for her.*"—Hermas Vision ii: vs. 31, 32, 33. Observe, 1. This proves that the Church was represented by a woman. So says St. John. 2. That she was created, in some sense, before the world was, because she was the first *of all the creation*, and the world was made *for her*. 3. If the Church, or the material of which it is now constituted, existed before the creation of the world, and the world was made "*for her*," and by Jesus Christ, the great head of the Church (he acting under the authority and in virtue of the power given him by the Father), it then follows, as a necessary sequence, that there was some such undertaking, agreement, or "*covenant*," between the Father and the Son before this creation.

All this may be admitted as legitimate and a necessary conclusion from the testimony as produced, but it may be replied that the witness is a stranger. We find no such name in the sacred canon. We should be exceedingly careful as to the credibility of all the testimony on which we rely in matters of religious faith, it is true. I also admit that no one should offer testimony which he does not consider entitled to all the credit he attaches to it.

This I have not done, and will not do. The testimony of a witness whom it is attempted to impeach, may be sustained, either by the evidence of those who know him well, that he is a good and truthful man, or corroborating circumstances proven by other witnesses of known and universally conceded veracity.

Having taken the liberty of offering the testimony of the meek and humble father Hermas, for the credence of those who are unacquainted with him, I feel in duty bound, in justice to his memory, to the reader, and to myself, to sustain him in what he has testified on that point. I have already referred to some of those who knew him best, and are themselves well known, and who consider him a witness whose evidence is entitled to grave consideration.

I will now proceed to the proof of a few facts and circumstances which tend to sustain the evidence of Hermas, and to do so by witnesses whose reliability will not be questioned. In speaking of the power and goodness of God, the Apostle Paul says: "Who hath saved us, and called us with an holy calling, not according to our works, but according to his own purposes and grace, which was given us in Christ Jesus BEFORE THE WORLD BEGAN."—2 Tim. 1: 9. If the grace whereby we are saved was given us by the Father, in and through the Mediator, Jesus Christ, "*before the world began*," how can it be other than true that He who gave that grace, He who was the Medium through whom it was conveyed, and we, the favored recipients of the Divine bounty, were all in being before that time?

It will be remembered that to constitute a gift, three things are necessary, a donor, a donee, and something which the one can bestow and the other receive. It may well be asked also, how and why it was that God gave us grace "*before the world began*," if we were not then in need of His grace? And how could we *need* that, or anything else, if we had no being? God, through His prophets, may have had reference to such a state of things as we are now considering, when He said: "Ye have sold yourselves for nought; and ye shall be redeemed without money."—Isa. 52: 3. If we are of those who were engaged under Satan, in that rebellion of his, it may with all truthfulness be said of us: "Ye have sold yourselves for nought." And if we are saved through Jesus Christ, it is equally true that we "shall be redeemed without money."

These things pertain to the mystery mentioned by Paul (and are worth searching out with all diligence), when he says: "And to make all *men* see what *is* the fellowship of THE MYSTERY, *which from the beginning of the world hath been hid in God*, who created all things by Jesus Christ."—Eph. 3: 9. "Who verily was foreordained before the foundation of the world, but was manifest in these last times for you."—1 Pet. 1: 20.

Note, Paul says "the MYSTERY was hid FROM the beginning of the world," but says nothing as to whether it was generally known *before that* or not. Peter says that Christ (as a lamb without blemish) "was foreordained BEFORE the foundation of the world." From all which we may infer that the things which have been "hid in God" (that is, by him concealed from us), *from* and *since* that time, as well as the most important fact for us to know, that a sacrifice for our sins was provided, were, or at least may have been, well known before the creation of Adam and Eve here. But more of that hereafter. I will, however, submit one question for the reflection of the reader just here. Christ was "in the world, and the world was made by him, and THE WORLD knew him not."—John 1: 10. Then, what does the following Scripture mean: "And in the synagogue there was a man, which had a spirit of an unclean devil, and he cried out with a loud voice, saying, Let us alone; what have we to do with thee, *thou* Jesus of Nazareth? art thou come to destroy us? I know thee who thou art; the Holy One of God. And Jesus rebuked him, saying, Hold thy peace and come out of him. And when the devil had thrown him in the midst, he came out of him, and hurt him not."—Luke 4: 33 to 36.

In support of the proposition that the *covenant* now under consideration was made before the creation of the world, a cogent argument may be drawn from the following words of St. Paul: "In hope of eternal life, which God, that can not lie, PROMISED before the world began."—Tit. 1: 2. Then God made that promise. To whom was it made? The most natural inference from this verse, considered alone, would be that it was made to man directly; but viewing this passage in connection with others already noticed, we must conclude that the apostle here refers to the "*covenant*" which was made between the Father and the Son for our benefit; and if so, we have the direct and positive evidence of that great apostle that it was made "before the world began." We are assured by the blessed Redeemer, that on the great day for which all other days were made, those who are found faithful shall receive the royal invitation: "Come, ye blessed of my Father, inherit the kingdom prepared for you *from the foundation of the world*."—Matt. 25: 34. By the expressions here used, are we to understand that the *kingdom*, which was prepared for the redeemed on earth, was made at the same time the world was or before? It could not have been prepared since, or it would not have been in readiness "*from* the foundation of the world." It certainly was not made at the same time, for we have a full account, in detail, of all that was then made, and nothing is there said about the "*kingdom*" mentioned in this text. Furthermore, if the commonly received opinion as to the nature of man is true, there was no necessity for such "*kingdom*" then; for Adam had not fallen, and was not subject to death. He was well provided for in Eden. If the theory of the writer is true, the preparation for such kingdom was a necessary part of the covenant for our redemption, and was therefore included in it. This view accords strictly with the language employed here, and with other Scriptures on the same subject, as well as with natural reason. Had we not better, therefore, so construe it?

In the ever memorable prayer of the Savior to the Father on the night in which he was betrayed, he says: "I have glorified thee on earth: I have finished the work which thou gavest me to do. And now, O Father, glorify thou me with thine own self, with the glory which I had with thee before the world was."—John 17: 4, 5. The Redeemer of the world had, as we are here by himself informed, glory with the Father before this world existed, and we also learn from the same remarks, that the Father had given him charge of the work which he was then bringing to a close; a work of no less magnitude than the redemption of those whom the Father had given him of this world. Was not the work which he had finished that of giving the "*eternal life*" which God had *promised* "before the world began?"

If so, this was done pursuant to agreement between the Father and Son; of course, one could not have assigned a work to the other, and the latter have accepted the charge and accomplished the work, without concert between them. That "eternal life" was promised "*before the world began.*" By whom was it promised? By God the Father clearly. To whom? The Son, as has been shown. For whose benefit? That of fallen man, as all believe. Where and in what condition was man then? Intimations from Revelation have been given already in answer to this question, but we hope to look into that branch of our inquiry more fully presently. It is expected that all who have examined the authorities cited in this chapter are satisfied, that after Satan and his angels were cast out of heaven, and before man was placed here, a *covenant was made for* OUR *redemption*, and in that confidence I here bring this chapter to a close.

CHAPTER X.

Covenant of Redemption—Condition of Fallen Angels—They as likely to Repent as we—Their Case Compared with ours—World Created by Jesus Christ—To Destroy the Works of the Devil—What Works of His are to be Destroyed—Lost Spirits to be Reclaimed—Who were Deceived by Satan—How far he is Chargeable—What Man is—Hopeful Future—When the World was Created—Its Perishing Nature—Better Adapted to a Temporary Use on that Account—Why it is so—What if Man had not Sinned—God never Disappointed.

Having argued in the preceding chapter (and with what success each reader is left to judge), that after the fall of Satan and his followers, and before the creation of this world, there was an agreement between God the Father and His Son Jesus Christ, by which pardon was to be offered to the fallen, on terms, I now propose to inquire whether it is true: "That pursuant to that divine covenant, and for the purpose of carrying it into effect, this world was created or adapted to its present use, and God "*made*" man and placed him here for probation."

It is universally conceded to be a legitimate mode of reasoning to begin with cause and trace it down to effect; or to start from things known to exist, and search out the producing cause. If any reliance is to be placed on the Bible writers, there was, at some time, and on some account, some sort of discord in heaven; and Satan and others, who were, previous to that time, angelic beings, were expelled from the immediate presence of God, and were put in a condition which is painful and tormenting, and where they were surrounded by the gloom of night and overwhelmed with black despair. These were all creatures of the same God who made us. They were misled, if not deceived, by the same arch deceiver who beguiled and deceived our first parents. And the Bible represents the great Author of the revelations, promises, and threatenings therein contained, as having wisdom, power, and mercy, with no bounds except those by His own divine attributes affixed to each other.

These fallen spirits are also represented as rational beings in a degree far above our own. If so, is it any less likely that they would regret their folly in suffering themselves led so far astray by a created being, such as themselves, and repent of their wickedness, committed under such circumstances, than that we shall bewail the folly of our first parents, and repent of our complicity with, on account of having descended from them; or, to put the case nearer in its true light, is it more reasonable that we, if newly created beings, should repent of our individual sins, committed in obedience to our natural desires, and under the direct and immediate influence of Satan (a being above comparison with us in wisdom and power), than that they should repent of their wickedness and sins, which were committed against their natural proclivities?

But it is assumed that God has no compassion or sympathy for them. Where do we find sufficient evidence of that? Why should His tender mercies not extend to them? They were not altogether without excuse. Adam, from whom it is said we inherit our evil dispositions, offered an excuse, which was not wholly unfounded, for his transgression. When called to account for his disobedience, he said: "The woman whom thou gavest *to be* with me, she gave me of the tree, and I did eat."—Gen. 3: 12. In that, he is sustained by one of the latest inspired writers: "And Adam was not deceived, but the woman being deceived was in the transgression."—1 Tim. 2: 14. He did not give any pretended reason in justification of himself; but owned up, like a man should, "*I did eat*," desiring the fact that his wife, whom he dearly loved, had given him the fruit, should be considered only in extenuation of his crime. He was, therefore, rather *misled* than *deceived.* That the angels who followed the lead of Satan in that rebellion were *misled*, there can be no question. And, to my mind, it is equally certain that both Adam and they were all deceived as to some of the consequences of their disobedient conduct. Sufficient evidence of that may be inferred from the fact that the penalties by each incurred would, if fully anticipated, have overawed, deterred, and prevented them from their acts of disobedience. They must, therefore, have all been, and alike, deceived by the devil. If we are a new race of beings, there are, certainly, two sets, families, or classes of degenerate backsliders and fallen creatures, who need, if we do not want, renewal, reclamation, and regeneration.

These are some of the facts as to the situation of an immense number of rational creatures of God, whether we are all of one or constitute two distinct families. A world has been created since the fall of, at least, one of these families, and is occupied by both. The question now before us is, for whose benefit was it intended?

Let us next inquire, by whom, when, and under what circumstances, other than those already mentioned, it was made.

It has been argued that after that rebellion, a covenant was made between the Father and the Son in heaven, and before the creation of this world, by which it was agreed that the Son would offer his mediation between the Father and the recusant angels who were cast out with Satan. And I proceed to show here, that this world was made pursuant to, and for the purpose of carying that covenant plan into execution, and that it was made by Jesus Christ.

If it can be shown that the Messiah created the world, and that it was not done directly by Jehovah, we will have found a strong, not to say conclusive argument, that the work was done in pursuance of the scheme of redemption embraced in that divine covenant, and for the benefit of those intended by it. Several texts of Scripture were quoted, but for another purpose, in the preceding chapter, which tend to prove that Jesus Christ, the promised Messiah, was the immediate architect of this terrestrial building, its inhabitants, and appurtenances; we will notice others; all which together, I think, will be acknowledged as conclusive as to that point.

In speaking of Jesus Christ, St. John says: "He was in the world, and THE WORLD WAS MADE BY HIM, and the world knew him not."—John 1: 10. "God, who at sundry times and in divers manners, spake in the past unto the fathers, by the prophets, hath in these last days spoken unto us by *his* Son, whom he hath appointed heir of all things, *by whom also he made the worlds*."—Heb. 1: 1 and 2. "All things were created by him, and for him."—1 Col. 1: 16. "But to us *there* is but one God, the Father, of whom *are* all things, and we in him (or for him); and one Lord Jesus Christ, by whom *are* all things, *and we by him*."—1 Cor. 8: 6. "He that committeth sin is of the devil; for the devil sinneth from the beginning. For this purpose the Son of God was manifested, that he might *destroy the works of the devil*."—1 John 3: 8.

These several passages have been selected from the large number to be found in the New Testament bearing upon this mysterious subject, and are presented at one view; so that the reader may be enabled to form a correct opinion from them, as to the true relations which exist between the Father and Son, so far as they have been revealed and comprehended by us, and which is sufficient for us to know for any practical purpose. And as much has been revealed as it was intended we should know of their divine relations, while here on probation, I preferred this course to any extended comments of my own, as the more prudent and safe for myself, if not for others. Just here are some of the *hidden things of God;* and the place where they lie concealed is sacred and holy ground, upon which our sin-polluted feet may not irreverently tread with impunity.

The following notes may, however, as I think, be safely made on these Scriptures: 1. John puts the question at rest as to who was the direct and efficient architect of this building, as will appear beyond all doubt or cavil to any one who will turn to and read the context from which the above quotation from him was taken. If read alone, it might, without any strained construction, be understood as giving the Son such full credit for this work as to deny the Father the glory to which He is entitled as the great moving cause; and in virtue of whose power, and by whose permission, and under whose instruction it was done. Our Savior was careful, however, not to detract from the Father any of the glory of the creation or the gratitude due from us for our redemption. St. John, no doubt, so understood the Son, for he, in another place, recorded the following words of the Savior: "I can of mine own self do nothing: as I hear, I judge: and my judgment is just; because I seek not mine own will, but the will of the Father which hath sent me."—John 5: 30. In teaching his disciples how to pray, he told them: "After this manner, therefore, pray ye: Our Father which art in heaven, HALLOWED BE THY NAME," etc.

That the Son should be revered as an object of our devotion, together with the Father, there can be no question. His extreme modesty and self-denial, nevertheless, forbade him so to teach directly. It is true, he spoke of himself as being *one with the Father.* But he evidently, in such remarks, had reference to the work of redemption, in which he was engaged, and of the union of purpose and common power which he and the Father had and held as connected with the mission of love on which he was sent. And he intended to be understood as using the term *one*, in that sense in which it is applied to others, having common interests or purposes, as when we say of husband and wife, *they are one.*

2. The quotations from the great apostle to the Gentiles should be construed and qualified (as is true of all Scriptures) by what he has, and other inspired writers elsewhere have said on the same subject. For instance, in one of the quotations from him above, he says of the Son: "Whom he hath appointed *heir of all things.*" From this, the apostle might be supposed to teach that Jesus Christ was to inherit all the glory due and to accrue, not only from this creation and man's redemption, but from all the mighty works the great Jehovah (by whom, and in virtue

of whose Almighty power all things were created) has ever done. Of which gross injustice that great apostle would have the best of reasons for complaining, for he expressly said: "The Spirit itself beareth witness with our spirit, that we are the children of God: and if children, then heirs; heirs of God, and JOINT HEIRS WITH CHRIST; if so be that we suffer with HIM, that we may be also glorified *together*."—Rom. 8: 16, 17. This sufficiently explains his meaning when he said that Christ had been appointed "heir of all things."

3. These authorities not only prove satisfactorily that Christ made this world, but show with equal certainty for what purpose it was created, when it is said: "He that committeth sin is of the devil; for the devil sinneth from the beginning. For this purpose the Son of God was manifested, *that he might destroy the works of the devil.*"

From this last quotation we also learn: 1. That *we sinners* are "*of the devil*"—of his followers—his disciples—his angels—such as they who were "*cast out with him.*" 2. That "*he sinneth from the beginning,*" that is, that he has been engaged in the commission of sin from the time he began his diabolical career which required his excommunication from the society of the holy and faithful angels in heaven; and that he is yet engaged in the same work of ruin. 3. And "*for this purpose*" (on that account) "the Son of God was manifested," that is, made known to us in his human form and divine attributes, "*that he might destroy the works of the devil.*"

What works of the devil are to be destroyed? Those mentioned, of course; and they are the works in which he has employed himself "*from the beginning.*" What are we to understand by the expression "*destroy* the works of the devil?" He has, so far as we are informed, created no worlds, built no cities or castles which might be burned up or otherwise *destroyed;* he has made no men or other living beings, who or which might be killed, and therefore said to be destroyed by our Savior. Then what works of the devil did Michael come to destroy? If we could ever learn to exercise the practical good sense to read and construe the Bible as we do any and all other books, we could readily conceive what *works* of Satan they are which are so to be destroyed. But we are too fond of mystification, when we read that holy book, to profit, as we should, by the plain simple statements of fact which are everywhere contained therein. And when we approach a question of the character of that before us (and which is involved to some extent in mystery), we can not accept statements of fact in the plain literal sense which is in most cases intended, but must hunt up some vague and unnatural construction which *turns light into darkness.*

If Satan has made nothing material or spiritual, which might be *destroyed*, we can not understand more as intended than the undoing something which has been done amiss; the refitting of something which he has wickedly torn down or marred, or the recovery of, at least, some of the wretched millions whom he has led astray. The Savior himself stated the object of his mission in these words: "The Son of Man is come *to seek and to save that which was lost.*"—Luke 19: 10. If we are here in a primitive, or first state of being, we must insist on a highly figurative and mysterious rendering of this apparently plain and simple statement of him who, as we have been fondly trusting, came for our salvation, or we can find no hope therein. For, if that be true, we have no interest in the atonement purchased by him, as literally stated by himself, as we were not brought into existence for near two thousand years after his time, and could not have then been *lost.*

But, if on the other hand, we become satisfied that we are of those *lost angels*, who were driven out of heaven with Satan, the plain literal meaning of the words used by the blessed Jesus is best for us. So believing, we can, with great confidence, apply all his gracious promises to ourselves, and feel rejoiced that, notwithstanding all our original and present sins, and the terrors with which we were oppressed during the long and dark night of our exile, we are now brought up from that horrid dungeon, in which we lay so long as prisoners confined, into a world of comparative light and liberty. And that we owe this divine favor to him whom we saw standing victorious on the battlements of heaven, denouncing the anathemas of an angry God upon Satan and his rebellious hosts, and to him, whom we then feared as the stern avenger of his holy Father's violated laws. We can not, therefore, doubt his ability to deliver us. O, if we could all so feel and believe, how happy we would be! Where is the human being, who understands his condition so to be, and is yet so blind to his own interest, so lost to all sense of gratitude, so far demented (even by association with the devil and his imps for more than six thousand years) as not to accept, on the first invitation, the great deliverance which Christ has purchased for us with his precious blood? This he offers as a free gift, if we will *only* repent of the sins we have committed, confess our faults, and give evidence of such our contrition, by observing the few, simple rules which he has left recorded for our guidance *back* into the immediate presence and restored favor of such a merciful God. But too much zeal has led me clear ahead of the argument, and I must return.

Taking the fact that Christ came "to seek and to save that which was lost," as our guide into the inquiring as to what works of the devil he came to destroy, and we have a starting point. And if we fail to find any other evil work that he had done, than that of deceiving and leading to overthrow and ruin certain angelic beings (then living, though lost spirits) and that which he had done, and is still doing, of deceiving our parents and ourselves, it is but natural and reasonable to conclude that he came to "*seek and to save*" those lost spirits and ourselves from his iron grasp. That would "destroy the works of the devil;" and that he could have done by the creation of this world, bringing them into our present state of being, meeting us here, and extending pardon to every one who had really been so misled and deceived by Satan, and restoring all such to the divine favor, their original purity, and celestial glory.

Angel spirits were out cast, Satan had misled them;
Our own race was also lost by his wiles in Eden.
If we are but sons of night, they sons of the morning,
Saving either were but half Satan's works undoing.

Whether such was the object of his mission or not, we may confidently affirm: 1. That in that way he would have destroyed the works of the devil. 2. That without the redemption of any one of God's creatures, who had been led into sin and rebellion against Him, by the cunning devices and artful practices of the devil, and against the unbiased desire, free will and consent of such erring spirit, whether done on earth or in heaven, *the works of the devil* WILL NOT HAVE BEEN DESTROYED. It would be no answer to this argument to say, that in this view of his mission, Christ could not succeed in destroying "the works of the devil," without the redemption and restoration of all who were "*cast out with him.*" For the devil was no more responsible for the wickedness of those who acted of their own free will, and who were wholly uninfluenced by him, than they were answerable for his defection; and, therefore, *their sins* could not, in any just sense, be said to be *his works.* And the simple fact of any one, and every one who does so, rejecting the salvation offered in this life, is evidence conclusive that he prefers the sinful course of Satan to the righteousness of Christ.

It is hard for us, I know, who are so proud, so vain, and so well pleased with ourselves as we generally are in this life, to admit that we are nothing other or better than the puny imps of the devil! But, if we rightly consider the matter, we will find that we have nothing to lose by such admission. For, if we are now lost spirits, and of the class of beings known as "*devils, or imps of the devil,*" it is not less true that we were, at one time, bright and shining lights in heaven, happy spirits, angels of God; and were received with welcome to His sacred presence, and joyfully sported about His dazzling throne. But all that consolation amounts to nothing, when compared to the glorious hope of full pardon for all our past errors and transgressions, whatever they may have been, and of final restoration to the favor of God and sweet communion with His saints and holy angels; and with the joy also of knowing, with the Apostle Paul, "that if our earthly house of this tabernacle were dissolved, we have a building of God, an house not made with hands, eternal in the heavens."

> "O glorious hope of perfect love!
> It lifts me up to things above;
> It bears on eagle's wings."

As to the time when the world was created, we learn both from the first of Genesis and John, that it was "in the beginning." What was meant by the word "*beginning*" has already been explained to my own satisfaction, whether to that of others or not. The creation of the world was most assuredly attended to at the proper time; when that was, depends on the purpose for which it was done. If for the probation of the prisoners who were held in custody for final judgment, and who on any account deserved the Divine sympathy, it was, of course, made after their fall and imprisonment, and before Adam was "*made*" and placed in the garden of Eden, *provided* he was one of those prisoners. Was this world created for the purpose of carrying into effect a "*covenant*," for the benefit of those which were lost, or for others who *knew no sin?*

Much light may be thrown on the pathway which we must tread in search for an acceptable answer to this question, by observing the nature and character of this world and of all the creatures, whether animate or inanimate found here. We will not disagree as to the ability of the Almighty to make all His works perfect and fully sufficient to serve the desired purpose; nor that all His works, so far as we have been enabled to judge of them, have been so made. To say that He had failed to carry out any of His schemes, according to His own will and original intentions, would be profanity. Would it not? To believe such a thing possible is to belie, at once and together, the Sacred Scriptures, the result of all observation and every dictate of natural reason, and to stultify ourselves. This would be going too far, even to sustain the most esteemed dogma we have. We must believe that God has hitherto, can, and ever will succeed in carrying into full and complete effect all His holy purposes, despite all the opposition of Satan or any other power. God having omnipotent power then, and foreseeing all things, we must believe His means are all well adapted to accomplish the desired end.

We find on the most careful observance of this globe itself, of man, who was put in dominion over all other living creatures here, of such animate creatures themselves, and of the trees, shrubs, and grass, everything that grows on it, and the very clouds that fly over us, that all, all are perishing, rapidly fading away. Are we too dull of understanding to learn anything from the very words of nature when she speaks out for herself, and of herself, with a clarion voice, second only to that of Gabriel's trump, which is to wake the dead at the last day!

If the world was designed to serve a temporary purpose only, it was well adapted to the end for which it was intended; but if it was made for the permanent home of Adam and his posterity, and they were intended to live forever, I can not perceive how it could have been pronounced a "*very good*" specimen of perfect work. It was a beautiful specimen of such work, if designed for nothing more than a temporary occupancy by the fallen angels, and for the purpose of extending to them an offer of reconciliation. The very fact that everything around them is rapidly dying—passing away—seems as so many living oracles, warning them that their stay is but short, and that what is done here, must be quickly done. If everything but ourselves had been of a permanent, everlasting character, a contradiction in nature would have been manifest, and which would have tended to deceive us. The plan, therefore, would have been much less adapted to the purpose intended than it really is in its ever changing condition.

Is it not, hence, more reasonable to conclude that this

world was intended to serve only a temporary use? Finding it well suited to one purpose, which, if desired, would have been a temporary one, and failing to discover any other for which it was, or probably could have been so well adapted in its perishing nature, is it not a necessary result that we must believe it was made for that use, to which all the known facts and reasonable inferences point with unerring certainty as the magnet to the pole? If so, this world must have been created for the benefit of those lost spirits, and pursuant to the plan of redemption which had already been devised and adjudged, in mercy, as right in the high court of heaven before it was made. Some who are wedded to preconceived opinions, and cling to them with a persistent devotion, equaled only by the fiendish hate which drives the devil further and further still away from his God, and from everything that is just, pure, or good, may, nevertheless, object to this mode of argument, and reply that man was destined to but a brief stay on earth, and therefore all these arguments apply as well to him as a new creature, as they do if his spirit is that of a fallen angel.

This is not the proper place for me to bring this proposition under general review, but it may not be amiss to drop a few hints, in passing, with reference to it. I am not unaware that the opinion of the Christian world, in a general sense, has been, that our first parents were originally created pure and holy, and that they never would have been subject to death but for having eaten of the forbidden fruit; and I am prepared to, and now do, fully and freely admit the truth of that proposition in its most full and literal meaning. But what of that? They did eat the inhibited fruit and died. Let us suppose they had obeyed the command of God—abstained from the deadly tree, and lived forever. What then? It is impossible for us to form a just conception of what the state of things would have been in this world by the time Adam would have become an old man, if he had lived till now, and still should live forever. I guess he would yet have been a buxom young fellow, if no one but himself and mother Eve had been allowed to remain in their neat garden home longer than their majority. The finite mind can not go out so far as to fathom the full length, breadth, and depth of *eternity*, much less to conceive of what condition things might have been in here, *afterwhile*, if the monster death had not interfered with the progeny of that first pair.

Whether the brute creation would have lived on and bred forever, but for the sin of man, is a question which I have heard debated but little; the general opinion seems to be that they would. Well, if they had, all I will say about it is, there would have been a *good many* animals here by this time. Snakes would have been plenty.

We will suppose the fruit untouched; that Adam and all his family had lived even up to the present time; all the little children who have died would have grown up to mature life, and bred and lived on, too; what would have been the present population of the world? No arithmetic can answer this question; neither can I. How could animal life have found food for its sustenance? I can not tell. As all will see at a glance, the number of human beings alone, to say nothing of other animals, would, in that case, have been sufficient to have covered the whole face of the earth, and to have piled up, one on another, mountain high; so that nothing would have saved them from starvation or suffocation, but that they could not die. This world would have been wholly inadequate to the purpose of its creation, if it was not intended that man should sin and die, as he did; and a most signal failure on the part of the Creator would have ensued. Such a mistake, if made by the most perfect tyro who ever sat on cobbler's bench, would have been looked upon as supremely ridiculous even for such an one to have made.

But it is said God knew man would sin and die, and the preparation for him was, therefore, sufficient. I admit that also. Did Adam do just what God intended for him to do? I answer, yes; others say, no. If he did that which it was desired he should not do, was not God disappointed? If he did that *only* which God intended him to do, should he have been punished for it? I answer, yes; for, although God knew he would do it, Adam was commanded not to do it, and he disobeyed the divine command, and that was sin in him; while it was just what God knew he would and intended he should do. Although Adam was doing only that which he was created to do, and was strictly fulfilling his destiny, *he did not know that fact*, and was, therefore, just as guilty, as if God had been thereby really disappointed in His great scheme of creation.

I hold that God made man and placed him here for probation; and that Adam, Eve, and Satan, all acted the part which God knew each would act in that awful tragedy in Eden, and which He intended each should take—just that much, and no more. And that if either had failed in the part assigned, God would have been disappointed, and His plans, to that extent, would have failed of success; a thing which never has, and never can occur. God is supreme, and His divine will can not be thwarted by man or devil, or all of each combined.

CHAPTER XI.

Seventh Proposition—The Soul of Man a Fallen Angel—If Taught in the Bible, why not Discovered before?—A Full Knowledge of our Condition would have Defeated God's Scheme of Probation—His Mercies Extended to the Penitent only—Some of Them may have Repented—Character of the War in Heaven—Different Shades of Guilt Probable—Revelation Progressive—Always just Sufficient—Why Secret Things should now be Revealed—Science Advancing—Revelation must keep Pace with it—If this be Error neither God nor Satan will Favor it—And why—If Truth, it will Prevail—A Safe Doctrine.

THE most important questions which it was thought best to notice, as preliminary to the main proposition, on which the theory herein presented to the Christian world depends, having been for the present disposed of, we have now arrived at the great and vital question—Is IT TRUE "That the body only was then created, '*formed*,' and the soul which was '*breathed*' into it was a pre-existent spirit—A 'FALLEN ANGEL?'"

I have endeavored, in the preceding pages, to prove that there is nothing in the Sacred Writings, or natural reason, inconsistent with this hypothesis; and from this point, propose to call attention to such Scriptures as tend to establish its truth. And, right here, a perplexing question may present itself to the mind of most, if not all, who attempt to investigate this subject. If a fact of such thrilling import is taught in the Bible, and so plainly, too, that evidences of it are everywhere to be met with in that Sacred Volume, and which consist with all else that is therein written, and one also, which more than any other, serves (as the first rays of morning light, to drive the darkness of the night) to open up to our affrighted vision a true sense of our awfully responsible condition in this life, why has it not been known, and our lives guided by that brilliant light all the time?

Before proceeding further, therefore, I propose, with the Divine assistance, to remove all difficulty arising in that direction.

This is, for us, a state of probation. All so consider it. The whole scheme was devised by the Father and Son in heaven. *There* was *wisdom* to plan *and power* to execute. Bear this constantly in mind. Failure was, therefore, impossible. Now, suppose I am right as to the nature and origin of the human soul, and that God had informed Adam and all his descendants fully of all the facts and circumstances connected with his and their history and fall, and His plans and purposes connected with their present state of being, so plainly as to admit of no mistake or doubt, would not the whole probationary scheme have proven a signal failure? If I am right, where is the sinner so hardened that he would not repent if he were placed as on Pisgah's top, and the whole panorama of the heavens above, the world around, and hell uncapped below, were at once open to his astonished view, where he could learn all for himself, as to where and what he had been, why and for what he is here, and how and on what terms he can be restored to all the bliss of the glory-world above; and why, on his rejection of such merciful pardon, *he must be* cast into the yawning gulf beneath him, "where their worm dieth not, and the fire is not quenched," there to abide forever! yes, *forever and ever!* I repeat, who, in such case, would have rejected the offered pardon?

What sort of probation (putting on trial) would that have been? Men may, and often do, deal in farce. But God, *never!*

What would we think of a temporal monarch, who should issue his edict against the crime of murder: for instance, prescribing the penalty of death against all who may be duly convicted of that heinous offense, and proceed, in the same paper, to say: "I wish all my liege subjects to understand, however, that I have no thirst for blood, but love mercy; and pledge myself now to extend my gracious pardon to all who may be so found guilty, and who will, at any time before they are executed, repent of their sin, believe that I can and will pardon and forgive them, and promise to do so no more?" Are not the cases parallel? In the one case, how many sinners is it likely would go to hell? and how many murderers would be hung in the other?

If man has ever yet committed such folly, history has failed to record it. That a Being possessed of foreknowledge of all future events, and power without limit, should have done so, no sane man will pretend.

In such case, instead of putting us on probationary ground, that which would have amounted to the same as an unconditional pardon would have ensued. If a general amnesty and full pardon of all, even the most active instigators and efficient leaders of that rebellion, had been intended, there could have been no necessity for the creation of this world, and putting us on a mere formal trial, as, under the circumstances supposed, this would have been.

We will not believe that the Divine Wisdom acted in this, or anything else, without a wise motive and benign intention. If any of the lost angels, for any reason, deserved pity, they received it. "The pity of the Lord" reaches all his penitent creatures, no matter what their fault may have been or their condition may be. We find no evidence in the Bible that the Lord does not sympathize with, or that he will not pardon any soul or spirit of His creation, who does sincerely repent of his or their sins, humble themselves, and bow down before the "*mercy seat*," and with deep contrition of soul and desire for restoration to His divine favor, seek for mercy and pardon at His throne of grace. But to the contrary, the whole tenor of that blessed Book teaches us that its divine Author is full of compassion for His rational beings, who, though they err, repent of their evil doings. And every page of the Bible beams with the resplendent light of God's undying love for all His holy or repentant creatures.

Were it not so, on what ground could the highwayman,

the midnight assassin, or he who betrays the confidence reposed in him by woman's love to her shame, hope for salvation?

Yet we all believe that by such sinners, mercy may be sought and pardon found.

If we are of those fallen angels, although reproduced here and surrounded by peculiar circumstances for a special purpose, is it not reasonable that we retain, at least some of the characteristics of our pristine nature? I think it most likely that the leading traits of our character are very much the same now that they were at the time of our overthrow. But I can not stop here to argue that question.

There can be no dispute, that if we are identical with them there must be some resemblance of what we then were in our present peculiarities. To assume no more than this, we may satisfy ourselves that all were not equally guilty in that rebellion. Then, if some were less at fault than others, may we not naturally imagine that some were so deeply involved in voluntary and premeditated guilt, as to preclude the belief that even the mercy of God could again reach them? And yet, that others may have been deceived by Satan, and betrayed into complicity with him, under such circumstances as, notwithstanding they were cast out and committed to prison for the present, with others, should excite the Divine sympathy. May not some, nay, many (when they saw the sad havoc they had contributed to make, and remembering the countless instances of God's love and kindness to them, and the manifold obligations they had been brought under to love, serve, and obey him), have gone down to *Tartarus*, not only penitent, but lamenting and bewailing their own folly and wickedness, and in such manner as to excite the sympathy of all beholders, except, perhaps, of Satan himself? But more of this hereafter.

Whatever the nature or extent of that disturbance in heaven may have been, in revealing the fact to us that such event had transpired there, the term "*War*" is used. We know what that term means as applied to the acts of men or nations, and we must infer that it was one well adapted to communicate to our understanding some just conception of that which was intended to be made known.

Many of us have had the misfortune to witness some of the realities of rebellion and war in this world; and hence, we know how such things are gotten up and carried on. To one who has been an eye-witness of these things, there is no use in saying that all who ultimately become involved in them so far as to be treated as participants, and held to answer for it in some way, and that justly too, were equally guilty, and therefore deserved the same punishment. *We know better than that.* If there is such difference in the guilt of those who are captured together in arms, and held to answer for the part each may have taken in the bloody tragedy just closed in this world, as that the guilt of one is not only above but beyond all fair comparison with that of another, there must have been some similar differences in the guilt of those who were engaged in any sort of procedure in heaven, which would be called "*War*" in revealing the circumstance to us. The very expressions used in the Apocalypse imply nothing less.

In view of all the facts and circumstances revealed and known, which should have a bearing on the mind in considering this subject, it can not be too much to assume that there *probably* were differences in the shades of guilt incurred by different individuals who were engaged in that "*War in Heaven.*" And that some may have been *cast out* on account of their complicity therein, who had not gone so far in sin and rebellion that the mercy of God could never reach them. No further concession is necessary for the purposes of the present argument. For, if we are satisfied that some *may* have still been embraced in the Divine sympathies (His *power* to save being conceded), the mind is sufficiently free from bias as that we can listen to argument tending to prove that what *may* have been, *really was the case.* And further, that God *may have* desired to extend to some such an opportunity to repent and return to him, and that this creation may have been intended for their benefit. And lastly, that the souls of men *may be* of that class of fallen angels. If a real, fair, equal, and liberal term for probation to those so circumstanced was intended, that our true condition should, during our term or trial, be to some extent concealed from us, is too plain to admit of debate.

We are met here by another question, which deserves our careful attention. If it was necessary to conceal from the world so long their true nature and condition, why discover it now?

To attempt a full and complete reply to this interrogatory would require more space than I think it best to assign it in this work, as brevity is intended.

I must content myself for the present, therefore, with offering a few general remarks, such as may be deemed sufficient to lead the mind of the reader to a correct answer, and with but little detail.

In the first place, it will be observed that men in this life are very unlike in various and distinguishing particulars. Some are more humble, others more vain and proud than the average of men; some are endowed with far greater mental capacities, and others with as much less than the middle class; while some of all classes specified, and of every grade in each, are naturally more inclined to venerate and worship the Great Creator than others. These remarks apply with equal force to men of every age and country of the world, and alike to Jews, Gentiles, Christians, and barbarians.

God has, as the great apostle to the Gentiles expressed it, "at sundry times and in divers manners," revealed Himself to men. We have the best of reasons to believe that He has, and will, in every age, and to every individual who is to be held answerable at the judgment, in one way or another, made Himself, His laws, and our relations to Him sufficiently well known, to give all a fair opportunity to know their obligations to their Maker, and the duties hence arising both to Him and their fellow-men, to enable each to choose advisedly between good and evil. In the first ages of the world, God communicated with men frequently through the medium of angels, who visited them and delivered their messages in person and verbally. He also and often advised, instructed, and warned them in dreams, visions, etc. He afterward employed the holy prophets as a common channel through which to reveal Himself to His probationers; by whom, also, He prepared the way for the introduction of Messiah and the more brilliant light of His gospel.

So that it is easy to perceive how it may be that all may have, and may have had, just that amount of light and knowledge which God saw was necessary to give each and all a fair and equal chance to avail themselves of the benefit of their probationary term.

And the Savior assured us that: "Unto whomsoever much is given, of him shall much be required."—Luke 12: 48. By reference to that chapter, it may be seen that all are to be held accountable according as each may have had more or less of the light of revelation and other blessings of this world conferred upon them. His gifts are, and will be so distributed, and the rules by which His judgments will be pronounced, so adjusted, that all will have a fair and equal trial when that grand assize shall come; and full and equal justice will be meted out to every one (but tempered with much mercy) by the impartial and infallible Judge who will preside over that august tribunal.

From the creation of the world down to the present time, the work of revelation has, in some way, been going on, and, as we are assured, will continue to proceed until the final end of the world and accomplishment of all the divine purposes for which it was made.

There are two separate and distinct classes of revelation: One of which is called *prophecy*, and was intended to be durable in its nature and general in its application, and for the benefit of all to whom they should be made known. The other is special, and designed only for those to whom they were, or are made, and perhaps their immediate families, friends, or associates to whom they should be communicated. The time for *prophecy* closed with the lives of the immediate disciples of Christ, as is generally supposed. Of this, however, there may be difference of opinion. Special revelations, for individual warning and comfort, have, as the Scriptures assure us, been made from the days of Adam to the present day, and will continue to be made down to the close of the "*Books*." The prophets often speak in figurative, sometimes in mysterious languages. This is especially true of the prophecies left of record by our Savior himself and those of the Apocalypse. Many of the old prophets predicted events running down through the whole stream of time, and can never be fully understood until they shall have been fulfilled. The New Testament prophecies also, point to events and teach lessons which will ever be transpiring and manifested to men until the return to earth of their divine Author.

The angel which appeared to the God-like Daniel (whose curiosity was no doubt excited to comprehend more fully the secret things represented by the vision which he saw and the words he had heard), said to him: "But thou, O Daniel, shut up the words, and seal the book, *even* to the time of the end, *many shall run to and fro, and knowledge shall be increased*." After the appearance of the "*other two*," and on hearing the great and mysterious words which they spoke, Daniel became so anxious to understand something more of the strange things he had heard, that he took the liberty to ask the interpreting angel: "O my Lord, what *shall be* the end of these *things?*" But he only received for answer: "Go thy way, Daniel: for the words *are* closed up and sealed till the time of the end," etc.—Daniel 12: 4, 8, 9.

From these Scriptures three sacred and pregnant facts are distinctly taught: 1. That the prophets did not always themselves understand the full import of the revelations which were made to and through them. 2. That God did not intend they should fully comprehend them. 3. That they should be better understood in future ages, and should stand as living oracles, teaching men more and more of the secret things of God "till the time of the end." That is, to the last age of the world.

The Savior was careful to impress it on the minds of his disciples, that they were not fully instructed in all things pertaining to our present state of being; and to encourage them that all the light which not only they but others after them should need, would, in due time, and in some way, be given them.

In Matt. 10: 26, we read: "For there is nothing covered that shall not be revealed; and hid, that shall not be known." See also Mark 4: 22; Luke 8: 17; and 12: 2, 3, to the same effect.

He had reference unquestionably to the important facts which are intended to be made known all in their proper time, and which have already been foretold by the prophets, himself included; but which are so mysteriously communicated, so "COVERED" up and "HID" in symbolical and other figurative language and dubious forms of expression, as to baffle all efforts on the part of the mere curious to expose their true meaning. These are the *hidden treasures, jewels of great price*, etc., which are reserved for the possession of those for whose benefit they were *covered* up and *hid away*. They are, no doubt, worth a "*great price;*" more than the banker, by his business tables, can compute.

The blessed Jesus has not left us without a friend to whom we may look, and, looking confidently, rely upon, for the fulfillment of his precious promise in reference to the heavenly treasures of which he spoke, as being *covered* up and *hid* from the sight and search of all but those for whom they were provided and so safely stored away. He says: "But the Comforter, *which is* the Holy Ghost, whom the Father will send in my name, HE SHALL TEACH YOU ALL THINGS, and bring all things to your remembrance, whatsoever I have said unto you."—John 14: 26, and 16: 13.

As to *how* the Holy Spirit was to teach, we are not here informed. But we are authorized to believe that he teaches "*at sundry times and in divers manners*," as God did of old. Nor is it material by what method he imparts his information, so that we, and all in their day, are enabled to know the sacred truths which have been withheld from those who have gone before, and are to be found uncovered and revealed to us and those who are to come hereafter. Is it asked why a fact, of the fearful import of this (if fact it be), should have been permitted to lie concealed so long, and at this particular juncture be made known? If so, it is sufficient, whether satisfactory or not, to reply that:

> "God works in a mysterious way
> His wonders to perform."

That this is a wonderful age has escaped the observation of none but the truly blind. All mankind appear to be under the influence of some great and general upheaval of nature. Advance, change, and revolution seem to be the watchwords of our era. Witness the political commotions, rebellions, wars, and revolutions which have afflicted, not only our own unhappy country, but, in a less or greater degree, the whole civilized world within the last decade.

The Christian Church, considered as one great family, has not escaped a full share of the evils arising from the all-pervading mania for change and universal spirit of disquiet, which has ruled and directed everything around her.

Notwithstanding all which, the rapid strides which have been made, within the same period, in the way of scientific discoveries, inventions, and improvements in the useful arts and sciences, have been truly wonderful.

But while this is marked, and justly so, too, as an age of advancement in science, it is equally entitled to distinction as an age of sin. "The abomination of desolation" appears to preside everywhere and over everything, the Church of Christ not excepted; and infidelity is threatening to make desolate her fairest fields and greenest pastures.

Should it be a theme for wonder, therefore, if God, in the wisdom of His pr[illegible]nce and plenitude of His grace, should *just now* manifest to this wicked and gainsaying generation, some one, or more, of the astounding facts which have hitherto (although revealed) been *covered* and *hid* from the uninspired mind of sinful man? This is emphatically *the age* of reason, as well as one of general discontent and desire for change.

There may be many as good by nature as others, who esteem the value of natural reason so highly, that they find it impossible for them to accept as true any proposition, although said, and with apparent truth, to be taught in the Bible, if, as understood by them, it is evidently unphilosophical and utterly unreasonable.

It may be true that other persons are now laboring under dark clouds of doubt and uncertainty, which amount to near the "blackness of darkness," and which arose in the same direction of those which so benighted the writer.

And if so, it may have pleased God to raise the screen, which excludes all but divinely approved light from our darkened vision a little higher, and permit us to look that much further into the things that have been concealed, and even to read a few more lines of our own dark history.

The time may have come when more Gospel light is necessary to effect the purposes intended in giving us this probation. The light of revelation must correspond with that of natural science. Evidence which may have been sufficient for an uncultivated heathen, or ancient Jew even, may now be wholly unsatisfactory to men who, though possessed of a devotional cast of mind, are nevertheless, well versed in all the learning and science usually taught in our schools and colleges, and who, withal, have been endowed, by that divine Being who made them, with reasoning powers of superior order.

If that be the case, more information may be intended, as but an act of justice to such persons, that they may be placed under circumstances which afford them equal opportunities of faith and salvation with others who have been less favored in respect to both natural capacity and mental cultivation, for, "God is no respecter of persons."—Acts 10: 34.

In view of all surrounding circumstances, it may be admitted, that in this advanced age of general learning, it is but natural to expect that new discoveries of biblical truth will be made; that more of the hidden riches of divine revelation may be brought to light. Yet it still may be a mystery to many, why, if God intended to reflect more light on the pathway which leads from earth to heaven, He did not make one of His learned Gospel ministers His instrument, by and through which to effect His benign intention.

If asked why it was not so done, I could only answer, *I can not tell.* But I can say: "*One thing I know, that whereas I was blind, now I see.*" It may, nevertheless, be true that I only "*see men as trees walking.*" If so, Satan has shown them to me, and he is entitled to full credit for the delusion. But, on the other side, if I see myself and my poor deluded fellow-men *as God sees us*, the glory is all His; for I know I am entitled to none of the praise due for such discovery.

It would not seem likely that the devil, notwithstanding his proneness to deceive, would desire to mislead us in this direction. What he would have to gain by it I can not perceive.

The only effect such error can have, if error it be, is to remove from the human mind the chief source from which the most dangerous doubts of the truth of the Bible arise, and to confirm the truth of the Christian religion.

If I am right then, as to the effect which the universal acceptance of this theory would have on the mind and conduct of men, the devil is not entitled to a tithe of the credit heretofore accorded him for shrewdness, if he has invented it or shall encourage its propagation. If an error at all, it can not, as I conceive, hurt the cause of Christ in its practical effects, but would and will, if established as true, prove seriously damaging, not to say ruinous, to that of the adversary.

This line of reasoning is, at least to my mind, one of the most convincing, outside of the Bible, in support of the theory under examination. If my views regarding it are well founded, they will, sooner or later, as God may direct, be generally adopted by the Christian world. And if I am deceived as to its foundation on scriptural evidence, and it should turn out to have been but a legitimate child of "fancy's dreary dream," it will speedily die a natural death.

The devil will not advocate it, whether true or false, because to do so could serve no purpose of his, and God will give it no countenance if false, for He hates all manner of falsehood and deception, and teaches nothing which is not true.

And if my opinion be erroneous, even on this vital question, still I am not left without consolation, for it is highly gratifying to know: 1. That if in error, I need not fear the taunts or ridicule of my fellow-men in this life, because none of them have, as yet, furnished or favored a theory which is more reasonable or scriptural. 2. I fear not the curses of any at the judgment on this account, for though damned they be, I can, with Macbeth, say, and in so saying speak the truth:

> "Thou canst not say I did it: never shake
> Thy gory locks at me."

And, which is of more worth to me than everything beside,
Christ knows that I am innocent of wish man to mislead;
That all my aim is for his good—his dying soul to save,
Hence, on God's grace can I rely, full pardon to receive.

CHAPTER XII.

The Same Continued — Scriptural Evidences — Mosaic Account Considered—Spirit Breathed into Adam one of the Lost—Man's Spiritual Eyes Closed and Memory Suspended—1 Cor. 15: *Considered in Connection with Mark* 4—*The Spirit Passes into the Body as the Grain of Corn into the Stalk, and so Becomes Identified with it—That the Soul is not a Newly Created Essence, but a Fallen Angel, Revealed to St. Paul—Never Spoken of by Christ but in Parables.*

WE will now refer back to the biblical history of the creation of man, and see what we find said there as to the soul, or vital part.

In the first chapter of Genesis, mention is made of the creation of man in a general way; but nothing is said there of his soul. But, in the second chapter and seventh verse, it is said: "And the Lord God formed man *of* the dust of the ground, and breathed into his nostrils the breath of life; and man became a living soul."

Here we have the whole question in a nutshell. What was it that God "*breathed*" into Adam? It was something which was in existence at the time it was put into him. Nothing is said of its having been made then, as is of the body. It must, therefore, have existed before; or, at least, that is the legitimate inference.

Mr. Henry, in this place, says of the soul: "It takes its rise from the breath of heaven, and is produced by it." And again: "It takes its lodging in a house of clay, and is the life and support of it."

Mr. Watson, under the head, Adam, and on this text, says: "It is manifest from the history of Moses, that human nature has two essential constituent parts—the BODY, formed out of pre-existing matter, the earth; and a LIVING

SOUL, breathed into the body by an *inspiration* from God." . . . "Whatever was then imparted to the body of man, already '*formed*,' and perfectly finished in all its parts, was the only cause of life; and the whole tenor of Scripture shows that this was the rational spirit itself, which, by a law of its Creator, was incapable of death even after the body had fallen under that penalty," meaning the penalty of death.

These authors are quoted for the purpose of showing the most commonly received opinion as to the union but different natures of the *soul* and *body*, and that it is not pretended the SOUL was then created, "FORMED."

From the use of the expression, "*It takes its lodging* in a *house of clay*," by the former, and "*was incapable of death even after the body had fallen*," etc., by the latter, it is evident that they considered the *soul* and *body* as being so perfectly separate and distinct, the one from the other, as to be comparable to a house and its occupant. This is the common, not to say the universally received view of the nature of the soul and body, as related to each other, by all who admit that the soul is immortal. It is, as I entertain no doubt, also, the correct view, as far as it goes. The only difference between the writer and others of the class of Henry and Watson is, that they stop here, and I proceed a few steps further, to see *what it was* that God *breathed* into that newly made body, and which had such wonderful effect upon it, and I find it was a *pre-existent spirit—a fellow angel!*

But some doubting *Thomas* may ask me, Is it not possible that YOU are mistaken *as to what it was?* To that interrogatory my answer would be, *I think not.* And, for further answer, I would propound this question: If it was not that sort of spirit, what was it? And before my suspicious friend could frame an answer to that, which would be satisfactory to himself, I could have some half dozen or more of the same sort prepared and ready for him.

Let us now look and see what Moses says about the soul of our Grandma Eve. But, as I am rather pressed for time at present, reader, please excuse me, and look that up at your leisure. And, should you fail to find it, we will take it as granted that she had a soul; for without it she would not have been "an help meet" for Grandpa. Her body appears to have been made of a *rib* taken from Adam's side, when he was asleep. But, should we fail to find it so stated by Moses, we will not suppose that her *soul* was made of the *same* rib. As well might God have made the soul of Adam "of the dust of the ground," as that of Eve out of one of his ribs. The *rib* was as much *matter* as the *dust*, and the soul of Eve, if she had one, was as pure *spirit* as was that of Adam; and, as God did not make the soul of Adam of the *same material* of which he made his body, we should not infer, in the absence of all evidence and without reason, that he did make the soul of Eve out of the same substance of which her body was made. Then, what and whence was her soul, and how was she possessed of it? I answer, it was a kindred spirit of the same origin and nature as that which was "*breathed*" into Adam, and was from the same place, or condition, taken by God, and "*breathed*" into her body, as was the former into his. Is not this the best hypothesis? If not, please, reader, give us a better.

The word "*breathed*," as used to convey the idea that man was endowed with a living soul, is quite a suggestive one, if we understand it as applied to one of the outcast angels. That which is said so to have been "*breathed*" in, Dr. Clark says, was, in the original, "*ruach chayam*," and literally signifies the "breath of lives."

The soul is the life—the breath—the living principle of man. It is *the* LIFE *of our* LIVES When it is said, then, that God "*breathed into man the breath of* LIVES, may we not consider it as equivalent to having said, *God breathed into him a soul that was living? or, one of the living souls?* I think it amounts to about the same thing. This view gains strength by observing the result of that breathing "into his nostrils," which was that "man became a living soul." A living soul! That expression requires modification. He was not *all* soul; for, in the nineteenth verse of the next chapter, we learn that God said to Adam,

"Dust thou *art*, and unto dust shalt thou return." The soul was not of *dust*, or, as we are elsewhere informed, liable to become dust, but was intended to live forever. Yet both these remarks are applied to the same creature, as one individual. By a fair and consistent rendering of these several expressions, we will find all difficulty as to the true intent and meaning of each entirely obviated. The words, "*and man became a living soul*," may safely be construed as if written, "and man became possessed of a never-dying soul." Or thus, "and the soul *which was* BREATHED INTO MAN *was a* LIVING SPIRIT." Then construe the curse, "dust thou *art*, and unto dust shalt thou return," as applying to the body only, and perfect harmony is secured.

The expression, "*breathed into his nostrils the breath of life*," is one divinely appropriate, if we imagine that when God had "*formed*" the body of Adam, and it was fully prepared and ready for occupation, He called the spirit elect for whom it was prepared, and bade him come and live; that quickly he, as the caged lark, which a whole, long, dreary winter a prisoner's life had lived, is on May-day let loose; quick up, as thought, she darts and flies away—high up she mounts, and higher still she goes, and soon is lost to sight—so, too, he quits his dark Tartarian cell, and on the wings of morn (rejoiced no less, but more, as his cause was more great), so mounted he, and up he fled away—away sped he—the further, faster still, till he in Paradise arrived, and with the first drawn breath of that new body, well and fitly made, softly, gently was, as man, "*breathed in*."

What a happy change was that! But in the wisdom and mercy of an all-wise Providence, he was not permitted to enjoy it to the full extent. His spiritual eyes were closed, and his memory suspended. He was only able to know what his physical senses taught him. His astonishment, therefore, at himself and what he witnessed around him, must have been bewildering indeed. The imagination of Milton, in his Paradise Lost, as to what he, Adam, thought, and said, and did, on that interesting occasion, I think well founded.

This may be thought but a loose rein of the imagination, and therefore of doubtful propriety, without some evidence to justify the remark that Adam's spiritual *eyes were closed*, and his memory *suspended.* And as this is an interesting subject of inquiry, and to some extent connected with that now under discussion, I will pause here and give it some attention.

We are not so well informed as to the amount of understanding which was allowed our first parents as we are as to that of their descendants. But from the fact that they were subject to be, and were deceived and led into sin by Satan, we must infer that they were of much less capacity than was their deceiver. In fact, the brief account we have of the transaction shows clearly that they did not understand the nature of the threatened penalty to be incurred by eating of the forbidden fruit. If they had known all the consequences of their transgression and had the *power* to resist the temptation (and which they indubitably had), it is not so much as probable that they would have yielded to the tempter.

Without belaboring the question further as to them, it would be safe to conclude that we are not so much unlike them as that they should have known and remembered all the thrilling incidents of the eventful state of being through which they had passed.

If God had put the question to Adam: "Where wast thou when I laid the foundations of the earth?" the day before or after his fall, he could not have answered it any more than Job could, as we have every reason to believe. And we have the same grounds for believing that the identical cause which disqualified the one from answering that interrogatory from the Divine lips would have been just as effectual with the other.

Job was informed in the same discourse why he could not answer it, when he was told that "*from the wicked their light is withholden.*"—Job 38: 4, 15. That they were both wicked, none will dispute. And that *their* light was withholden is just as clear. From the pronoun *their*, preceding the word LIGHT, we can not infer less than that some light which they had once enjoyed was referred to. For why otherwise could it be considered "*their light?*" Such passages as the following are frequently met with, both in the Old and New Testament Scriptures: "The Lord openeth *the eyes of the blind.*"—Ps. 146: 8. "In that day shall the deaf hear the words of the book, and the eyes of the BLIND shall see out of OBSCURITY, and out of DARKNESS."—Isa. 29: 18. "And I will bring the blind by a way *that* they know not; I will lead them in paths *that* they have not known: I will make DARKNESS LIGHT before them, and crooked things straight."—Isa. 42: 16. "Let them alone: they be BLIND LEADERS OF THE BLIND. And if the blind lead the blind, both shall fall into the ditch."—Matt. 15: 14. "And he spake a parable unto them, Can the blind lead the blind? shall they not both fall into the ditch?"—Luke 6: 39. To the unbelieving Jews, Paul said: "And art confident that thou thyself art a guide of the blind, a light of them which are in darkness."—Rom. 2: 19.

Again, of the Patriarchs, he said: "These all died in faith, not having received the promises, but having seen them afar off, and were persuaded of *them*, and embraced *them*, and confessed that they were STRANGERS and PILGRIMS on the earth. For they that say such things declare plainly that they seek a country. And truly, if they had been MINDFUL of that *country* FROM WHENCE THEY CAME OUT, they might have had opportunity to have returned."—Heb. 11: 13–15; see Lev. 25: 23. With but few remarks on these Scriptures I pass on.

The condition of man in this world is represented as that of being *blind*. It was promised that the eyes of the BLIND *should see out of obscurity and out of* DARKNESS: that the blind should be brought by a way they know not, and led in paths that they have not known. They were not literally blind, and we must, therefore, receive such passages as figurative. It is most reasonable to believe that the blindness attributed to us is a comparative one. Then to what is it compared? To that dazzling light which shines about the throne of heaven? That will not do, for the light promised was to shine on our pathway to that upper kingdom. It must then refer to a light which we have known and enjoyed ourselves. It is distinctly stated that the Savior spoke "*a parable unto them,*" when he asked: "Can the blind lead the blind," etc. Then to what is it more likely that he referred than to their own blindness which, in some way, had resulted from their sin? If this were our first state of being, he could not be understood to mean that we are more blind than we ever were before.

Men are said to become more wise as they grow older. Again, he had reference to the blindness of the unbelieving Jews. He could not, therefore, have had reference to a greater amount of light which they should realize in a future state; for, from the way he denounced their hypocrisy, unbelief, and sin, and warned them of the penalties thereof, he certainly did not refer to any celestial light which was to be enjoyed by them hereafter.

The quotations from Paul above are very plain in their application; indeed, I can not see how but one construction can be put upon them. He was speaking of the wonderful consequences of their faith, and went back so far as to include Abel, Enoch, and Noah. It can not be said, therefore, that he referred to any other *country*, which they or their ancestors had previously occupied in this world. They were, nevertheless, "*strangers* and PILGRIMS on the earth." In what good sense could they have been considered "strangers and pilgrims" in this world, if they had never lived anywhere else? They were not, as he represented them, "MINDFUL OF THAT COUNTRY FROM WHICH THEY CAME OUT." Of what country had Abel come out? or Enoch, or Noah, and to which they could not easily have returned? According to Paul, their *memory* of the past had been at least *suspended*, and if their spiritual eyes had not been closed, they would have seen and known all the rugged way by which they had come on their pilgrimage. And, with the liberal offers made them, could easily have made their way back. Enoch, we know, and the others we have good reason to believe, "*returned*" home; and that by a much nearer and better route than that through which they came to this "*country*."

In the fifteenth chapter of Corinthians, a great deal of light is *made to shine* in this dark place. In verse twenty-two, the apostle says: "For as in Adam all die, even so in Christ shall all be made alive." The first question I will notice here is, what is meant by the expression, "as in Adam all die?" It has some valuable meaning, or it would have found no place here. In what sense do *all die in Adam?* Not in the most literal one, certainly. For if they did, when we die we would all go into our common ancestor, and become one with or find our home in him—*die into him;* or we would have to understand that many were in him when that letter was written, all of whom die in him. No literal construction will do. We must look for a figurative one. On entering the search for a construction of this singular passage, we should bear in mind that Adam is, in some sense, spoken of by the sacred writers as the common representative, or federal head of all our race; and that Christ is also considered our federal head in another sense. The term *sleep* is used by the same writer as emblematical of *death*. To say that one *died*, or that he *fell asleep* means the same thing. The present tense, also, is sometimes used as covering the whole probationary term of Adam and his posterity, as is evidently done by the apostle in this instance.

Now, let us try the following figurative construction of this text, and interpret it as though it read thus: For, as the spirit of Adam fell asleep, and on entering his body become as if dead to all knowledge of his responsible situation, even so, in virtue of the redemption purchased by Christ, shall all be quickened, and made alive to a true sense of their condition.

If this construction be looked upon as being too liberal, I must call to my assistance the following from the same chapter: "36. *Thou* fool, that which thou sowest is not quickened, except it die: 37. And that which thou sowest, thou sowest not that body that shall be, but bare grain, it may chance of wheat, or of some other *grain:* 38. But God giveth it a body as it hath pleased him, and TO EVERY SEED HIS OWN BODY."

Here we have a beautiful emblem of the union of the soul and body of man, in which is represented the necessity of the death (sleep or torpor) of the soul on entering the body, that it may be restored to full life by the quickening spirit and regenerating power of Christ. And a clear revelation of the fact, that God gives to every spirit *his own body*, one prepared especially for his own use and occupation. The seed which is sown represents the *spirit*, which, it is said, must *die* before it can be quickened, restored to real life. The nature of the death of the soul, on entering the body, is illustrated by the change which a grain of corn undergoes on being sown into the ground, vegetating and passing into a new life. The stalk into which the life of the seed passes represents the body of man, in which the soul lives while he tabernacles here. And the uncertainty which exists as to whether the seed sown will, in due season, be reproduced through a new body (trial or probation), or whether it will blast, mildew, or otherwise go to ruin, represents the uncertainty as to the result of our probation.

The husbandman who prepares the ground and sows his seed represents the God who made the world, which is his field; and, as it requires a very great number of seed to sow a field of wheat, "*or of some other grain*," we learn that God has a like large number of spirits whom He has promised, in Christ the Mediator, a probationary term in this life, and who are to have bodies prepared for them. But, as there is a point at which the emblem ceases to represent that which is emblemized, care is taken to point out when that likeness ceases, and to guard against the danger of leading us into error on that account. It is well known that many seed on being sown fail to vegetate, but decompose in the earth, or are destroyed by insects, birds, etc. But, as God intends to preserve all the "*seed*" he has prepared to sow in this field from loss or destruction, before entering into a body, and having the benefit of this life, the apostle assures us that God will give every seed a body, "*and to every seed his own body.*" His seed shall not perish in the earth, but spring forth into a "newness of life."

The apostle illustrates this matter, but in the same figurative style, throughout the remainder of that chapter. By a careful study of what he there says, and viewed in this light, much may be learned on this interesting subject. To prove conclusively that I have not misconceived that inspired apostle in this particular, I call attention in this place to what Christ said on the same subject:

"And he said, So is the kingdom of God, as if a man should cast seed into the ground; and should sleep, and rise night and day, and the seed should spring and grow up, he knoweth not how. For the earth bringeth forth fruit of herself; first the blade, then the ear, after that the full corn in the ear. But when the fruit is brought forth (or ripe), immediately he putteth in the sickle, because the harvest is come."—Mark 4: 26 to 29, inclusive.

Observe, 1. He was avowedly teaching in parables. 2. This is not the parable of the sower, which he explained to his disciples to mean: "the field sown is the world and the seed is the Word of God," or the Gospel. He had both given and explained that one, before he uttered this, as is shown by the same chapter. 3. That he evidently intended to teach something else of importance. 4. And that he did not expound this one as he did the other. 5. This must, therefore, be classed with the things which are *hidden, concealed, covered up;* and which he promised should, in due season, be *manifested, made known, uncovered, and brought to light.*

The Apostle Paul, with the permission of the Savior, *removed* some, nay, nearly all the covering by which this treasure was concealed and hidden; and St. John, in Patmos, was permitted to see both what and where it was, as it is likely; and certainly to intimate to us so closely the whole "*secret,*" that by reasonable search we also could find it.

On this subject I feel in duty bound to make a suggestion to general Bible readers, and which may strike the mind on a first impression as decidedly strange, not to say paradoxical, or even absurd, and I had as well do it right here probably as anywhere else. It is this, that the astounding fact that the soul of man (and which is the man) is not a newly created ESSENCE, but a *fallen angel*, was not, so far as we are informed, fully comprehended, if conceived at all, by any of the patriarchs, prophets, or apostles, save Sts. Paul and John; and not by the latter, prior to his vision in the Isle of Patmos, if then. Christ, of course, knew all about it, and often had reference to it in his acts and sayings, but taught it, though in various forms of speech, yet always in parables. Paul, on his way to Damascus, had a vision; he saw a light from heaven which shined about him, and which oppressed him so that he fell to the earth; and he heard a voice speaking words which overwhelmed him. Of all that he saw and heard on that occasion, and under circumstances so alarming, he has informed us but little. It was enough, however, to "make a believer" even of the mighty "*Saul of Tarsus*," who was the leading champion of the persecution then so cruelly prosecuted against the disciples of Christ. He was not only convinced, but his towering ambition was subdued, and he became at once as meek and humble as a little child. He no doubt did hear "*unspeakable words which it is not lawful for man to utter.*" See Acts 9: 3, *et seq.*, and 2 Cor. 12: 4.

Notwithstanding he was not permitted to tell *all* he saw and heard, he was granted the privilege of making a "*right-about-wheel*," to repent of all his evil doings, seek and find pardon, and to abandon every earthly interest, and devote his capacity, energies, and days to the service of his Divine Friend, who was so gracious as to forgive him. And he was also allowed to make such references to things he then learned, as would, in the providence of God, tend to the *increase* of *knowledge* in the earth, as circumstances should, from time to time, require.

It is true that intimations are thrown out, and remarks

often made by patriarchs, prophets, and other apostles, which have reference to this great truth. But, from the way in which it was done, it would seem that they only spoke as the spirit gave them utterance; and, although they spoke truly, as they were commanded, and said just what God intended they should say, there is no sufficient evidence that they fully comprehended the whole scope and intendment of all that they heard and uttered. Indeed, we have positive proof that Daniel did not understand all that he heard and wrote; and that Paul and John did not tell all they knew.

Begging pardon for this digression, on the ground that it occurred to me as best to make it, I now proceed further to notice the parable above copied.

In what respect did the Savior intend to be understood as comparing the "kingdom of God" to the sowing of seed, and the reproduction of corn therefrom? I must confess that I should find this question one hard to answer, but for the light which he has been pleased to throw on the subject since he propounded it for our solution. But, with the help of what the Apostle Paul said about it, the mysteriously wonderful revelation to St. John, and the many allusions, more or less pointed, but all in the same direction, which are everywhere to be found both in the Old and New Testaments, the problem has become an easy one.

He clearly meant precisely the same thing which Paul did in first Corinthians fifteenth, as far as his parable went; but that of his apostle, when considered altogether, goes much further than Christ himself went; so that I need say but little more in explication of this than simply to refer back to what I said there. In short, I understand the Savior as if saying to this generation: As a man sows his seed in the ground, and it comes up and grows, while he sleeps and wakes, night and day, he knows not how, for the earth appears to bring forth fruit of herself, first the blade, then the ear, and next the grain, and when the harvest comes he cuts down and gathers his wheat into his barn; so it is that God populates and orders His earthly kingdom. He plants His *seed*, which are the *souls* in the *bodies* of men, although their souls and bodies appear to grow up together, night and day, being first little children (the blade), then infants (the ear), and after that into mature age (the full corn in the ear), they know not how; and when His fruit is ripe, He cuts it down and gathers it into His garner, even as the farmer harvests his grain.

And by which He has given us light to understand that by His *seed* He intends the *eternal spirit;* for the probation of which the world was created, and the body of man "*formed*." And that our spirits, although very differently capacitated before, are, on entering our bodies reduced to the torpidity of mind or intellect of the little child, the newly born babe; that it gradually expands and grows into the advanced state of infancy (minority), and "*after that*" matures into that of the adult man or woman. And that as the Divine purposes for which we were brought into this state of being have been accomplished as to each, the fruit is ripe, and then Death, with his sharp scythe, cuts down the body (the stalk), and the emancipated spirit is wafted home to heaven or driven away into eternal darkness, as the fruit has proven good or bad. I have introduced this parable of the Savior, in this place, not so much to prove the origin of the human soul as to sustain the position that the spiritual *eye is shut*, and the *memory* of the past *suspended*, when the soul enters the body.

This it does successfully. Not so much by furnishing additional reason for it, or evidence that such is the case, however, as by showing that my construction of the fifteenth Corinthians is well founded. The figure presented by Christ is, in substance, the same, and, so far as is necessary for this argument, identical with that of St. Paul. They both represent the *spirit given by the seed sown*, and the passing of the seed into the stalk, by which the union of the two is produced, and the maturity of the fruit, in the same way, although in different words. To carry out the simile of either, the spirit, the seed, must pass into and through a condition which may, in parabolical language, very properly be indicated by the terms *sleep* or *death*. The reason why this should have been done has already been shown. That God has the wisdom to contrive and power to execute such a plan, no one will deny who recognizes the cardinal truths of Christianity.

If, then, there was good reason why some such plan should have been adopted, and God could have done so, and there is strong scriptural evidence that he did, we may, in the absence of any good reason, and all proof to the contrary, believe that such is our fearful situation in this life.

Does it not seem wonderful that such minds as those of Solomon, Luther, Webster, and Bascomb, to say nothing of others, ourselves, or those we personally know, should have been at one time as *torpid*, *insensible*, *dead*, as is that of the unconscious nursling—*a little babe!* Strange though it may appear, it is no less true than strange. So we all began our earthly career. We enter this life as one passes into a dream—a trance—and from which state we return to sensibility slowly but gradually and regularly. And from the foot round, we ascend the ladder of science, higher and higher, until met by Death, whose unrelenting hand cuts the brittle cord which binds us here; *then* again we "shall be as gods, knowing good and evil." Well and truly did Job say, that God "doeth great things past finding out; yea, and wonders without number."

CHAPTER XIII.

The same Subject Continued—Parables of Luke 15 Noticed—To whom Addressed—The Surrounding Circumstances—Followed by those of the Unjust Steward and of the Rich Man and Lazarus in Chapter 16—Parable of the Lost Sheep Construed—That of the Piece of Silver—Of the Prodigal Son—Figurative and Literal Meaning of Days—Secret Things—Reluctance of Man to Repent—Other Scriptures compared with these Parables—Manner of Christ's Teaching—Care with which Opinions on Leading Subjects should be made up—Our True Status in this World.

BEFORE leaving this branch of the subject, it is deemed best to call attention to a few more of such Scriptures as bear directly upon it.

And in doing so, I call the reader's attention, in the next place, to the parables of which the whole of the fifteenth chapter of Luke consists. And as I have not the vanity to think I could fill the same space with any argument of my own which would be comparable with what the Savior taught there, I copy the whole chapter here, that these several parables may be read in the light reflected from this stand-point, and, considered together, as they were delivered by the Messiah in person:

"1. Then drew near unto him all the publicans and sinners for to hear him.

"2. And the Pharisees and scribes murmured, saying, This man receiveth sinners, and eateth with them.

"3. And he spake this parable unto them, saying,

"4. What man of you having an hundred sheep, if he lose one of them, doth not leave the ninety and nine in the wilderness, and go after that which is lost, until he find it?

"5. And when he hath found *it*, he layeth *it* on his shoulders, rejoicing.

"6. And when he cometh home, he calleth together *his* friends and neighbors, saying unto them, Rejoice with me; for I have found my sheep which was lost.

"7. I say unto you, that likewise joy shall be in heaven over one sinner that repenteth, more than over ninety and nine just persons, which need no repentance.

"8. Either what woman having ten pieces of silver, if she lose one piece, doth not light a candle, and sweep the house, and seek diligently till she find *it?*

"9. And when she hath found *it*, she calleth *her* friends and *her* neighbors together, saying, Rejoice with me; for I have found the piece which I had lost.

"10. Likewise, I say unto you, there is joy in the presence of the angels of God over one sinner that repenteth.

"11. And he said, A certain man had two sons:

"12. And the younger of them said to *his* father, Father, give me the portion of goods that falleth *to me.* And he divided unto them *his* living.

"13. And not many days after, the younger son gathered all together, and took his journey into a far country, and there wasted his substance with riotous living.

"14. And when he had spent all, there arose a mighty famine in that land; and he began to be in want.

"15. And he went and joined himself to a citizen of that country; and he sent him into his fields to feed swine.

"16. And he would fain have filled his belly with the husks that the swine did eat: and no man gave unto him.

"17. And when he come to himself, he said, How many hired servants of my father's have bread enough and to spare, and I perish with hunger!

"18. I will arise and go to my father, and will say unto him, Father, I have sinned against heaven, and before thee,

"19. And am no more worthy to be called thy son: make me as one of thy hired servants.

"20. And he arose, and came to his father. But when

he was yet a great way off, his father saw him, and had compassion, and ran, and fell on his neck, and kissed him.

"21. And the son said unto him, Father, I have sinned against heaven and in thy sight, and am no more worthy to be called thy son.

"22. But the father said to his servants, Bring forth the best robe, and put *it* on him; and put a ring on his hand, and shoes on *his* feet:

"23. And bring hither the fatted calf, and kill *it;* and let us eat and be merry:

"24. For this my son was dead, and is alive again; he was lost and is found. And they began to be merry.

"25. Now his eldest son was in the field: and as he came and drew nigh to the house, he heard music and dancing.

"26. And he called one of the servants, and asked what these things meant.

"27. And he said unto him, Thy brother is come; and thy father hath killed the fatted calf, because he hath received him safe and sound.

"28. And he was angry, and would not go in: therefore came his father out, and entreated him.

"29. And he answering, said to *his* father, Lo, these many years do I serve thee, neither transgressed I at any time thy commandment: and yet thou never gavest me a kid, that I might make merry with my friends:

"30. But as soon as this thy son was come, which hath devoured thy living with harlots, thou hast killed for him the fatted calf.

"31. And he said unto him, Son, thou art ever with me, and all that I have is thine.

"32. It was meet that we should make merry, and be glad: for this thy brother was dead, and is alive again; and was lost, and is found."

Observe, 1. These parables were addressed to a mixed multitude, consisting of scribes, Pharisees, publicans, and sinners, as well as to his disciples. 2. That the Pharisees had "*murmured,*" saying: "This man receiveth sinners and eateth with them;" and that it was in part for the purpose of showing why he did so that they were uttered. 3. That immediately after he closed the last of these parables, he turned to his disciples and addressing them (chapter sixteen), delivered that of the unjust steward, and which, by the way, if I interpret it correctly, was the most severe specimen of sarcastic irony with which I have anywhere met. The Pharisees seem to have suspected as much and became highly incensed, and thereupon Christ gave them, as the only consolation he had to promise them, as they were then acting, the parable of the rich man and Lazarus, that they might digest the two together at their leisure.

In the vastly different manner in which the Savior treated his own devoted and beloved disciples and those vain and proud Pharisees on that occasion, we have, in juxtaposition, and in bold contrast, a striking illustration of the love of God for the righteous on the one hand and of His wrath against the wicked on the other.

Let us now notice these parables separately, and in the same order in which they were delivered. I interpret that of the lost sheep in this way: The "*man*" whose sheep it is supposed was lost represents God whose creatures we all are; the "*lost sheep*," a rebellious spirit that was cast out of heaven with Satan; by the "*wilderness*," is intended this world, into which the fallen angels were sent and where they are pursued, and in which *some* of the lost sheep *are found and recovered.* To give this verse (4) any satisfactory solution, we must transpose the words "in the," which precede "*wilderness*," and place them, with it, after "*and go*," so as to read "and go in the wilderness." The reason for this is obvious. A shepherd would not be likely to leave his *ninety and nine* sheep *in the wilderness* and *go out of it* to hunt the one that was lost. For this, two reasons are apparent: 1. The sheep which had strayed off would be more likely to wander further into the wilderness, in hunt of the flock, than to return to the fold, as all who know anything about that animal will attest. 2. If he had supposed the lost sheep had gone off, clear out of the wilderness, he surely would have first taken the flock back to the fold and secured them, and seen whether the lost one was there, and where it most probably would have gone, if it had left the wilderness entirely; and not left the ninety and nine there unprotected, and to take care of *themselves*, as best they might, and wandered off *himself* somewhere (neither he nor any one else could have imagined where) in search for the lost one.

It is natural for us to rejoice more over an article, although of small comparative value, which had been lost, but which we have just found, than over others of much greater value that have not been lost.

Note carefully the seventh verse: "I say unto you, that likewise joy shall be in heaven over one sinner that repenteth, more than over ninety and nine *just persons*, which need no repentance."

Here we have conclusive evidence that I have thus far properly applied the figurative language employed in this parable.

The joy which the owner of the lost sheep is represented as feeling on finding it, represents the rejoicing which the repentance of a sinner here causes in heaven.

But, it may be asked, what are we to understand by the last clause, "more than over ninety and nine JUST PERSONS which need no repentance?" The "*ninety and nine*" sheep that were not lost, represent the faithful and holy angels who did not fall away after the manner of Satan. And they are the "JUST PERSONS which need no repentance."

I am aware that objection has been made to construing the term "persons" as applying to the holy angels; but I am glad to have the authority of such a man as Dr. A. Clark to sustain me in saying that such objection is wholly unfounded. If it does not refer to them, I ask, in turn, to whom or to what does it apply? I know of no class of beings, other than men, or angels, who could have been intended. It certainly is not applicable to men, for the best of us, who move at all, go blundering and stumbling along like a drunken man, and say and do things daily of which we should (and if we are what we ought to be, do) repent. "If we say that we have no sin, we deceive ourselves, and the truth is not in us" (or we are deceived as to ourselves, or else speak that which is untrue knowingly).—1 John 1: 8. This was the experience of that disciple whom Jesus loved, frankly confessed, when a very old man. How many of us could, with like sincerity, say the contrary? I could not. Let him who can, speak out, and then go read 1 Cor. 10: 12.

So it is that Jesus Christ and the angels of heaven are made to rejoice more over one lost spirit who repents of his folly and wickedness, and returns to the allegiance due to God and his Christ, than over ninety and nine others who have never gone astray.

What a beautiful illustration of that which was intended in this view! It is perfectly symmetrical in all its parts, and easy to be comprehended by every one. In the parable of the piece of silver, which a woman is supposed to have lost, and after "diligent" search found again, at which she was so overjoyed that she called in her friends and neighbors, and asked them to rejoice with her, the same precious truth is, in another form, impressed upon the believer's mind. It is scarcely worth saying, this illustration being so plain, that the woman here represents Christ himself, and the piece of silver one of the *lost*, whom he came "to seek and to save." And the "friends and neighbors," who are called to join in celebrating the gladsome event are of the "*morning stars* (which) *sang together*," when the plan for our recovery was first perfected.

After but one brief sentence, in the way of application, the Savior proceeded to the parable of the prodigal son:

"And he said, A certain man had two sons." Here, God and the whole family of heavenly angels, of whom some apostatized and others did not, are represented by the figure of a man having two, and only two sons. "The younger of them" stands in the picture for those who fell. For this, two reasons strike the mind at once: 1. They are said to be the "*younger*," because they proved themselves to have been the weaker, less stable, having suffered themselves deceived and led away from the path of duty, as the others, their elder brethren, did not. 2. They were the lesser portion of the family—more remaining steadfast than fell into sin. It is quite natural, therefore, that the holy angels—the elder brethren—should warmly sympathize with their erring brothers in their horrible dilemma, and feel to rejoice over every one who repents and receives pardon. "He is coming home again!" What a joyous time they have had up there ever since righteous Abel was restored.

But I must not follow my own inclination here lest I lose sight of my argument entirely, and dash off on a theme which is so much more inviting. Reader, we too may, *if we will*, realize some of that heavenly bliss which is now but faintly conceived by our sin-clouded imagination. We *may* get there *in time* to witness the arrival of many yet.

"Father, give me the portion of goods that falleth to me." In this, by an appropriate allegory, we may learn that the universal desire of young men when they first grow up, is to become masters of their own fortunes and builders of their own destiny. And by it we may also learn the more valuable and glorious truth, that God's children *are all free* to act for themselves; and, at the same time, the alarming fact that we are held to strict account for all we say and do! This solemn truth St. Peter enforces with all his inspired ability in his second general epistle, wherein, with other illustrations, he says: "God spared not the angels that sinned, but cast *them* down to hell (Tartarus), and delivered *them* into chains of darkness, to be reserved unto judgment."

As our heavenly Father is more perfect in all His divine attributes than are our earthly parents, so is He more indulgent to His children as long as they observe His statutes; and to the same extent is He more strict in holding the wayward to just account for their transgressions. "And he divided unto him his living." Made them, in each case, masters of their own will, and permitted them to go at once into the full enjoyment of the fortunes He had in store for them, and which, in the one case, included all the rich treasures of heaven; but, in the other, consisted of such worldly trash only as our earthly parents can provide for us. What a contrast! The pictures are none the less life-like, however different they appear, as opposed to each other; and the original from which each is so easily drawn is a most apposite one to the illustrations intended.

"And not many days after the younger son gathered all together, and took his journey into a far country, and there wasted his substance with riotous living." The word *day* is often used by the sacred writers in a figurative sense. "One day is with the Lord as a thousand years, and a thousand years as one day."—2 Peter 3: 8. And it is also employed in its literal meaning at other times. It is possible that the Savior may have used it in this place to express both a thousand years and one of our days. If so, in the first view it relates to the time the fallen angels remained steadfast; and, in the second, to the time the younger son remained under the paternal roof after receiving his patrimony, and before "he took his journey into a far country;" and we may infer that the stay which, in each case, was made at home before leaving, was as so many thousand years is to the same number of days. But as no definite number of days is given, and inasmuch as some profligate young men abide at home after receiving their outfit longer than others, we could, were we presumptuous enough to try, arrive at no result which would probably approximate the truth from this data, as to how long we enjoyed the celestial bliss of a home in heaven before we fell into sin, and were cast out into the earth.

This pertains to the secret things which are known to those above alone. Each "took his journey into a FAR COUNTRY." Here we have the contrast again. As the earth is further from heaven than one country of this world is from another, so was the *journey* taken by the fallen angels greater than that of the prodigal son. "And there wasted his substance in riotous living." The prodigal wasted his trash, trifled it away as things of no value: even so the ungrateful soul of man underrates and trifles away the rich treasures which Christ has purchased for him "*in riotous living.*" O how ungrateful! how unwise!

This prodigal, it seems, never became penitent on account of his wicked ways, while he was squandering his means, nor even after his "*substance*" was gone, until "there arose a mighty famine in that land." When gaunt starvation began to stare him in the face, his pride was to some extent humbled, but not subdued; he would not return to his affectionate father, whose kindness he had so much abused, and beg his pardon, and seek shelter again under his paternal roof. No, rather would he go into the employ of a heathen of that country, in the most degrading of all service, and especially to the proud Jew, of a *swine-herd!* Never, until he had exhausted every other expedient, did his pride fully give way. But when his poor wages had proved inadequate to sustain animal life, "and no man gave unto him"—he could not beg—"he came to himself." No wonder that he did!

Thus far the parallel runs smoothly along the downward road traveled by the lost spirit and the prodigal of this world. No sign of relenting is manifested by either until driven to the last extremity. The rebellious spirit follows the deceptive lead of Satan, not only until he is cast out of heaven with him, but (so far as we are informed) until he is overtaken by the Holy Spirit in this life, and his utter destitution and helpless situation are so plainly revealed to him, that he is made to see that all is lost with him, and not so much as a delusive hope is left of anything better than death—eternal death awaiting him—unless he humbles himself before his Father, God, confess his sins, and seek for pardoning grace. Just as it was with the prodigal son.

But here the parable ceases to apply to all prodigals, and the Savior extends it to none but those who, though late, repent before too late. To such as resist all the proffers of mercy in this life, no consoling promise is to be found in this parable or elsewhere in the Word of God.

Although that prodigal son, with great reluctance, resolved to return to his father, and felt so guilty that he would not presume to ask so much as full pardon and restoration to his favor as a son, but would be happy to get the place of one of his hired servants, his affectionate parent did not set so low an estimate on his own fatherly love and forgiving spirit. "But when he was yet a great way off his father saw him, and had compassion, and ran, and fell on his neck, and kissed him." What a welcome surprise to the son was that, though prodigal he had been! The father's heart was made too glad on seeing his son alive, whom he had mourned as dead, to prolong the unpleasant conversation about the wicked road he had walked. He saw he was penitent, and that was enough. Without any reply in words, he ordered the best robe put on him, "a ring on his hand, and shoes on his feet;" that the fatted calf be killed, and a family festival be had: "For this my son was dead, and is alive again; he was lost and is found." So it is with our heavenly Father. When one of His sons, who "*was dead* (*lost*) *is found*," although with great trepidation of soul, he ventures to approach Him with sincere contrition, and asks pardon through Christ our Redeemer, he not only receives a welcome, which overcomes him with a sense of gratitude, but a great rejoicing is made by the whole family of heaven "over one sinner that repenteth."

How different is it with us in this sin-polluted world. The only brother of this relenting son, on hearing that he had returned to the bosom of the family, after an absence so long that he was supposed to have been dead, so far from rejoicing, as do our brethren in heaven when one of us returns, when he heard the cause of the merry-making going on in the house, positively refused to go in where his brother was. His envy was excited; probably his fears also, that his father might *give him something*. How superlatively selfish and *mean* the love of money makes some people in this world.

In what true sense was it said, "*my son was dead*," as applicable to the soul of man, if he never had been alive? All so understood it. And if it does not refer to the human soul, no one has yet (so far as I know) been able to assign it any valuable meaning. Again, how can that be called *lost* which never had a state of being more perfect than it now has? How could it be said that the soul of man is both *dead* and *lost*, if it never had been in existence until it entered this life, and while it is now present in the body, and advancing in knowledge and rising in the scale of being every day? To believe that Jesus Christ would apply such epithets to a being which never had any other state of existence, to say the best of it, requires a great stretch of credulity.

But to construe all these parables as applying to fallen angels, who are now here in the form of men, and in a state of probation, preparatory for that judgment to which they are reserved, and nothing is more easy than to comprehend fully all that was intended by each and all of them, whether considered separately or together. No satisfactory solution of the mystery in which these parables are involved having hitherto been found, and as this rendering gives them such application as it is reasonable to believe was intended, and is consistent with all other Scriptures, we may safely so construe them, and should do so, until a better application of their meaning shall be discovered. And if this is the true one, as it certainly must be, that will never be done.

Let us now compare these views with other passages of Scripture, and especially with some other remarks made by the Savior, and see whether the last foothold for doubt as to what he meant by the parable of the "*lost sheep*," the one of the "*ten pieces of silver*," and that of the son who "*was dead and is alive again;* was *lost and is found*," will not be removed. I will first call attention to a remark which Christ made to his disciples before he delivered these parables, and which is full of meaning and bearing directly on this point: "*Ye know not what manner of spirits ye are of.*" That was true, and not only so, but a matter of grave import to them, or he would not have said it, and with such emphasis as he did. He "rebuked them and said, Ye know not what manner of spirit ye are of."—Luke 9: 55. Whatever else may have been intended by that remark, it is certainly true that he designed to put his beloved disciples on notice that there was some important fact connected with their spirits of which they were ignorant.

According to St. Luke, after giving them that notice, and on another occasion, he said: "For the Son of man IS COME to seek and to save that which WAS LOST."—Luke 19: 10. Mark the phraseology, "IS COME," "WAS LOST." Can anything be inferred from what he there said, less than that he intended to inform them that he came to seek and to save those who *were lost before his advent* as Mediator in this world? That it will not do to say that he had reference to our having been lost, in consequence of Adam's fall and our descent from him, has already been shown. St. Matthew says our Savior spoke in parables, "That it might be fulfilled which was spoken by the prophet, saying, I will open my mouth in parables; I will UTTER THINGS which have been kept SECRET from the foundation of the world."—Matt. 13: 35.

It is but fair to admit that Matthew knew why it was that Christ taught in parables, and that he informs us correctly as to what his motive was, and that one of his objects was to *utter things* which had been *kept secret from men* up to that time.

Now, starting from this point, if he did not intend, by the parables found in Luke 15, to instruct us more perfectly as to what "*manner of spirit*" we are possessed of than was known to his disciples at that time, I ask, in all reverence, *what did he intend to teach by them?* He had some motive for giving *utterance* to those mysterious parables. We will not suspect that he failed of his purpose.

To give them a literal construction, they taught nothing new. Everybody knew then, as well as now, that if a man should lose one out of his flock of sheep, it is usual for him to go and hunt it up, and that he is glad when he finds it; that a woman, who had but ten pieces of silver, on losing one of them, would search diligently for it, and feel proud when she had found it, no one who knows anything of woman's care over her little treasures would doubt; and that a profligate young man might wander off a long way from home, fall into dissipation, and thereby squander his property, and when no alternative is left but go back to his father's or starve, that he will return home, and that his father on seeing him coming should run out to meet him, fall on his neck and kiss him, and clothe him in his best attire, give a dining party, and call in his friends to rejoice with him, is but natural. And that even a scion of the Shylock species, in the form of a selfish, groveling, penurious brother, should feel more sorrow than gladness on his brother's return, are all things which were then and still are well known.

That the Savior intended by these parables to teach some important lesson, all Christians agree. What that lesson is, has been a question of much interest among divines, and on which a great diversity of opinion has prevailed. Commentators, perhaps, most generally construe those of the lost sheep and prodigal son as intended to illustrate the love of God to man; and that of the piece of silver as designed to impress on the mind the intrinsic and true value of that salvation which Christ came to purchase with his blood.

While I do not pretend to deny that valuable lessons of that sort might have been gleaned from them, if necessary, yet I can not believe that such was the object he had in view at that time, or the prime motive for which they were "*uttered.*" The time allotted for his ministry was quite short. His manner was to court brevity and force of style, and not to go over his work time and again without effecting any improvement on what he had done already. Nor did he teach that so mysteriously as to render it next to impossible to understand his meaning, which he intended to make so plain that none should fail to know what he meant, as he did elsewhere, teach the love of God, and the worth of the soul. If I am right in this, it is impossible that he should have intended nothing more by these parables than has so been generally understood. For both of these precious truths were plainly, by him, on other occasions, taught so clearly and illustrated so forcibly, that to have attempted to teach and explain them, in the form of the parables referred to, would have been no better than to "*darken counsel.*" And that our divine Master never did.

For proof of what I say, the following only, of the many other passages of like clearness on these points, are offered: "God so loved the world that he gave his only begotten Son, that whosoever believeth in him should not perish, but have everlasting life."—John 3: 16. There is no proof so strong, or illustration so clear, of the love of God to man in either of those parables, as to admit of grave comparison with the manner in which it is manifested in this text, and the subsequent fact of Christ's death. If nothing more was intended to be expressed in them than that one truth (although it towers above all others in worth to us), no possible good could have resulted from speaking them. The only effect would have been to mistify that which was plain; and to believe which, would be to deny their claim to a place in the Bible. That we must not, can not believe, was his intention. The love of God for man, though fallen and sinful now, is not of the "*secret things,*" but is the most prominent, as well as the most precious truth taught in the Bible; the light of which is reflected from every page of that blessed Book, from the first of Genesis to the last of Revelation.

Of the value of the soul's salvation, Jesus said: "What shall it profit a man, if he shall gain the whole world, and lose his own soul? Or what shall a man give in exchange for his soul?" It is not really necessary, I presume, but to prevent possibility of error here, I remark, the last clause quoted should be understood as if it read thus: Or what *should not* a man give in exchange for his soul, *if its salvation could be* BOUGHT WITH A PRICE?—Mark 8: 36, 37.

Here we are informed that one immortal soul is worth a price, with which this world, with all her glittering show of honor, wealth, and pleasure, is not to be compared. Is it not utterly unreasonable to suppose, that after saying that our blessed Redeemer compared the salvation of the soul to the value of a *piece of silver* which a woman lost, and which would not probably have paid for a night's entertainment in the meanest hotel in all that country?

In making up an opinion as to the true intent and meaning of the Sacred Writings on any given subject, we should diligently compare what has been said by each and every one, and by the same teacher or writer in different places on that subject. It would not be safe to hazard our eternal interests on a faith which is of sufficient importance to control, in a good degree, the conduct of our lives, on a mere *impression*, which has, although vague itself, grown with our growth and strengthened with our strength. Nor should we hastily form an opinion, especially on a question of the enormous dimensions of the one now under consideration, but carefully examine everything connected with, or bearing upon it. A conclusion arrived at with such laborious and anxious care deserves to be called *an opinion.* Nothing short of that should be accepted as satisfactory when relating to matters of such moment.

The writer has investigated this subject with that sort of labor, care, and anxiety; the result of all which is, that he has become satisfied that we are not in our original state of being here, but in a secondary and transitory one. That we are of the rebellious spirits which were cast out with Satan from heaven, and that we are here on trial under circumstances well adapted to that end. And that, when we pass out of this life, we but continue in the fulfillment of the eternal career on which we entered when first created. And, which is of more importance still, that when we leave this world, we will be restored to the paradise of God, redeemed, regenerated, and re-admitted to the Divine favor, when we will be as happy as before our apostacy, or that we will be forever cast out from the presence of God and His holy angels, and doomed, by the justice and mercy of God, to dwell eternally with devils and damned spirits such as ourselves.

It is true, my faith is not based alone or chiefly on any construction of the parables we have last been considering. But I do think this great truth was that to which Christ had reference when he uttered them. We should remember that we are oft assured by the sacred writers, that there are great and important facts, and in which we are interested, that we do not fully comprehend; and further, that the Holy Spirit is to instruct us in such truths. This he could do in divers ways, but none would appear more consistent with the known dealings of God with us, than that on all important matters of this sort, He should reveal them fully through his prophets, but in such mysterious way as to prevent their being comprehended until the time should come when, in his providence, they should be known. And then, let them be found only after such careful and diligent search as that by which the *piece of silver* was found. We should not forget the important truth either, that if we are not informed of our true nature and origin, and hence, of the full weight of the responsibilities resting upon us in this life, by the class of Scriptures relied on to sustain this hypothesis, we are nowhere in the Bible enlightened on this, to us a most important subject. I had intended to present some other views which strike my own mind with great force, and produce the Scriptures on which they are based, under this head, but as I fear the reader's patience is already well nigh or quite exhausted, I decline doing so; and reserve such as seem most valuable for a place under a subsequent division, and where they may be introduced in a connection as much, or perhaps more, to the satisfaction of the reader than if here presented.

CHAPTER XIV.

Eighth General Proposition Stated—The Relations of the Soul and Body to each other—May Exist Separately—Samuel, Lazarus, and others Raised from the Dead—Miracles Considered—The Soul is to the Body what the Operator is to a Factory—The Angel which Appeared to St. John in Patmos—The Spirit of one of the Older Prophets—The Spirit of Elijah the Prophet and of John the Baptist probably the Same—Eighth Chapter of John noticed—Soul does not Descend with the Body from Father to Son.

PURSUANT to arrangement for the discussion of this subject, I have now reached the eighth proposition, to-wit: "That the bodies, not the souls, the physical, not the spiritual part of subsequent generations, were created in Adam." This, as will be observed, is closely allied to the preceding proposition, and may be said to grow naturally out of it.

If the body only of man was created when the world was, and the soul which was sent to occupy it as a mere tenement, was a "pre-existent spirit," a number of interesting questions arise as to the relations of the soul and body to each other. Some of the most prominent of which I now proceed to notice.

First, then, attention is invited to their capacity of separate existence. Is it true that the soul and body can exist entirely distinct and apart from each other? I answer, it is.

If my theory is well founded, it is necessarily so. For, suppose the body of Adam to have been made, and the whole machinery necessary to the performance of all the functions of animal life, as well as the apartment for the residence of the proprietor, the operator, all to have been prepared, manufactured, and set up in perfect running order, before the spirit entered the house of his tabernacle, and that the soul existed before that as a separate, distinct, and rational though miserable creature, of course they both were in existence before they were united together.

As we may conjecture, the body may not have been brought into even animal life, but lay, as if dead, on the ground. If that be so, yet he was in a state of *existence* no less real, before animated by "*the breath of life*," than he was afterward. So we find the soul and body of the first man actually did exist altogether distinct and apart from each other, at one time.

Let us see if we can find scriptural authority for saying, that the essence of the body and soul is so perfectly distinct, the one from the other, that the spirit may depart from the body and remain absent days at a time, and then return to his late home, enter the body again, and set all his machinery in motion, and run it as successfully as before. If we can so establish that fact, we will be enabled to report progress in proving their capacity for separate existence.

The first authority to which I will refer, is that found in 1 Samuel 28. There we learn that when King Saul was hardly pressed by the Philistines, and in a perfect agony of fear, and wholly at a loss as to what he should do (his former friend and counselor, good old Samuel being dead), as his last hope, went in disguise to the Witch of En-dor, and tried to prevail with her to "bring me him up whom I shall name unto thee." The woman refused, on the ground that all who had familiar spirits had been ordered by the king to leave the country, and she feared to exercise her black art on account of the danger to which she would thereby expose herself. Her unknown patron having, however, given her satisfactory assurances that she could safely grant his request, she assented.

11. "Then said the woman, Whom shall I bring up unto thee? And he said, Bring me up Samuel." She called him, and he arose from the dead. When she saw

Samuel she was alarmed, and cried with a loud voice. The King said to her, "Be not afraid."

"14. And he said unto her, What form *is* he of? And she said, An old man cometh up; and he *is* covered with a mantle. And Saul perceived that it *was* Samuel, and he stooped with *his* face to the ground, and bowed himself."

"15. And Samuel said to Saul, Why hast thou disquieted me, to bring me up?"

They then proceeded with the conversation for which he returned. How long Samuel had been dead, we are not informed; but from the narrative of passing events, it must have been two or three years. His body had, probably, been kept in such way as that it had not decomposed materially. Be that, however, as it may, his body and soul had existed apart, in some form or other, during the time which elapsed from his death to that of his being raised to life again, and that is sufficient for the present purpose.

I will next refer to the case of Elijah, who raised the son of the poor widow: 1 Kings 17: 21. "And he stretched himself upon the child three times, and cried unto the LORD, and said, O Lord, my God, I pray thee, let this child's *soul come into* HIM AGAIN."

"22. And the Lord heard the voice of Elijah, and the soul of the child *came into him again, and he* REVIVED."

The prayer was that "*this child's soul come into him again.*" The answer was: "And the soul of the child came into him AGAIN, *and* HE REVIVED."

How very much like the account we have of the first union of the soul and body of Adam. Of that it is said: God "breathed into his nostrils the *breath of life, and man became a living soul.*" Suppose Moses had gone on, and afterward said, that Adam became sick and died, and Eve prayed and said: O Lord, my God, I pray thee let this (*man's*) soul come into him again, and the soul of the man came into him again, and he revived; would we not have understood that the soul entered the body the *second* time *just as it did the first?* Certainly we would. And from the words, "and he REVIVED," we would have thought of nothing else but that he lived on, soul and body together, precisely as before he died, as was the case with the child.

But I am wandering off again. I will pause here only to say further of this case, that it is another instance of the soul and body existing apart. The case of Jairus' daughter, who was raised from the dead, is another in point. Her soul and body had a separate being and re-union, after they had once been united and separated.—Mark 5: 35–42.

The reader's attention is next invited to the death and resurrection of Lazarus: John 11. He had been dead and lain in the grave FOUR DAYS. Yet, at the bidding of Christ, his soul returned into the body, he arose, came out of his grave, and lived on as before his death.

Now, it will be observed that the soul of Lazarus was as perfectly distinct from his body immediately before it re-entered it, as was that of Adam just before entering his body. Why could God not have made another body for Lazarus as easily as he made that for Adam? It will be conceded that he could have done so. Then there is no difficulty in comprehending how it was that a spirit which existed before Adam's body was made, could have entered and occupied it.

And as the soul of Lazarus existed while absent from the body, in some real and intelligent condition, or otherwise he could not have heard and obeyed the command of Christ, "Lazarus, come forth," we find no cause of wonder at being told that the spirit of Adam existed in the same way before animating his body. The death and resurrection of Christ himself proves conclusively that the soul and body can exist apart, and that *a living spirit* may animate *a dead body.*

But to all this it may be replied that the cases cited were all miracles. Oh! were they? Well, I reply, the first one of these "*miracles,*" is said to have been wrought by "*an old woman.*" And what is the existence of this world, of man, beast, and every other living creature that lives upon it, but so many miracles? All wonderful things are miracles. Everything we see around us is, to the man of thought, a subject for wonder and admiration. The very bodies in which we live, move and have our being, were said by the Psalmist to have been "*fearfully and wonderfully made.*" God "*worketh wonders.*" It is no valid objection, therefore, to anything which God is said to have done, or which it appears that He did, to say that it is wonderful, miraculous, or anything of that sort.

He has said to us: "As the heavens are higher than the earth, so are my ways higher than your ways, and my thoughts than your thoughts." While everything may appear mysterious and wonderful to us, nothing is so to Him. The difficulty with us, in this life, is that our minds are so beclouded, and our capacity so limited, that there are but few things we can fully comprehend; and hence it is, that we meet with so many wonders, mysteries, and miracles. It is to be hoped that a brighter day awaits us.

Whether we can understand how it is or not, there is nothing more clearly taught in the Bible than that the soul and body may not only exist apart, but that they can be separated and united again just as they were before.

Indeed, it would seem that the soul could, with God's permission, just leave his body at any time, remain absent as long as desired, and then return, and move on as if he had not left at all (provided his establishment has not dilapidated too much during his absence), as conveniently as the operator of a cotton-mill can stop his machinery, close up, and go abroad at pleasure, return at will, and fire up, raise steam, and go to work again, precisely as before he left.

Certain it is, our Savior could have done so, for he says of his life: "I have power to lay it down, and I have power to take it again."—John 10: 18. It is not so with us, however, for we are here as prisoners, and confined each within his own cell; but he was not a sinner or prisoner, as we are, but came and abode with us voluntarily.

That the soul can live without the body, and that after death it is restored to an order of being far above anything conceived of while in this life, we have proof conclusive in the Bible. Passing by a great variety of passages in which this is intimated very clearly, I will call attention to one authority only, and which is sufficient within itself. "And I John saw these things, and heard *them.* And when I had heard and seen, I fell down to worship before the feet of the angel which showed me these things. Then saith he unto me, See *thou do it* not: for I am thy fellow servant, and of thy brethren the prophets, and of them which keep the sayings of this book: worship God."—Rev. 22: 8, 9. The same thing is referred to in Rev. 19: 10, where John says plainly: "I fell at his feet to worship HIM." From this Scripture we learn: 1. That John was deceived as to who it was that had been talking to him. He most probably thought it was Christ in person. 2. That it was an angel of God, one who was admitted to the divine presence, and shared His confidence and favor; for he says, he was sent *from God*, therefore, he must have been *with Him*, and having been charged with a message of so much importance, he must have had the confidence and favor of his God. 3. That he was *the departed spirit of a man*, who had served his probationary term here, been redeemed by Jesus Christ and taken home to heaven; for he said: "I am thy FELLOW SERVANT and of thy brethren THE PROPHETS, and of them WHICH KEEP *the sayings of this book.*" To whom but a redeemed human soul could all these descriptions be applied? A "*fellow servant*" of St. John, "*and of thy brethren the prophets,*" as John also was, and, at the same time, one who kept the commandments which God gave to men. And below, in 22: 16, we read: "I, Jesus, have sent mine angel to testify unto you all these things in the churches." He calls him "*mine angel.*" This must have been one whom the Father had given Christ, as the price of that blood which he so freely shed for our ransom.

Here is food for thought, and a feast for the soul. By this we learn where the redeemed spirit goes after death; that it does not sleep with the body until the judgment, but returns at once to God, is restored to His favor, and becomes one of the gladsome throng, who worship about His throne while it is day and when it is night here. And that he is permitted, yea, commissioned to return to earth, in the capacity of a ministering angel, to instruct, warn, and encourage the loved ones he left behind him. He is not then shrouded in darkness, or confined to his prison, as before; but his spiritual eyes are again opened, his ears are unstopped, and the walls of his prison thrown down. Then he, with others like himself, in pairs—by tens—hundreds—or as many less, or more, as wish, together go, and make the voyage of heaven, can mount on angel wings, and soar aloft at will, through God's vast domain of worlds; and see and hear, or from others learn, all that has been, will be, and is transpiring here and there and everywhere. And still the more he sees, the more he learns, the more he loves his maker God, the happier he becomes. Could we at all times, and in the unsuspecting confidence in which the little child receives the fond sympathy and cheering assurances of a kindly affectionate parent, drink into our oft desponding souls, and in full measure, the buoyant hope and triumphant faith which the Word of God, as to the glorious future which awaits us, should inspire, then could we, as did the Apostle Paul, challenge death and the lonely grave: "O death, where is thy sting? O grave, where is thy victory?"

Before leaving this branch of the subject, I will invite the reader's attention to several things which have been said, by the sacred writers, of the Prophet Elijah and John the Baptist, and which do not seem to have attracted the general attention of theologians. This I do reluctantly, because I have to confess that I have not given the subject that attention myself which its importance demands, or which is necessary to enable me to form an opinion which is entirely satisfactory to my own mind.

The Scriptures referred to come very near amounting to proof conclusive, that the same spirit inhabited the bodies of both; and that, therefore, as the soul is the man, *they were but one and the* SAME. By reference to 2 Kings 2: 11, it will be seen that Elijah did not die, as men usually do, but was translated, soul and body together, up into heaven; and that Elisha, who was with him, *saw him no more.*

Malachi prophesied of the coming of Messiah and his forerunner, thus: "Behold, I will send my messenger, and he shall prepare the way before me: and the Lord, whom ye seek, shall suddenly come to his temple, even the messenger of the covenant, whom ye delight in; behold, he shall come, saith the Lord of hosts." . . . . "Behold, I will send you ELIJAH THE PROPHET before the coming of the great and dreadful day of the Lord."—Mal. 3: 1, and 4: 5.

The Jews confidently expected this prophecy would be fulfilled by the *reappearance* on earth of Elijah, who had been so translated, and that he would be the "*messenger*" who should prepare the way for the Messiah. And the supposed nonappearance of that prophet with them, before the advent of Christ, and as his forerunner or herald, was one of the chief grounds on which they rejected the Savior.

Of John the Baptist, the Savior said: "But what went ye out for to see? A prophet? Yea, I say unto you, and MORE THAN A PROPHET. For this is *he*, of whom it is written, Behold, I send my messenger before thy face, which shall prepare thy way before thee. Verily, I say unto you, Among them that are born of women, there hath not risen a greater than John the Baptist: notwithstanding he that is least in the kingdom of heaven is greater than he. . . . And, if ye will receive *it*, this is Elias which was for to come."—Matt. 11: 9–14.

By reference to that chapter, it will be observed that these remarks were made while John was in prison. After he was beheaded, Christ, in reference to him, said further: "And his disciples asked him, saying, Why then say the scribes, that Elias must first come? And Jesus answered and said unto them, Elias truly shall first come, and restore all things; but I say unto you, That Elias is come already, and they knew him not, but have done unto him whatsoever they listed. Likewise shall also the Son of man suffer of them. Then the disciples understood that he spake unto them of John the Baptist."—Matt. 17: 10–13. See also Mark 9: 11–13. The New Testament writers always call Elijah, "*Elias*," as is generally known.

The angel Gabriel, when he informed Zacharias of the coming of John the Baptist, said of him: "For he shall be great in the sight of the Lord, and shall drink neither wine nor strong drink; and *he shall be filled with the Holy Ghost, even from his mother's womb.* And many of the children of Israel shall he turn to the Lord their God. And he shall go before him in the spirit and power of Elias, to turn the hearts of the fathers to the children, and the disobedient to the wisdom of the just; to make ready a people prepared for the Lord."—Luke 1: 15–17.

"There was a man sent from God, whose name *was* John. The same came for a witness, to bear witness of the Light, that all *men* through him might believe. He was not that Light, but *was sent* to bear witness of that Light."—John 1: 6–8.

These things were said of John the Baptist by others. Now, notice what he said of himself: "There COMETH *one mightier than I* AFTER ME."—Mark 1: 7. "John bare witness of him, and cried, saying, This was he of whom I spake, He that cometh after me is preferred before me: for he was before me."—John 1: 15. "He it is who COMING AFTER ME is preferred before me, whose shoe's latchet I am not worthy to unloose."—27. "This is he of whom I said, After me COMETH a man which is preferred before me: for he was before me."—30. "And I knew him not: but he that SENT ME to baptize with water, the same said unto me, Upon whom thou shalt see the Spirit descending, and remaining on him, the same is he which baptizeth with the Holy Ghost."—33.

As no argument is intended here, I will, with a few suggestions, as to the manner in which these Scriptures strike my own mind, pass on.

Observe the peculiar phraseology of the Prophet Malachi: "Behold I will send my messenger;" and the Lord "shall suddenly COME." "I will send you Elijah the prophet." If I say to my reader, *I will send* you my servant, agent, or messenger, he, or she, will understand me as promising to send one *from where I am*, when I send him to where the reader is, when the messenger arrives. The Jews knew that Elijah had been translated to heaven, and expected he would have been sent *from there to Judea*. Was not that a reasonable construction of the language used? St. John expressly says: "There was a man *sent from* God, whose name was John." Not *sent by*, but *from* God. If he was right, that prophecy was fulfilled to the letter. The disciples asked the Savior: "Why then say the scribes that Elias must first come?" To which he replied: "Elias is COME already." John the Baptist said of himself and the Savior: "Then cometh one mightier than I after me." "He it is who coming after me is preferred before me." This form of expression is oft repeated, as will be observed from the above quotations; but I will not recite them all again. He, the Baptist, says again: "*I knew him not*, but HE THAT SENT ME to baptize with water, the same SAID UNTO ME," etc. By such expressions, so often met with, and applied alike to John the forerunner and the Savior himself, as *sent* from God, and one *coming before*, and the other *coming after*, it would seem that it was intended such remarks should convey the idea that they were not only both *sent by* the same divine authority, but *from* the same place; and that each existed before he was sent. Is not this the most natural inference?

But this is not all. Zacharias the prophet said of John the Baptist, "*And he shall be filled with the Holy Ghost, even from his mother's womb.*" This is *very unlike* the way in which the condition of the rest of us, when we came into the world, is described in the Bible. To say that one is filled with the Holy Ghost *from his mother's womb*, is equivalent to saying that he came into the world holy, just, and good—a child of *God;* such as the angels of heaven, and as the regenerated and translated souls of men are. What less could have been meant?

And the Savior is *reported to have said* himself, of his herald, that he was "*more than a prophet*," and that, "*This is Elias which was for to come.*"

From the reading of these Scriptures, and in fact of the

whole Bible, with the exception of *one*, and *only one*, little monosyllable, I would entertain no doubt of their spiritual identity. There is nothing unreasonable in it; but, on the contrary, it is easy to perceive why one who needed not baptism, or regeneration, of which it was the sign, himself *should have been sent* to introduce that ordinance, by baptizing the Master and his immediate disciples.

Now, for that little monosyllable. In our translation of the Bible, by some means, I know not what, the Baptist is made, not only to deny his identity with Elijah, but to omit saying a word about his coming in the *spirit* or *power* of the old prophet; as it was so plainly and fully declared by others, both that he *should* and *had* come. I refer to the circumstance, which is recorded in John 1: 19–28, of the Jews sending to inquire of him, "*Who art thou?*" The messengers who were sent reported (with divers other questions put by them and answered by him), the following: "*Art thou Elias? And he saith, I am not.*"

The *not*, although but a very little word, becomes one of no small significance as found here. If it has the *right* to occupy the position there assigned it, it has the *power* to deny and make null and void all the authorities referred to, as having been spoken by the prophets, the Savior, and of him who was reported as having so answered that question.

It is not too much to say, that there is something wrong about that report of the "*Priests and Levites.*" Wherein that error lies is the point referred to, as one which I have not investigated sufficiently to have formed an opinion which would be worth anything to others. The truth is, I am so well satisfied that some mistake, or omission, has been made, either by some copyist or translator of that paragraph, that I have cared but little to know when, or by whom it was done.

If that *not* were found in a will or deed, when up for construction before a court of chancery, and surrounded by so many, and such clearly inconsistent and contradictory clauses, occurring both before and after that, it would tumble out, *on motion*. And the chancellor would not waste time to inquire how it got there. Nor will I. But for the benefit of those who have the time, means, and inclination to look into it (and it should be done), I will suggest, as a starting point, that the error may, and most likely is to be found in the nineteenth or twentieth verses. St. John may not have intended to say that the report which those infidel "Priests and Levites" made of what the Baptist said of himself, was *true;* but simply wished to put on record the *report which they made*, or were said to have made. Many other falsehoods, perpetrated by the same wicked crew, were preserved for future generations by the New Testament writers. If the difficulty lies in either of these verses it may have arisen simply from an omission of the translators to throw in such explanatory words as are necessary to express the true meaning of the original text.

To reconcile this paragraph with the whole Bible, nothing more is necessary than to insert after "And," in the twentieth verse, the two little words, "*they said,*" italicized (as the translators always did such explanatory words, when thrown in to give the true meaning by themselves), so as to read, "And *they said* he confessed," etc.

If these words were found there, no doubt would be left that Elijah and John the Baptist, although appearing at different times, and occupying different bodies, were the same. The only connection this question has, however, with the argument before me, is, that the account given of the birth of the body and origin of the spirit of John the Baptist, proves conclusively that his spirit was not "*created in Adam,*" and was not produced by or from his (John's) parents, as his body was. And, for that purpose, it is immaterial whether he ever heard of Elijah the prophet or not, as his spirit certainly was *in being* before it "*was sent*" or "*come*" into his body.

Inasmuch as it is desired to speak of the union of the spirit and body of Jesus Christ in another place, I pass that interesting subject for the present, and leave my readers to make up their own opinion or opinions, should they differ, as to whether *his spirit* and *body* descended together from Adam through his parents.

The eighth chapter of John reflects much light on the subject of our present inquiry.

"23. And he said unto them, Ye are from beneath; I am from above: ye are of this world; I am not of this world."

Here are two distinct apothegms announced, both of himself and us; and which indicate with unerring certainty, that neither he, nor we, was, or are, in an original or *first state* of existence in this life. "Ye are FROM BENEATH," are the words of Christ, and have meaning. "*Ye are of this world*," are from the same divine source, and of like worth.

Now, apply the first to our spirits, and the last to our bodies, and the import of both, though grave, is plain. The affirmations of himself, "I am from above," "I am not of this world," apply to his own spirit and body in the same way.

Our bodies are but fruits of ordinary and natural generation, and are, therefore (as well as our souls), like others of this world; his body was produced by an extraordinary cause, and not as ours were: and hence, *was* not a natural production "*of this world*."

"38. I speak that which I have seen with my Father: and ye do that which ye have seen with your father."

"44. Ye are of *your* father the devil, and the lusts of your father ye will do."

Observe, Christ compares that which *he had seen* with his Father to that which the vain Jews, who were immediately addressed, had seen with their father. What could he have meant, by what they had seen with their father the devil? We certainly see nothing *with him* here. One moderately fair glimpse of that long venerated sire of ours now, would put the most of us in a condition not to recollect much that we saw WITH HIM.

We must, therefore, conclude, that the Savior referred to something which they had seen *with him* when they were on terms more familiar (if not more agreeable) than those existing between him and them in this world; and, if so, then they and he existed somewhere else, and under different relations, before they came into this life. And, again, as their bodies were of this world, their spirits must have had being before their bodies were born, and apart from them. "For the love of Christ constraineth us; because we thus judge, that if one died for all, then were all dead: And *that* he died for all, that they which live should not henceforth live unto themselves, but unto him which died for them, and rose again."—2 Cor. 5: 14, 15. If all of this generation for whom Christ died were "*dead*" before his crucifixion, we must have lived before, as one must live before he dies; for we were not living as human beings then. In any other view, as he atoned for only those who were dead then, we could claim no interest in his salvation. And the very text quoted says, "*he died for all.*"

The preceding argument has been entirely negative, as the reader has already observed. This is a common, and sometimes the only way by which we can prove the truth of a hypothesis, and is often no less satisfactory on that account. If it has been or can be shown that the souls of men existed before and at the time the body of Adam was made, it follows, as a necessary sequence, that they were not *created in him.* And as the Bible furnishes no account of the creation of the souls of men, or of the angels of heaven, but does affirm the existence of both, it is an open question which was created first, the soul, or the body of man; and it is one which should be examined in the light of such facts as are recorded there, and which tend to illustrate the one now under consideration.

There is a class of texts from which, as it would seem, some have thought we have evidence that the souls of all were created in Adam, and that they are procreated from generation to generation just as are the bodies. Of such are the following: "And the Lord appeared unto Abraham, and said, Unto thy SEED will I give this land."—Gen. 12: 7, and 35: 11, 12. "And God said unto him (Jacob), I *am* God Almighty: be fruitful and multiply; a nation and a company of nations shall be of thee, and kings shall come out of thy LOINS. And the land which I gave Abraham and Isaac, to thee I will give it, and to thy SEED after thee will I give the land." And again, 46: 26, 27: "All the souls that came with Jacob into Egypt, which came out of his LOINS, besides Jacob's sons' wives, all the SOULS *were* threescore and six. And the SONS of Joseph, which were born him in Egypt, *were* two SOULS: all the souls of the house of Jacob, which came into Egypt, *were* threescore and ten." "I will set up thy SEED after thee, which shall proceed out of thy BOWELS, and I will establish his kingdom."—2 Sam. 7: 12. In this promise, which was made to David, both Solomon and Jesus Christ were referred to, as the context shows.

"The Lord hath sworn *in* truth unto David; he will not turn from it; of the FRUIT OF THY BODY will I SET UPON MY THRONE."—Ps. 132: 11. That by *seed*, *souls*, the issue of the *loins*, *bowels*, etc., as found in the above, and all similar passages, the bodies and not the souls of men are intended, I think, is too clear to require any serious argument. The disciples of Christ, most indubitably, understood all such expressions as applying to the body. St. Peter said of King David: "Therefore, being a prophet, and knowing that God had sworn with an oath to him, that of the *fruit of his loins*, ACCORDING TO THE FLESH, *he would raise up Christ to sit on his throne.*" Hear St. Paul, who understood all these things much better than we do: "Concerning his Son Jesus Christ our Lord, which was made of the SEED of David ACCORDING TO THE FLESH."—Rom. 1: 3. "What shall we then say that Abraham our father, as pertaining to the flesh, hath found?"—Rom. 4: 1. "For I could wish that myself were accursed from Christ for my brethren, my kinsmen ACCORDING TO THE FLESH."—Rom. 9: 3. (Note, nothing is said as to whether they were his kindred ACCORDING TO THE SPIRIT, or not.) "Servants, be obedient to them that are *your* masters according to the flesh."—Eph. 6: 5.

Confidently believing that no one who has heretofore understood such Scriptures to teach that the human soul is nothing more than a spiritual essence, emanating from our common parents, will fail to be convinced of error in that vital particular, on a review of them for him, or herself, I pass on, at least, for the present.

CHAPTER XV.

Mosaic History of Creation, both Literal and Figurative—Why it was not Full in the Figurative Sense—Several of the Symbolical Features Noticed—Union of Soul and Body of Adam—The Garden of Eden—Trees of Life and Death—The River Which Watered the Garden—The Employment of Adam—But One Rule Prescribed for His Observance—Creation of Eve—Her Soul—The Temptation and Fall—The Shame and Fear Thereby Produced—The Excuses Offered—The Curse on Satan—On Eve—On Adam—The Coats of Skins—Who Were Present—Expulsion from Eden—The Cherubims and Flaming Sword—Other Scriptures Prove the Account of the Creation Figurative—A Passing Remark.

Our ninth proposition is: "That the account given in the Bible of the temptation and fall of man in Eden, although literally true, is also a clear symbolical and allegorical representation of his real temptation by, and fall with Satan in heaven." It was not the covenant plan for the probation of man, as has already been argued, that he should be put in possession of a full knowledge of his nature, and of the responsibilities which rested upon him in this life. To have so informed him, would have defeated the very object of the creation of this world, and of giving us a fair opportunity to repent our rebellious conduct in heaven, and return to the service of God and His Christ. To the accomplishment of that divine and merciful purpose, it was necessary, however, that we should know something of ourselves, and of the importance of a strict observance of the laws of our Creator.

That amount of light has been given to every generation which has lived on this earth up to the present time, and we have every reason to believe the same liberality will be extended to all who are to come after us. And, perhaps, in none of God's dealing with man, has His infinite wisdom and loving kindness been so beautifully displayed and universally manifested as in the various ways in which that heavenly light has been reflected upon the pathway of all, whether Jew or heathen, Christian or pagan, of every age and country, and of whatever condition, from the creation of Adam to the present time. It is impossible to conceive of any other way in which so many hidden things of God could have been at once placed within the compass of man's limited capacity, and yet done in such a way that they could only be comprehended one by one, as his necessities should require and heaven's providences permit; and at the same time furnishing a fruitful and profitable field for reflection and explanation, by the cultivated and pious mind of all ages of the world, than that by which it was done in the symbolical and allegorical account of the creation as it is recorded in Genesis.

Of the interesting circumstances narrated in that brief history, which present to the thinking mind subjects of anxious inquiry as to what each is intended to represent and teach, are the following:

1. The formation of the body of Adam, of that which was seen, and "breathing" into that body "*the breath of life*," a thing unseen, yet no less real, and of far more value than was the visible man. 2. The planting of the "*garden eastward in Eden*," so beautiful and lovely. 3. The placing of two trees, unlike all others, in the midst of it—the tree of life, and the tree of death. 4. The river with four heads which flowed "out of" the garden to water it. 5. The putting of man in the garden "*to dress and keep it.*" 6. The command given directly by God to man in person: "Of every tree of the garden thou mayest freely eat; but of the tree of the knowledge of good and evil, thou shalt not eat of it, for in the day thou eatest thereof thou shalt surely die." 7. The causing Adam to *fall into a deep sleep*, and taking from his side a rib, and "*closing up the flesh instead thereof;*" and the making that rib a woman. 8. The manner in which the serpent deceived the woman, and

Adam was led into sin by and with her. 9. The shame and the fear of God caused by their sin. 10. The very poor excuses rendered by each for their voluntary violation of the only law prescribed by their Maker. 11. The several curses pronounced upon each. 12. The putting enmity between the serpent and the seed of the woman, and the foretold result of it. 13. The making "coats of skins," and clothing them therewith. 14. The driving *the man* out of Eden; and, 15. The placing "*at the east end of the garden*," cherubims and a flaming sword, which turned every way to keep the way of the tree of life." These are all so many life-like pictures, and vivid representations of man's true condition in this life, of his original purity, present depravity, and of God's sympathy with him even in his present fallen condition, as well as of His wrath against the wicked. All this, *and more*, is represented by the divine Artist, with an unerring and skillful hand, within a space so small, and yet it contains a perfect epitome of the whole history of our temptation and fall in heaven, our expulsion thence, the preparation for, and our probationary state here, and a promise to the obedient of redemption by blood and eternal life. Well may that work have been pronounced "*very good*."

In a treatise like this, nothing more can be attempted than a brief reference to and application of the most striking outline features of this divinely traced picture. If I had the descriptive powers of a Shakspeare, Milton, or anything approximate to those of either, but which I have not, and the requisite leisure which I could devote to the task, there is, perhaps, no labor of like magnitude in which I would take more pleasure, than in making a full explication and explanation of such parts of that mysterious narrative as *I think* I understand. I can not, however, attempt anything of that nature here. The very thought of such huge undertaking reminds me of Virgil's hyperbolical description of the wooden horse which the Greeks led into Troy, and of St. John's vivid conception of the enormous mass of books it would have required to contain and illustrate all our Savior taught during his brief ministry on earth.

1. The body of Adam was "*formed of the dust of the ground.*" By this we are informed that even his body was not what it once was, and that as the body of man, that is, the material of which it was made, was elevated in the scale of being by having been so changed, right here the idea of an upward tendency is presented. Into the body which had been so formed, God "*breathed the breath of life.*" Here we find an inanimate body animated by a living spirit. The body was a thing physical, substantial, but of recent formation; the soul was spiritual, invisible to the natural eye of man, and yet had the quality of infusing life into the earthly body which it entered; and was something which was in existence when the body was made. Man, then, was a compound of two separate and distinct natures; one new and physical, subject to be changed into different forms or conditions of being; the other metaphysical, spiritual, eternal. And from the condition of the body before the soul entered it, and the wonderful change which was caused in it the moment the spirit entered and took possession of his edifice, we learn that the soul is the vital, the living, thinking, acting, and, therefore, *responsible* part of man, as constituted by the union of the two.

It should be remembered that Adam was not "*formed*" in the garden, but outside of it, and before the preparation of the little paradise intended for him. The soul had entered the body, and the *man* was fully constituted in a place much less desirable than was his future home. The garden was also planted "*eastward in Eden.*" The sun, the fountain of light, rises in the east; it is there the first dawn of light appears, which is soon to drive the darkness of night away. The word Eden denotes *pleasure, delight.* From this we should learn that God has something better in store for us than the poor pleasures of this sinful life. That He has a home prepared for us "*eastward,*" where is the fountain of light and perfection of life—an Eden of spiritual pleasure—soul delight.

3. But we are, in the next place, warned of dangers which lie before us. In that beautiful and lovely garden, into which God was soon to remove Adam, there were two trees growing, not only unlike all the surrounding shrubs, vines, and trees, but the fruits of which were as far different in their effects as is a life in heaven from a death in hell. So is the pilgrim's life in this dark and mysterious world a succession of hopes and fears. One moment our hopes are so highly excited that we imagine we can almost see our seats ready prepared and waiting in heaven; and the next, an ominous doubt strikes the mind, our fears are alarmed; the spiritual light, which but now shone so brightly above and around us, is gone as the lightning's flash. The whole soul is overwhelmed in darkness and crushed with fears. Nothing less than the still, small voice of the Holy Spirit: "*Fear not! I will not forsake thee*," could, under such trying circumstances, save us from hopeless despair.

4. A river is often used by the sacred writers as a symbol of eternal life; as in Rev. 22: 1—"And he showed me a pure river of water of life, clear as crystal, proceeding out of the throne of God and of the Lamb." By the river that "*went out of Eden to water the garden*," is represented that eternal life which was provided for those who were to inhabit that beautiful and lovely place which was provided by his Maker for Adam, and who was its first and for a time sole occupant.

5. "And the Lord God took the man and put him into the garden of Eden, to dress it and to keep it"—2: 15. The business of Adam was to keep and dress the garden; although it is not at all likely that there was any necessity for the labor of man to support himself in that garden (for the earth produced spontaneously an abundant supply of food for both man and beast), yet man was not intended for, or adapted to a wholly inactive life; but moderate exercise was a requisite to the enjoyment of his life then as now. And we can conceive of no physical employment that would be more agreeable to a man in his state, before the fall, than that of pruning his young trees and shrubs, training his tender vines, and trimming and dressing his flower plants in the

cool of the morning, and again late in the evening. From the fact that Adam, even in a state of innocence, was charged with a duty requiring activity and care, we should learn that in no condition of life ought we to remain idle; but that some laudable occupation is necessary to our happiness here, as well as to our well-being hereafter. The very conformation of our bodies and natural proclivities of our minds furnish proof enough that we were intended by our Creator for activity, both of body and mind. We have a work to do here, as well as had our common father. He had an Eden to lose by the violation of God's law; and we have souls to save by the observance of His commands. Let us not be idle or slothful in the completion of our task, lest, ere we are ready, the night of death overtake us, and then it will be too late.

6. No duty was required of Adam but that of making himself happy all the time by attention to his garden. And but one restraint was laid upon his utmost liberty to do as he pleased, and to eat, drink, sleep, wake, work, or rest, and to go where and return when he chose. In everything else he was as free and unrestrained as the morning breeze which wafted to his waking sense the cheering notes of his whole winged band of minstrels sweet, when first they piped their matin songs.

What more could man have asked? What less could God have required? For there must be a limit set, even to the indulgence of the most innocent pleasures, or else the appetite will cloy, and that which should be sweet will turn to bitterness and loathing. And if a boundary is best for him who knows but one restraint, there must be one whose right it is to give, and another whose duty is that law to keep. The law which was given Adam was but little more than a piece of friendly caution and advice. God advised him of the presence of that poison-tree and of the danger of partaking of its deceptive fruit. There was no threat of death as a penalty to be imposed on Adam, by another, for eating of that fruit; but he was simply put on notice of what would be the natural effect of partaking of it. "In the day thou eatest thereof, thou shalt surely die," simply meant that he would die, as was proven by what the serpent said to Eve, "*Ye shall not surely die*," and which was verified. It was, however, given and received in the nature of a law, although expressed in as mild a form as anything which could be considered a law could have been. It was delivered directly to Adam by his Creator before man had learned to fear, and caused no alarm when given.

The comparatively free and happy circumstances under which man was placed in Eden, is a feeble though faithful representation of the estate which he enjoyed in heaven before he was led into the ways of sin and folly there. His faith in his Creator appears to have been unwavering, and at the same time he seems to have felt no more alarm, or disquiet of any sort, in the immediate presence of God, than a favorite son does in the society of his father.

7. "And the Lord God caused a deep sleep to fall upon Adam, and he slept: and he took one of his ribs, and closed up the flesh instead thereof; and the rib, which the Lord God had taken from man, made he a woman, and brought her unto the man."—Gen. 2: 21, 22. Note, Adam was in "*a deep sleep*," when the rib was taken from him; sleep is an emblem of death. When his soul entered his body, he lay as a newly-molded lump of clay fresh from the potter's hand. He can not be said to have been dead, for he (his body) never had lived. When the rib was taken from him, he lay *sleeping, as if dead*, and was unconscious of what was going on until the rib had been taken from his side, the flesh closed up, healed sound as before he fell asleep, and had been fashioned into woman. The rib, after it was detached from the body, of which it had been a component part, was as dead—as void of animal and spiritual life—as is the foot or hand which has been, by the surgeon's skill, amputated from the body; or, as a bit of butcher's beef as it hangs in the stall. Was it not?

The statement is not, that God made the woman *of, or out of the rib;* but it is, "and THE RIB *which the* LORD GOD *had taken from man*, MADE HE A WOMAN." That is, by His wise creative power God caused the rib to expand, grow out, and assume all the forms and qualities of which the human frame consists, and adapted to the performance of every function necessary for the purposes of her creation. Here we observe that God works in ways and by means unknown to man. We must believe that Adam was as ignorant as any Hottentot of the means used by God in removing his rib, healing the wound, and, by a simple touch of his miraculous power, causing a single rib of his to bound up in a twinkling of the eye, and stand erect before him—a full grown and mature woman—in form and feature far excelling himself, and clad in the witching charms of maiden loveliness.

No human eye has been permitted to witness the entrance of the soul into the body, and observe the effects of that union. When Adam was made, there were none to see and scrutinize the process by which his earthly man was converted into a living, thinking, active creature; when Eve was made he was in "*a deep sleep*," and saw, or knew nothing of it. And from then till now, no one has been allowed to know anything more of how that mysterious union is effected, or at what moment it is done, than what we can learn from the Sacred Scriptures, and observation, guided by human reason thereon.

It is a fact worth serious consideration, that not a word is said in the Mosaic history about the soul of Eve. Whether she had one, if she had, what was it, whence it came, when and at what stage of the process of her formation and maturity it took possession of her body——all these, and other matters of interest connected with the miraculous manner of her creation, are left by the sacred historian wrapped in Egyptian darkness. This was most assuredly done for a purpose. Then why were we left in utter ignorance concerning a matter of so much value to ourselves? There is a good and sufficient reason why that delicate matter was left untold. If all had been revealed, the whole object of our creation would have failed, as has already been shown; and even if a vague or delphic account had been recorded, as to *forming the body* of Eve, and *breathing* into it *the breath of* LIFE, whereby she "*became a living soul,*" as was done in the case of Adam, a clue, a starting point, would have been given—a dark lantern furnished the curious adventurer, by and from the help of which he could have groped his way around and through the dark aisles, and up the devious stairways of revelation, and thus have entered the secret chamber wherein the hidden things of God are kept concealed, much sooner than it was intended man should know the true character and origin of his own soul.

The soul being a pre-existent spirit, of course no account could have been given of its creation when her body was; and if the historian had particularized the circumstances with the same and no more distinctness than he did as to the formation of Adam—something in this way: "And the Lord God formed (*the woman of the rib, which he took from the side of man*) and breathed into (*her*) nostrils the breath of life, and (*woman also*) became a living soul;" a great deal more light would have been reflected on that which is involved in so much darkness and uncertainty.

Three distinct facts would thereby have been revealed that were left concealed: 1. That Eve had a soul as well as Adam. 2. That it was not made of the same material of which her body was "*formed;*" and, 3. That her soul, as that of Adam, was some spiritual essence which existed before. But some one may inquire, was not her soul made of the *same rib* of which her body was made? To that question I should reply, *I guess not!* The rib was but a dead bone, as remarked already. Adam had but one soul ("*so far as we are informed*"), and that was a spirit which was breathed into his body. If that had gone out of him with the rib, he would have been (*minus a rib*), just as he was before his spirit animated his body. It will hardly be insisted that the soul is divisible as is the body, and that a *small portion of the soul remained in the rib*, and was made a whole one as the rib became a whole body. If a part of the soul of Adam was in the rib when taken from the body, sufficient to have become a whole soul as the rib became a whole body, then the soul and body are so commingled and identified that neither could exist without nor survive the other; and, therefore, the soul dies with the body, and is shown not to be immortal, as we have hitherto been informed that it was. Too many absurdities follow such a hypothesis to justify the argument of it further.

From the fact alone, that nothing is said about the soul of Eve, we have very good reason to believe that it was not made then. For a clear, though short history of the origin of her body having been given, and that being of so much more comparative worth than was her body, it would be indeed wonderful, if it was made at the same time, that nothing should have been said about it; as we can, in that case, conceive of no reason why there should have been any concealment of the fact that the soul was made, or how, or of what it was made.

The most reasonable inference, from a view of all that is said of the creation of our first parents, is that the facts connected with the creation of Eve are correctly narrated so far as they were different from those relating to the creation of Adam, and that nothing further is said about it, because they were, in all other respects, the same in both cases. If I am right in coming to this natural conclusion, it follows, as a matter of course, that her spirit was "*breathed*" into her, just as Adam's was into him, and that they were both of the same class of spirits. That, I have no doubt, is the true solution of the whole problem. And having noticed this subject partially under another head, I will pass on.

8. In the third chapter we have an account of the temptation and fall of man. Now, reader, get your Bible and read that chapter, then read Rev. 12, and compare the two carefully together, and see if each does not reflect the light of the other, as certainly as the mirror reflects the general contour of your own face. The style of both is chiefly allegorical. I have already explained the figures used in Rev. 12, and will now offer a few remarks in explanation of this, and but few, as I think a mere suggestion that they both point with magnetic certainty to the same events will be found sufficient.

Dr. A. Clarke speaks of this as one of the most difficult things in the whole of the Sacred Writings to understand, and says: "The whole account is either a *simple narrative of facts*, or it is an *allegory*." I am satisfied that it is both together.

There is no sufficient reason to disbelieve that the whole narrative is literally true; nor is there any, why we should not believe it true, in an allegorical sense, as applying to another transaction with which the one recorded was intimately connected, and, in fact, out of which this grew. As already remarked, there was perhaps no other way in which the original transgression of Satan, and of man under his influence, could have been recorded so as to have served all the purposes for which this figurative account was intended.

What sort of an animal it was that appeared in Eden and held that conversation with Eve, is a question about which the most learned commentators have failed to agree; but, so far as I know, there is no difference of opinion between them as to who or what was the moving cause, and intelligent actor in the matter. The same circumstance has been referred to so often by the sacred writers and by our Savior himself, and all pointing directly to Satan as the real deceiver, no matter in what form he appeared on that occasion, that we have no reason to doubt his being the party described as the "*serpent*."

We have here, then, as in Revelation the same *deceiver* identified as *Satan*—that "deceiveth the whole world." It has been shown satisfactorily (to myself at least), that the fallen angels were the parties deceived by him in heaven, and that the spirits of men are of the same; and that they were again made his dupes here, and are now the sufferers for having followed him.

The deceptive .means used were the same in both instances. It was not done by direct falsehood alone, if at all, but by misrepresentations of that which was, in a certain sense, true, and by a suppression of truth. Eve, no doubt, had believed that, if she ate of that fruit, the consequence would be that she would die a natural death.

Satan told her that was not so, but that by eating of it she and her husband would become "*as gods, knowing good and evil.*" That proved literally true. They did become "*as gods, knowing good and evil,*" but at the same time they violated the law of God, and subjected themselves to a spiritual and eternal death, which was, beyond all comparison, worse than the death she had feared. Satan knew well what God meant by His remark, that "in the day thou eatest thereof, thou shalt surely die;" but he carefully suppressed that truth. If he had told her all he knew of the sad consequences of what he encouraged her to do, *he would have failed of his purposes* most signally. So would he have failed to have deceived and misled the holy angels in heaven, if they could have foreseen the fatal result to themselves of their folly and wickedness in following his lead.

He deceived Eve by flattery, and appeals to her pride and vanity: "Your eyes shall be opened; and ye shall be as gods," said he. That was a thing highly gratifying to her pride, and very desirable food for her vanity. She was, doubtless, wonderfully well pleased with the idea of being so much elevated in the scale of being. That was a weak point at which to assail a woman. Many, very many of her daughters have been, by the same enemy, deceived and led down to perdition by the same kind of flattery. Adam was, in part, influenced by the same deceptive assurances; but was also, as the account justifies us in believing, very much controlled by his devotion to his wife. He, too, thought a literal death would result from eating the fruit of that tree, but suspected nothing worse; and on being informed that Eve had already partaken of it, he expected she would die, and without her life had but few charms for him, and probably he would have preferred a physical death to the grief which the loss of his companion would have brought on himself.

The same cause—pride, vanity, and consequent envy—led to the rebellion of Satan and his angels in heaven, as it is purposed to show hereafter.

The parties concerned as deceiver and deceived, both in

Eden and in heaven, were the same; the artful practices were the same, and the consequences were, in an allegorical sense, the same, as will appear presently.

9. In the shame and fear produced on the minds of Adam and Eve, we have proof that what Satan told Eve would be the consequence of eating the forbidden fruit was true. Their eyes were opened and they became as gods (beings superior to themselves), "*knowing good and evil.*" They saw their nakedness—helpless condition; knowing they had done wrong, they feared the wrath of God. They had enjoyed all the felicity of familiar intercourse with their Maker. They loved and revered Him as their creator, benefactor, and friend; He had loved them as the creatures of His power and the objects of His favor. They had known "*good*" with Him in heaven, they then knew a *little* of the "*evil*" of sin. "*They sewed fig leaves togethcr and made themselves aprons.*" What a shallow device to hide them from the ALL-SEEING EYE! It may be, that some of us may, even now, be trying to hide from the vengeance of an angry God behind *aprons of fig leaves* —*the name Christian*—when our hearts are far from Christ. What beautiful emblems we have here!

10. The excuse rendered by our venerable grandfather was but poor, I admit; but it was manly, honorable, and highly creditable to himself; and at the same time, he made no disparaging reflection on the conduct of Eve. When called to account for his violation of the command of God, he owned up like a man, and told the truth, to the shame of the devil: "The woman whom thou gavest *to be* with me, she gave me of the tree, and I DID EAT." And poor old mother Eve, in that trying moment of her checkered life, sustained herself quite as well: "*The serpent beguiled me, and I did eat.*" That was the truth, the whole truth, and nothing but the truth. When held to account by Michael in heaven for their rebellion against the laws of Jehovah God, they had, doubtless, similar but no better apologies to offer. It is easy to conceive the analogy between the two cases, but impossible for us now to know all that occurred there.

Notwithstanding their honesty and frankness, we can but see that they were not only alarmed, but they were *humble, penitent, and believing.* They were just in that condition required by Christ of us all, when ministering in person with us, in order to receive pardon and be restored to eternal life. They *believed, confessed, and repented.* When Christ witnessed the afflictions of the family and friends of departed Lazarus on account of his death, it is said he "*wept.*" And, if clothed with a body capable of generating tears, when he saw the deep contrition and anguish of soul evinced by that unhappy pair, on that ever-memorable morning in Eden, he then, too, *would have* "*wept!*" Do not say I err in this, because they were driven out of Eden and punished with the curse *after that.* It is true they were punished *after that*, but it is as certain as that the Bible is true, that *they were not punished for that*, after that sad and solemn interview. Their punishment *for that sin* was already sufficient. Tell me not that our Redeemer, who had already undertaken our redemption at the cost of his own life and blood, and whose arrangements had then been made for the execution of his benign purposes, and on account of which he was there on the morning of that eventful day, felt no sympathy on that occasion for those he loved so well. He had the power to forgive, and I entertain no doubt but he *did* freely forgive them. He knew all and pitied their blind and ruined condition.

> He knew them long, had known them well;
> He knew them in their purer state,
> And knew them in their fall.
> He pitied them, who, once so great,
> By Satan led to their sad fate,
> So humbled had become.

No, reader, they were not further punished for that transgression. That was but a symbolical representation of the real sin for which they and we were all to answer.

11. "And the Lord God said unto the serpent, Because thou hast done this, thou *art* cursed above all cattle, and above every beast of the field; upon thy belly shalt thou

go, and dust shalt thou eat all the days of thy life," etc.—Gen. 3: 14. A pretty severe penalty was that, even on the devil, by the way, if for but one day's work! This verse is a pure allegory. By the *serpent*, Satan was intended; by that which he had then done, his deceptions and revolt in heaven are represented. He was cursed above all "*cattle* and *beasts of the field;* the cattle and beasts here stand for the others who were involved in that transgression with him; and, as he was to be punished more than any other, we are to understand that he was the most guilty. His humiliated condition is represented as that of one who must crawl upon the ground and eat dirt all his life. "*What a fall was there, my countrymen!*"

The woman, having first yielded to the tempter, was cursed the more severely; her sorrows should be multiplied (made many), and especially should she sorrow on account of her children. Her fondness for her husband should be so binding that she could not break away from him, and yet, as the tyrant rules his slave, so could he, at will, "*rule over*" her. Woman, being deeply involved in the heavenly rebellion, was required to perform the duties of a painful office, which became necessary to the work of redemption. Adam, although acting, to some extent, under the influence of Eve, is evidently treated as the party most responsible, and the head of his race. It was for his sake that the *ground was cursed.* And in sorrow, heavy drudgery, and the consequent sweat of his face, he was doomed to procure his food while he should live; and that, in fine, he should die, and his body molder away, and become as the dust of which it was made. In that, he was informed that he was but a sojourner here; yet from whence he came, and whither he should go, he appears to have been left in total darkness.

12. "And I will put enmity between thee and the woman, and between thy seed and her seed; it shall bruise thy head, and thou shalt bruise his heel." The most valuable lesson taught by this verse, as is most likely, is that which is generally considered its full meaning. I have nothing to do in this place, therefore, more than to offer another;

and it is one which I am well satisfied was purposely included also. It is this, that by the *seed of the woman bruising the serpent's head*, and *the serpent bruising his heel*, is meant that those who repent their folly and wickedness in being seduced by the cunning and deceptive devices of Satan, and their participation with him in that "*War in Heaven*," and return to Christ in this world, will curse that wise but wicked *head* of his for having so deceived them; and that, in turn, Satan will curse the *heel* of him who owns he was deceived, and flies away to Christ for pardon, and salvation too, on meeting with him here.

13. "Unto Adam also and to his wife did the LORD God make coats of skins, and clothed them."—21. It will be observed that the name *Lord*, as printed in our Bible, is sometimes, as here, expressed in small capital letters, to denote the fact that in the original it is Jehovah, and that by the expression "*Jehovah God*," the Father is intended and not the Son. We are elsewhere informed by the Sacred Writers that this world was made by the Son, who was, for that purpose, sent by the Father, and clothed with His wisdom and power.

The language used here is "the LORD God made coats," etc. We must, therefore, look for some other than a literal rendering of this passage; for if God the Father made nothing else here, by his own immediate act, we will not do the sacred historian the injustice to charge him with saying, that he did so make those "*coats of skins*." If, then, the most literal construction is not to be accepted as the true one, we should next look for the most reasonable one that consists with the text. What is that? It is, that He who made the world and man, made the "*coats of skins*" also; and that He made them precisely as He did other work of a similar nature. Then, how was that? By the agency of man; as he wrote His Book, and baptized those who became His followers. All that can be fairly inferred from this Scripture is, that God endowed Adam and Eve with the capacity and skill to prepare for themselves that particular clothing; bade them do so, and they obeyed His command, and made them. If they were so made, it was properly and truthfully said that the "LORD God made them." It was done in virtue of His wisdom and power, by His creatures, whom He had a right to use as His servants, and in obedience to His command. And, "*what one does by the agency of another he does by himself.*"

I have digressed from my line of illustration to relieve this passage of a very unfair criticism, to which it has been subjected; and I beg pardon of the reader for having done so, and return:

To procure the skins, of which to make the "*coats*," the animals whose skins were to be used must have been slain, and the skins taken off for that purpose. For, it will be remembered, that before that time no flesh had been used for food by man or beast. To have killed and skinned the animals, blood must have been shed. "It is the blood that maketh an atonement for the soul."—Lev. 17: 11. "And without shedding of blood is no remission."—Heb. 9: 22. Here, then, we have a beautiful symbolical representation of the redemption of man by the shedding of the blood of Christ; and by whose immediate order the blood was shed, to procure a covering for the sin-smitten bodies of Adam and Eve. As their bodies were covered, and their shame concealed, by the shedding of the blood of beasts, so were their souls to be covered and their sins atoned by the shedding of the blood of the God who made them; and that, also, by his own free will and consent, as the blood by which it was symbolized was shed.

The nakedness of man, when first created, represents the nakedness of the soul. By reason of transgression he had been stripped of that "*white robe*" in which, as a holy angel, he had been clothed in heaven, and driven down to earth, *poor*, *blind*, and *naked*. And before he can be permitted to return, his sins must be expiated, and his soul reclothed as before. All this our gracious Redeemer undertook to do for those who might prove themselves worthy of pardon on his liberal terms. He has made the sacrifice for sin, and has promised to provide each a robe of righteousness; that is, to give them (the sons of Satan) *power to become the sons of God*, who come to him as directed.

14. "And the Lord God said, Behold, the man is become

as ONE OF US, to know good and evil."—22. Enough is said, in this place, to awaken anxious desire to know more; but we are not permitted fully to gratify such a wish, although it is a laudable one, or it would not have been excited *on purpose*, as it was evidently done. How many, and who were they that witnessed this, the most melancholy scene of the whole tragedy? Christ, *our best friend*, was there we know; and that others were with him we know; and they must have been our friends and sympathizers also, or he would not have allowed them to be present.

The number may have been large, yet Adam and Eve not so much as suspected the presence of any, save him who made himself visible to them. The common notion of the three persons constituting the Godhead, and no other, being present, and conducting the conversation, will not do. If no other rational being, and capable of talking, was there, on that idea of the unity of the Godhead, all that was said amounted to no more than a *soliloquy*. And to assume that as true would involve a degree of irreverence sufficient to shock the moral sense of all but the atheist. The most agreeable inference to ourselves, and one which is probably as well sustained by the facts narrated as any other, is, that many of our old friends and boon compinions were there by permission, possibly on invitation, to witness that painfully interesting ceremony.

"*So, he drove out the man*" from Eden, as "*he was cast out into the earth*" at first.—Gen. 3: 24; Rev. 12: 9. That the Mosaic account of the temptation and fall of Adam in Eden, and of his having been driven out into the world at large, is the antitype of his temptation and fall in heaven and of his being "*cast out into the earth*" is, to my mind, so self-evident, that I must think nothing more is necessary than to call the attention of others to the striking analogies which run all fours clear through both narratives, to satisfy them that such is the fact.

In the case typified, Satan stands at the head of the picture, as the great leader as well as the prime mover in the transgression; just so he stands in the antitype, as the moving cause and chief offender in the fall of Adam. In the first case, it is said that *Satan was cast out*, and his angels were cast out WITH HIM; so, in the other, he was punished first, and, beyond all comparison, the most severely; then the others received their several sentences in the order of their transgression. Again, in both cases, strong intimations are given that the sufferers with Satan in his sinful ways and deceptive practices are to be offered pardon and restoration; but no such encouraging promises are, in either instance, extended to him. And the same Michael, who drove Satan and his followers out of heaven, met with him and them again in Eden, is *the friend* who was to purchase (and in the same way) redemption for those whom he was, in both instances, and, at the same time, punishing.

15. "And he placed at the east of the garden of Eden cherubims and a flaming sword, which turned every way, to keep the way of the tree of life." By "*cherubims and a flaming sword*," we are to understand a strong guard of mighty angels, who were stationed at the east of Eden to guard the way, that is, prevent any access to the tree of life. The angels so armed are emblematical of the Almighty Power, which prevents the return of any who were punished by being "*cast out*" of heaven, without the permission of Him who drove them away from His divine presence. Observe, the guard was not placed at or around the tree of life, which would have been sufficient to prevent any improper use of the fruit by any one; but it was placed at the east side of the garden, that the outcast should not re-enter the garden for any purpose, without pardon and leave to do so. That the garden of Eden is an emblem of the Paradise of God—the happy place prepared for the redeemed of earth—is generally, if not universally, conceded.

From the fact a strong guard was stationed to prevent the banished from a present return to the sacred spot where the living tree grew, it is manifest that at some future time, they or some others were to enjoy the privilege of entering the garden and partaking of the fruit of that life-giving tree; for if not so, the tree itself would have been of no more value, and it being much more convenient to have killed the tree (as was done in the case of the barren, and therefore worthless, fig tree), than to have kept a perpetual guard to prevent the use of the fruit, the tree itself would have been instantly killed, and the guard relieved of a most irksome duty.

That there was something figurative in the Mosaic account of the creation and fall of Adam, the Apostle Paul puts beyond a doubt.

He says: "Wherefore, as by one man sin entered into the world, and death by sin; and so death passed upon all men, for that all have sinned."—Rom. 5: 12. And in the fourteenth he continues: "Nevertheless death reigned from Adam to Moses, even over them that had not sinned after the similitude of Adam's transgression, who is the figure of him that was to come."

In 1 Cor. 15: 21, 22, he says: "For since by man *came* death, by man *came* also the resurrection of the dead. For as in Adam all die, even so in Christ shall all be made alive." He says further of the figurative language of the Old Testament Scriptures, in reference to the two sons of Abraham, one of a bond, and the other of a free woman: "Which things are an allegory: for these are the two covenants; the one from the Mount Sinai, which gendereth to bondage, which is Agar. For this Agar is Mount Sinai in Arabia, and answereth to Jerusalem which now is, and is in bondage with her children. But Jerusalem which is above is free, WHICH IS THE MOTHER OF US ALL."—Gal. 4: 24, 25, 26. These several passages from St. Paul are presented together so that the reader will, seeing their drift, gather the true import without the necessity of any lengthy comment in the way of application here. This course is the more desirable, as I may have occasion to refer to the subject again in comparing this theory with others.

Observe, 1. He says: "And so death passed upon all men, for that all men have sinned;" and again: "Death reigned from Adam to Moses, even over them that had not sinned after the similitude of Adam's transgression, who is the figure of him that was to come." Here we are told with sufficient clearness, that Adam's case is a figurative one; that *all have not sinned as he did*, in eating the forbidden fruit, yet that we *all have sinned.*

2. He represents Adam as a type of Christ, and each as a representative head of a class. Adam, as the figurative head of the dead, and Christ that of the living, and says: "As in Adam *all die*, even so in Christ SHALL ALL BE MADE ALIVE." That is to say, as the spirit of Adam, on entering his body, became *as dead*, so, or to the same extent, "all die" who come into the world, and even so *in Christ* shall all *be made alive*," meaning, that in virtue of his power, or by him, all shall be restored to rationality, capacity to think and act for themselves as responsible creatures, or, as better expressed, become "*as gods, knowing good and evil*," and, in fine, be made alive, or to live again, as creatures possessing the same degree of intelligence as before each came into this life. Then, indeed, will Christ have *restored all things*, and left all in as good condition as they were before he brought them into this state of being, and whether they accept or reject the salvation which he has purchased for them.

3. In Gal. 4, the apostle construes the Mosaic account of Isaac and Ishmael as intended, figuratively, to represent the same classes, and as in the same relation, although by a different figure, and then proceeds to say: "Which things are an allegory, for these are the two covenants" (or represent the two covenants), as quoted above. He then draws another, of the same import, from Hagar, the mother of Ishmael, and Mount Sinai (from which the two tables of stone were taken on which the law was written), and says that Mount Sinai "answereth to Jerusalem which now is, and is in bondage with her children." He evidently intended to represent the Jewish city of Jerusalem, which was then in bondage, as an emblem of the holy city of God which is free, "*the mother*" who cast us off, and the place where the covenant for the redemption of man was made, and of the "*New Jerusalem*" which St. John saw "coming down from God out of heaven," and which should have "*many more children*" than their then present

city. For her family is to embrace all the redeemed, both of the bond and of the free woman. Compare this allegory of his, and the letter of which it is a part, with Isa. 54, from which he quotes, and Rev. 21: 2. Those who are elsewhere indicated by such terms as *dead* or *living*, he represents in this place as the *bond* or the *free*, and which are but different symbolical representations of the same condition of beings.

He does, too, in this place distinctly say, as I should remark before passing away, that "Jerusalem which is above is free, *which is the mother of us all.*"

That England should be called the *mother* of a man who was born and raised there, although he had afterward emigrated to France, America, or some other foreign country, and still remains abroad, is natural and common; but how it can truly be said that Jerusalem, the celestial city of God, "*is the* MOTHER *of us all*," IF WE WERE NEVER THERE, I am free to confess, I can not comprehend. I, therefore, must leave my readers, who believe we were made as entirely new creatures in this world, to investigate this matter for themselves, and, if possible, reconcile this Scripture with the truth on some other hypothesis.

CHAPTER XVI.

Tenth and Last General Proposition Stated—The World not Destroyed, but Renewed at the Judgment—The Precise Time Concealed, and Why—Devils and Men All Judged Together—The Ungodly Prosper in the World—The Righteous are Punished Here — Necessity for Future Retribution — But Two Classes Formed After Judgment—Various Questions Asked—A Story and a Moral—Christ Able to Save All—Willing to Save the Penitent and Faithful—Which the Most Wicked, Angels when They Fell, or Men?

I HAVE now reached my tenth and last proposition, to-wit: "That this arrangement will be continued until all who were embraced in that divine antemundane covenant have, or shall have had, a probationary term here. Then will come the final judgment; when all will be restored to their primeval favor with God, or doomed to that final punishment which is due for individual sin by each committed."

This head admits of subdivision into three parts: 1. As to the duration of our race, under present circumstances, on earth. 2. That there will be a general judgment, before which all men and devils will be brought. 3. That a final separation will then be made between those who return to Christ and live, and those who reject his salvation and die. All of which have been, to some extent, anticipated in the preceding pages of this work, or follow as natural and necessary consequences of facts and arguments already presented.

If it be true, "That pursuant to that divine covenant, and for the purpose of carrying it into effect, this world was created or adapted to its present use, and God made man and placed him here for probation, "as shown under the sixth general division, it follows, as a necessary sequence, that it must be preserved until the object for which it was made shall have been accomplished. No further evidence or argument is deemed necessary to establish this branch of our present proposition.

That, at the judgment, there will be a destruction of every perishing creature, both animate and inanimate, which may be found here at the time, the Scriptures fully assure us, and so plainly, that I do not think it best to trouble the reader here with any discussion of that subject. If the world was created out of pre-existent matter, or rather of that which existed before, but in a different form, as modern scientific discoveries prove very satisfactorily was the case, it would not follow that the matter of which it consists should be destroyed, in order to verify all that is said about the burning, destroying, etc., of this world at the judgment. It is far more reasonable and consistent with the truth of the Bible, to believe that God will then "*make all things new*," as it is said he will (Rev. 21: 5). What new form earth will assume, what new dress she may put on, by whom thence occupied, I can not tell. There is reason to believe that she will be converted into one grand *Paradise*—ever fresh and always green—of which Eden was a picture in miniature, and become the happy home, or a favorite resort, of those who will be renewed with her. But these belong to the "*hidden things*," which we can not fully comprehend ere we enter "*into that within the vail.*"

At what *precise time* this revolution will take place, God in His providence has seen fit to conceal, not only from men, but from His beloved Son also, while he tabernacled in the flesh. This concealment was most assuredly intended for our benefit. He has, however, assured us that such time will come, and to all except the generation who may be here when it comes, it is wholly immaterial when it may arrive. So far as we are concerned, our destiny is fixed, and the great future which awaits us is present and meets us at death. It is easy to see why the "*day and the hour*," on which Gabriel will summon the dead to arise and come to judgment, and that awful conflagration will take place, should not be foreknown to the last generation of men; but for which consideration it is most likely that the *precise time* of the second advent of the Savior would have been distinctly revealed, and all the mysterious prophecies as to the first and second resurrection, the millennium, etc., would have been delivered in the most plain and simple language.

That all men who may then, or have theretofore lived on this earth, as well as the angels who apostatized in heaven, and were thence cast out to earth, and are now known as devils, are to be together brought before the same judgment, and at the same time, we have the most conclusive evidence in the Sacred Scriptures.

Were there no judgment and no punishment to be inflicted after death, the wicked of this world would go entirely unwhipt of justice, and escape punishment not only for such minor offenses as the well intending too often commit, and for which they are severely punished by the providences of God in this life, but in many instances for the most flagitious crimes. "Behold, these *are* the UNGODLY, WHO PROSPER in the world; they increase *in* the riches."—Ps. 73: 12. "Wherefore do the wicked live, become old, yea, are mighty in power? Their seed is established in their sight with them, and their offspring before their eyes. Their houses *are* safe from fear, neither *is* the rod of God upon them," etc.—Job 21: 7, 8, 9. "Righteous *art* thou, O Lord, when I plead with thee: yet let me talk with thee of *thy* judgments: Wherefore doth the way of the wicked prosper? *Wherefore* are all they happy that deal very treacherously? Thou has planted them, yea, they have taken root: they grow, yea, they bring forth fruit."—Jer. 12: 1, 2.

So much as to the forbearance of God with the wicked in this world; but how is it with the righteous? "Blessed *is* the man whom thou chastenest, O Lord, and teachest him out of thy law."—Ps. 94: 12. "For whom the Lord loveth he correcteth; even as a father the son *in whom* he delighteth."—Prov. 3: 12. "As many as I love, I rebuke and chasten: be zealous therefore, and repent."—

Rev. 3: 19. "For whom the Lord loveth he chasteneth, and scourgeth every son whom he receiveth."—Heb. 12: 6.

Such being the rules by which God deals with men in this life, it would seem that there *should be* some distinction made in the world to come. Now, let us see what is said about that: Paul said it was "Because he hath appointed a day, in the which he will judge the world in righteousness, by *that* man whom he hath ordained."—Acts 17: 31. "Who will render to every man according to his deeds: to them who by patient continuance in well doing seek for glory and honor and immortality, eternal life: But unto them that are contentious, and do not obey the truth, but obey unrighteousness, indignation and wrath, tribulation and anguish, upon every soul of man that doeth evil, of the Jew first, and also of the Gentile; but glory, honor, and peace, to every man that worketh good, to the Jew first, and also to the Gentile: For there is no respect of persons with God."—Rom. 2: 6–11. And he who has been so "*ordained*" our judge has notified all parties interested of the form and effect of his sentence upon those of each class on that *day*. He says he will say to the one: "Come, ye blessed of my father, inherit the kingdom prepared for you from the foundation of the world;" and to the other: "Depart from me, ye cursed, into everlasting fire, prepared for the devil and his angels."—Matt. 25: 34, 41.

And, to prevent all manner of mistake as to the severity of the punishment which the wicked will suffer there, he, on another occasion, said, and repeated it twice in precisely the same words: "There shall be wailing and gnashing of teeth."—Matt. 13: 42, 50. From the two facts alone, that all who are to be judged on that occasion are to be committed to the place for punishment which was "*prepared for the devil and his angels*," and that the Bible says nothing about any other final judgment or place for punishment having been appointed for either, it would, to my mind, if to no other, appear pretty clear that all men and devils for whom that punishment was "*prepared*" would be judged at the same time. But we are not left alone to inference, from the above and similar remarks of Holy Writ, for information on this momentous question. So far from that, St. Peter and St. Jude distinctly say, in passages which have already been quoted in another connection: "For if God spared not the angels that sinned, but cast *them* down to hell (Tartarus), and delivered *them* into chains of darkness, to be reserved unto judgment." "And the angels which kept not their first estate, but left their own habitation, he hath reserved in everlasting chains under darkness unto the judgment of the great day."—2 Pet. 2: 4; Jude 6.

Now mark, Jude says, that those recusant angels "*he hath reserved unto* THE JUDGMENT OF THE GREAT DAY." Can there be any misunderstanding here? To deny what St. Jude says (in language virtually as plain as any other that could have been used), that men and angels are all to meet at the same judgment, is to make an *issue of fact* with that disciple and apostle of Jesus Christ, which can properly be tried by none but a jury of the peers *of the parties* so at issue. And as one of them has no peer in this age of the world, the case can not be tried; and, therefore, all must be left to form their own opinions as to which of the parties is entitled to the most credit.

In fact, the Savior is but little less distinct in his expression of the same thing than Jude, when he says the impenitent will be required to "*depart* into everlasting fire prepared for the *devil and* HIS ANGELS." And the reader will find but little difficulty in arriving at a correct opinion about this matter, if he will recall to mind the other Scriptures which have already been referred to, and which bear upon this subject, and especially that which says: "And the great dragon was cast out, that old serpent, called the Devil, and Satan, which deceiveth the whole world: *he was cast out into the earth, and* HIS ANGELS *were cast out with him.*"—Rev. 12: 9. And further (passing over all other Scriptures, some of which have and others have not been introduced in the preceding pages of this work, but many of which are but little if any less pointed), if we bear in mind *but one other passage*, it would seem that no room for doubt would be left in the mind of any as to the fearful truth, that the angels which were cast out with Satan, and the souls of men, are one and the same family of *lost spirits* which Christ "*came to seek and to save.*" I refer, a second time, to the noteworthy remark of St. Paul: "But Jerusalem, which is above, is free, which IS THE MOTHER *of us all.*"

If we all sprang from the same *mother*, we are but one family; and if to be brought before the same judge, and at the same time, to answer for transgression, it must be for some vice or sin which is, or was, common with us all. But again, our judge has also notified us that he will divide all who are to be brought before that general assize into but two lots, "as a shepherd divideth his sheep from the goats." And he shall set the sheep "on his right hand, but the goats on the left." And that he will then say to all that stand on his right hand: "Come, ye blessed of my father, inherit the kingdom prepared for you from the foundation of the world;" and then to them on the left hand: "Depart from me, ye cursed, into everlasting fire, prepared for the devil and his angels."

So we see that but one of two destinies awaits us all who are to be there judged ,whether now known as angels, devils, or men. The "*sheep*" all go up to heaven, and the "*goats*" down to hell. Now, if men and devils are of different families, but are nevertheless to be judged at the same time, and after they have been sorted and divided, "as a shepherd divideth his sheep from the goats," the men on one side and the devils on the other, and all of one class are to go to heaven, and all the other to hell, as the judge says he will conduct the trial and pronounce his judgments as to each and all, one of two results will be realized: of course either all the men will go to heaven and all the devils to hell, or all the devils will return to heaven and all the men go to hell. Is not this true?

But, rather than admit that all men will go either to heaven or hell, or that any lost spirit can be restored to heaven, some may prefer to believe that they never had any existence in heaven, hades, or anywhere else; that they never were angels, devils, or anything else, either better, worse, or different from what they now are; that their bodies and souls just grew up together, they know not how, and that the lost angels have been detained in prison for over six thousand years, waiting our judgment (in which they have no interest), they know not why.

For the benefit of such persons, I propound a few questions, which, I think, are in point, and some of which may prove difficult for them to answer to their own satisfaction. Our Savior says the impenitent shall be required to depart "into everlasting fire prepared for the devil and his angels." If we are not of his angels, why are we, if not redeemed, to be sent to *the place* of punishment which was "prepared for the devil and his angels?" There is no intimation given that it was prepared for us, if newly created beings. And, if our sins are none but those committed in this life, it would, at least, be a remarkable coincidence that they should be so nearly, if not precisely like theirs, as to justify *the same punishment* on both; and the more so, when we remember that theirs were committed by angels of light in heaven, and ours by creatures of darkness on earth. Would it not?

The kingdom to which Christians are to be invited, it is said, was "*prepared*" for them "from the foundation of the world." It is reasonable to suppose that the future home for the "*devil and his angels*" was prepared as early as that kingdom. Then why were not these rebellious spirits sent directly to that hell, which was prepared for them, at once, if they were denied all mercy and chance for repentance? Why reserve them so long before passing sentence on them, if they had no possible chance to escape the doom which had already been decreed against them? Or, if there probably was some reason for that, but which we are unable to comprehend, why was the devil and his angels turned loose, right here among us, a newly created, innocent, unsuspecting set of creatures (as is supposed), who did not know *good from evil?* Or, if that wily old deceiver eluded his guards, and escaped to this world against the knowledge or consent of the Almighty (and which is not a supposable case), and betrayed our first parents into sin before he could be recaptured and removed thence, why were they, and all their posterity also, held responsible for what they did under those circumstances? Our guilt, in this view, was not to be compared to that of Satan; yet, it is said, we must all go to the same hell, and burn there forever for our sins, as well as he for his. God is said to be wise and just, and that He is I entertain no doubt; but how such treatment of His creature man is just, if the facts are as here supposed (but which they can not be), I do not understand. Can you, reader? Or, if Satan and his angels had been cast out of heaven, and were here on earth (as most assuredly was the case) before the creation of man, and if we are entirely a different family of creatures from them, why were we not permitted to fill the places in heaven which they had been required to vacate? It will be no answer to say that we were not wise or good enough to associate with the holy angels in heaven, for that may be conceded, and then the question naturally arises, why were we not made as wise and as good as they? We are all the workmanship of the same divine Architect. They were made before man was *created here*, and it is not to be supposed that He had lost any of His skill as a master builder. It will not do to allege a necessity of putting us on probation here (if new creatures who knew no sin), before taking us up to heaven, that we might be tried, and our fitness for a more exalted position ascertained by experiment before our promotion. To do so, would be to deny the wisdom of God to know what we would do before giving us a trial, and His power to make us any more wise and good than we are. Would it not?

The novice in a wood, tin, or potter's establishment, may have to *try* his work before he can determine certainly whether it will serve the purpose for which it was intended; but we must not suspect that All-wise and Almighty Being who created the heavens and the earth of defect, either of capacity to know whether His work will answer any particular aim, without making an actual experiment, as a mere apprentice has to do to find out whether his will do or not; nor dare we question His ability to have made man sufficiently perfect, in every respect, to have filled successfully the place and position of Satan himself, much less of any of his followers before their apostacy. Or, if God had some wise and benign purpose to accomplish by creating us as new creatures, and putting us on probation preparatory to a better or worse eternal future, why were we placed here with Satan and all his hosts of damned fiends, where we were subject to be tempted and led into transgression and sin by him or them? And, if it were either necessary or desirable, on any account whatever, to keep those rebellious spirits here for a time, or for eternity, His domains are wide enough to have furnished Adam and his race a home on some other planet; or, if they were already fully tenanted, He could, by a simple wave of His creative wand, have brought from the womb of wild chaotic space another world of equal worth with this, and there, secure from all outside, unfair, and evil influence, a safe abode for him and his have had.

If we, and the other devils who inhabit this mundane sphere, are of no akin, but entirely different sorts of creatures, it is not likely that it was the original aim of the Creator of them and us, that this should be the common inheritance of both families. Then it becomes an interesting inquiry, who has the better right? Who the intruders are, or which a welcome guest is made, as sister makes a brother? As unredeemed men and devils must, as all admit, receive *the same "recompense of reward,"* it is fair to infer that our natures, or crimes, are not so enormously different as that the fallen angels should be judged without mercy, and punished in hell for a term without an end, and that we should be favored with the blessed privilege of repentance and salvation. While we are all sojourning together here, and they are waiting for their judgment, it would have been but little inconvenience, and caused no delay, to have extended a like opportunity to them. Why were they not permitted, on some terms, to repent, reform, and so escape that awful doom which awaits them all alike, *deceiver* and *deceived?*

Satan is said to be the enemy of God. St. John says, Christ came into the world that he might "destroy the works of the devil." It is, perhaps, by far the most commonly received opinion that all savages, heathen, idolators, and the unconverted of Christian nations will go, in mass, to hell; the Scriptures assure us that a large majority of Adam's posterity will find a lodgment there. That the devil has accomplished the ruin of the finally lost of our race, none deny. This is all his work. Now, if Satan is to safely keep, as his own, all the angels who were cast out with him from heaven, and will also get, at least, nine-tenths of the newly created race of spirits from this world, it would seem that Christ is not likely to "*destroy the works of the devil*" very soon! In this view of the case, do not the present signs of the times appear to forebode, with fearful certainty, that, without some great change of success, Michael will sustain a defeat on earth but little less signal than that with which Satan was overwhelmed in heaven?

The position in which such friends of the Savior as hold these popular notions, place him (unintentionally, I know), is not altogether unlike that in which the boy found himself, who tried to cipher another out of the well. I refer to an old field school story, and which (in hope of the reader's pardon) was about this: The master one morning gave a little boy, who was quite vain of his skill in arithmetic, and as a problem worthy his genius, the following: "A boy fell into the well, which is seventy feet deep, and in his efforts to get out, he can climb but ten feet a day, and he slips back eleven feet at night; how long will it take him to get out?" The little fellow took his seat and went to work with a will. After having nearly filled one side of his slate, he was seen to rub it all out; but, nothing daunted, went at it again, but making his figures much less than before. So he passed the morning hours. Play-time came and went; and Ike, refreshed, went at his work again. Late in the afternoon the master observed that he was still—his head bowed down, as if absorbed in deep study. His slate was full, but the answer was not reached.

He was called: "Ike, bring me your slate; have you got that boy out of the well yet?" "*Out!*" says Ike. "Yes, out?" "Out!!" rejoined he, in amazement. "O-u-t, indeed!! If my slate had a bin a little bigger I'd a had 'im *in hell long ago!*"

This little anecdote is not told in irreverence to our gracious Redeemer. Far from it! It is, in all reverence, called to my aid for the sole purpose of impressing on the mind of the reader, in the most durable way that I know how, and to fix and fasten it there, a correct appreciation and lasting remembrance of the utter absurdity of all such unreasonable and anti-scriptural notions, opinions, and dogmas concerning the merciful schemes, providences, and power of God. To *doubt* the power of Christ to *save*, is to *damn* the doubting soul. He had the power to expel both Satan and his angels from heaven; and that he should not have the power to restore such of the latter as become sufficiently penitent to justify such special favor, would be wonderful. To dispute that the mercies of God extend to all his repentant creatures, is to deny the most precious promises contained in the Bible, the only ground for hope of our own salvation. To deny that any of the lost angels repented the sins which worked their overthrow, is to charge God with the injustice of holding His creatures to account for crimes they did not have capacity to commit. For, if creatures of no more sagacity than men of the lowest grade, who are held amenable to criminal law, when they saw the sad consequences of having followed Satan in his rebellious practices, they must have sorely repented their own participation with him. And the rule is, even in the most bloody penal code of any civilized state, that no idiot, lunatic, or other person who is *non compos mentis* (literally of not sufficient mind), shall be punished, as a criminal, for any act whatever. Is God less merciful than man?

But it may be alleged that the angels, who were cast out of heaven for rebellion, are worse, more wicked than men are. Well, if they are, I pity the devil, who is charged with their government and control in future! Crimes have been committed by man, in the name of our holy religion (to say nothing of others for which no such covering was claimed), which, if proposed in Pandemonium, would have cost the mover his seat in the most unsaintly council ever held within her gloomy walls, and which, if *tolerated* in hell, would disgrace the devil!

> Boast not, vain man, as better thou
> Than the worst sinner God has made;
> But know thyself, as worse by far
> Than when, leave heaven, our God us bade.
> Up to that moment, he had borne
> With all the evils we had done;
> But since from him we were cast off,
> From Satan we have learned enough
> Deceitfulness, falsehood, and sin,
> To make us swear we ne'er have been
> As vile as those we left with him,
> For this vain world, to live as men.
> Our vanity and pride, so great,
> Since a Tartarian home we left,
> Make us disown, deny, forget
> Our betters, who were less at fault.
> Their equals we have never been;
> On them we looked as maid on queen;
> Whom God withholds for brighter days,
> The last millennial thousand years.

"Blessed *is* he that waiteth, and cometh to the thousand three hundred and five and thirty days."—Dan. 12: 12.

CHAPTER XVII.

This Theory Compared with Others—Pre-existence of the Soul as Held by Heathen Philosophers, and Some of the Christian Fathers—The Most Consistent with Our Sinful Nature—Erroneous Opinions of Jews and Christians as to the Heathen—Reasons why the Gospel Should be Preached to Them—Idol Worship—Persecutions—The Holy Ghost Teaches by Mental Impressions—Has so Taught in All Ages—The Effect of the Light Granted to Heathens and Christians Virtually the Same.

HAVING gone through the ten chief heads into which the subject was divided at the outset of this investigation, I proceed to compare the theory now under consideration with those which have been heretofore, and still are, held by others who admit the immortality of the soul.

That man is immortal, I know, is denied by a few, even of our own age of the world. But I feel constrained (for the present, at least) to leave that subject as presented in the second chapter, with the sincere hope that the suggestions made, and authorities there cited, will prove sufficient as beacon lights to direct the earnest inquirer to a speedy and correct conclusion on that vital question.

I now proceed to notice each of the old theories, in contrast with this, in a brief way, so as to direct the reader's attention to some of the most prominent points of objection to the old ones, as well as to a few of the more scriptural and reasonable grounds on which the one herein presented rests. Nothing like a general argument against either will be attempted. The design of this writing forbids anything more than a brief reference to the leading scriptural authorities, which, I think, were designed by the Almighty Wisdom, at the proper time, to reveal the true origin, nature, and character of the human soul, with the most potent objections to old theories; and to make such suggestions, in the way of application and argument, as appear necessary to direct others along the mystic path which leads to a satisfactory conclusion, that man is nothing worse than a fallen angel, and no better than a devil; and that he is both the one and the other.

The first theory, in the order in which they stand, as borrowed from Dr. Knapp, in the second chapter, is, in substance, that "God, at the beginning of the world, created the souls of all men, which, however, are not united with the body before man is begotten or born into the world." And of which he says: "This doctrine of the pre-existence of the soul is, however, almost entirely abandoned, because it is supposed irreconcilable with the doctrine of original sin. And if the mystics be excepted, it has been left almost without an advocate ever since the time of Augustine." Here we have, in a nutshell, what that faith was, and why it was so generally abandoned. If that doctrine had gone a little further back, and stood on the ground that the souls of men were lost angels, and instead of the vague idea that they were created at "the beginning of the world," insisted that the *world was created for them*, it would not have fallen, on the ground that it did not consist with that of "*original sin*." For it is, in fact, the only theory yet presented on which the doctrine of original sin, as clearly taught in the Bible, can be accounted for.

The hypothesis of the pre-existence of the soul, although it did not go far enough to drink of the spring from which the stream of human life flows, yet it went in the right direction, as far as the light of divine instruction had reflected her most glimmering rays, at the time and place of its adoption. This appears to have been the most ancient theory of the soul, as entertained by heathen nations. It was, perhaps, first presented in a systematic and logical form by the learned Pythagoras—of whom it is also said, that he spent a number of years and traveled in many countries, for the purpose of getting all the information which could be collected from ancient tradition concerning the nature of the gods and of the immortality of the soul. All the crude ideas of the most cultivated heathen nations, he, no doubt, industriously collected and philosophically digested into a creed, or rational system of theogony and heathen theology. Plato, who was the most distinguished Grecian philosopher of his age, and who lived about four hundred years before Christ, adopted the views of Pythagoras on this subject, and pressed their investigation and improvement as far as his giant intellect, or probably that of any uninspired mind, could have gone at that time. The wonder would seem to be how any human creature approached so near the truth, on a subject which was involved in so much mystery, without the aid of the written revelation from God. And, strange as the remark may appear, I must be permitted to say, that I have no idea that Pythagoras, Plato, or any other man, ever did advance so far *without light from above.*

I wish to say a few things about God's dealings with his creatures, who have not been and are not favored with the inestimable blessing of His Written Word; and I had, perhaps, as well pause right here to do so as anywhere else.

The Jews of old were the most favored people of their Creator. They should, therefore, have become the most humble and faithful in the observance of His laws. Instead of that, however, they became and were, perhaps, in morals, the most vain, arrogant, and disobedient people of their age. Since the advent of Messiah, Christian nations have been the recipients of the choicest blessings of heaven, and are, on that account, under the more obligations to humble themselves, worship and obey the God who has so favored them above all other people. But, as were the Jews, so are we; instead thereof, with proper exceptions, the most self-conceited, proud, and rebellious of all men.

The Jews conceived themselves as about all of God's creatures for whose well-being He had any care. So it is with Christian nations. Each in their day looked, and look, on heathen people as the offcast of their Maker, and as deserving but little of His favor. Some of each, however, thought, and now think, their heathen cousins were, and are, not altogether undeserving the sympathies of themselves, although very inferior beings and but far-off relations to them.

These proud, selfish, and egotistic notions have given rise to one of the most palpable and grave errors, and into which the most enlightened people of each age have fallen. I refer to the very generally prevailing belief, of both Jews and Christians, that all heathens and pagans will be lost; and that all the sweets of heavenly bliss are reserved for their own noble souls. To my mind, nothing is more clear than that this is, and was, a most egregious error. The only reason, in my judgment, why the proud generation of Pharisees, who rejected and crucified the Savior of the world, did not meet with legions of the poor, God-forsaken, and hell-deserving heathen, as they esteemed them, in heaven was, because they failed to get there themselves. And such, I fear, has been, and will be, the sad cause why a great many self-relying, soul-deceiving, so-called Christians have failed, and will fail, to meet those whom they consider idolators in that glory world, and in like large numbers.

Some may ask, why, then, what good is to be accomplished by sending the Gospel to the heathen, if they can be saved without it? I answer, much, every way. The heathen are greatly blessed by the preaching of the Gospel among them in this life. Their souls are also elevated, and adapted to a more perfect anticipation of the glories of that New Jerusalem, which awaits the redeemed of earth. They are thereby enabled to worship God more acceptably; and are, therefore, the better qualified to appreciate the ecstatic joys of that heavenly city on their arrival and during their eternal abode there. But a much more important reason to us why Christians should use all reasonable care to Christianize the whole world is, because Christ has charged us with that duty.

And it will be no sufficient excuse for us to render at the judgment for not having obeyed the solemn injunction charged and enjoined upon us: "Go ye into all the world, and preach the Gospel to every creature," that they could have been, and, in fact, many of them will have been, saved without the help of our humble instrumentalities. We are just as guilty as though they had all been lost, if we utterly disregard our duty in this respect.

God can, and doubtless will, extend that divine mercy to each and every one of His creatures which He has reserved for them, whether you, reader, or I, lend ourselves as His willing instruments, in the accomplishment of His mission of love. But if we refuse to obey His calls upon us, as the more favored of His people, we will be held to strict account for our disobedience.

I have no thought that any soul will be lost, on account of the dereliction of any other of his fellow-men; no more than I have that any one of us could save another, or even himself, by any power or virtue which has been given us. Christ can and will save all who approach him in penitence and faith, whether of Christian or heathen lands, in the best way they can. If we have the light of the law and Gospel, we must come to him in the way he has pointed out therein. But if we have the lesser light only, which shines into the benighted heathen soul, we will be accepted just as certainly, if we grope our way as best we can up to the mercy-seat, by the help of the little knowledge we may have of the narrow way which leads to it. Every man must die for his own sin, or live in virtue of the faith which God gives him; proven by his own obedience to His just and merciful commands.

To whom much has been given, of him will be the more required; and of him who has received but little, so will less in proportion be required. See Luke 12: 47, 48.

There is also a great mistake about idol worship by heathen and Pagan nations. The strange notion obtains generally, among Christians, that they *adore and rely upon* graven images, and mere blocks of wood, stone, or gods made of gold, silver, brass, or something of that sort. Nothing is more unnatural, unreasonable, or untrue. I have no idea that any man, who had sense enough to take a goose to water, ever worshiped an idol of that sort since the world was made. Certain it is, that no one of capacity sufficient to be held responsible for his conduct ever did such a thing.

And, which would appear more wonderful still to one who had never heard of the fact, if there were such an one, a very large number of as good Christians as any, charge, and no doubt honestly believe, that the oldest and most numerous family of Christians on earth do the very same thing; and that, too, regardless of their most positive denial of any and all such folly. Idolatry, I know, is denounced by the Sacred Scriptures as perhaps the most odious sin when committed by Jew or Christian. For that, a sufficient reason is found in the fact that God has revealed Himself more fully to them, and taught them that in their devotions they should address Him *directly*. And the first commandment of the decalogue is: "Thou shalt have no other gods before me."—Exod. 20: 3. This I understand as if it read thus: "Thou shalt have no other gods" *between me and thee;* that is, we should employ no image as a medium, but make our wants known immediately to our Creator and great Benefactor. The heathen have not been so instructed, or had any such law given them, and, therefore, when their work is performed in the best way known to them, they have done the best they can. And their offerings are accepted as no less deserving the divine favor than those of others who are better informed.

It may well be feared by those of us, whose lot has been cast in Christian lands, that we practice idolatries much more real and offensive to the Almighty than do the heathen, on whom many of us look with more contempt than pity.

Just think of it! What can be more absurd than to believe that a man who has the capacity and ingenious skill, to make some of the beautiful images used by Pagans, believes that it has, when finished in the most exquisite style of the art, *in and of itself*, the ability to save the soul or body of him who made it from the power of the great evil spirit whom they all so much fear!

The wonder is that any sane man ever considered another capable of such consummate folly. The error arises from our own bigotry. We are wont to esteem ourselves about as much above our own true value, as we depreciate the worth of others below theirs.

It may be, and in fact is, easy enough for persons who can not work the single rule of three, or for others who have enjoyed liberal educational facilities, but who have never thought the Bible worth reading, to believe that such men as Socrates, Demosthenes, and Plato, of Greece, and Brutus, Cicero, and the twelve Cæsars, of Rome, were stupid enough to worship a block of wood, stone, or some other image, or thing, made by man, believing that it was the God who created the universe of worlds and made them what they were.

The murky minds of many who assume so to sit in judgment of the capacities of such distinguished orators, warriors, and philosophers, would contrast no better with the brilliant intellect of any one of them than would a bit of unpeeled Irish potato, if set as a jewel in a royal diadem, appear beside the most sparkling diamond of equal size.

One of them—and who is considered the greatest philosopher who had lived in any former age (Socrates)—became wise enough to feel, and had the manliness to say, that he "knew nothing." Many of his self-constituted censors, on the contrary, believe, that what they do not already know, is not worth finding out. Solomon says that "folly is joy to him that is destitute of wisdom."

It was well for the Apostle Paul that he had a more perfect understanding of what was called idolatry, or idol worship, than many of our day possess. For, if when he went to Athens, and entered freely and publicly into conversation with her Epicurean and Stoic philosophers about God and His worship, he had charged them with holding such ridiculous opinions of the images which they kept in their temple, instead of the courteous invitation which they gave him to address them on these questions in their Areopagus, and of the patient and respectful hearing with which they honored him there, if "tar and feathers" were then in vogue in that classic city, he would have received the just compliment of a heavy dressing of that material, and therewith been granted leave of absence during his own pleasure.

He committed no such folly, nor offered any (even the least) offense. On the contrary, he was careful to explain to them that he was not a "setter-forth of strange gods!" because he preached to them "Jesus and the resurrection." After saying that he had seen the inscription, "To THE UNKNOWN GOD," on one of their altars, he went on and said: "Whom, therefore, ye ignorantly worship, him declare I unto you." His object was to declare to them something more of the God whom they worshiped ignorantly. And meaning by the word "ignorantly," without the light of that revelation which God had made to his countrymen, the Jews, and nothing more; as all, no doubt, understood at that time.

And he did not content himself with that, but explained further, that he worshiped the same God they did, by reminding them that "certain also of your (their) own poets have said, For we are also his offspring"—the offspring of the same God whom they worshiped. The great apostle was not there either to preach any new or strange God, or insult the world-renowned philosophers who sat before him, by charging them with general ignorance, or putting their trust in idols; he went for the glorious purpose of making them acquainted with some of the great truths which that God whom they all professed to serve, had revealed to His people, the Jews, and to no others; and, over and above all other considerations, he wanted to preach to them on the subject of the advent, teaching, crucifixion and resurrection of Christ; and, if possible, to convince them that he was the Messiah promised by God, through their prophets, who was to redeem all, whether Jew or Gentile, who came to him in faith. See Acts 17: 16--34.

His mission was one of love. Christ was his King; and from him he had received the royal commission, under which he was sent to that refined city. The success which crowned his brief labors there prove both propositions most conclusively. For he planted the standard of the Cross so firmly in that ancient city, the nursing mother of the polite arts and sciences, that Satan and all his hosts have not been able, from that day up to this present writing, to pull it down.

The popular error, as to idol worship, grows out of a misconception of the use made of images, emblems, etc. The heathen and pagan nations, who are said to worship idols, have not been favored with the better knowledge of God, and of His manner of dealing with His creatures, which was communicated to His peculiar people the Jews, and which, with the clearer light of the Gospel, has been transmitted to all Christian people.

They have, in the absence of the Bible, only a sort of general belief in the existence of a great and good spirit, which created all things; of another great and evil spirit, the enemy of the other and of all his creatures. That there is a future state of existence, in which all men who love and serve that good spirit in this life, by a virtuous and holy walk before him, will be happy with him forever, and that others who act wickedly, and thereby serve and please the evil spirit in this world, will be doomed to an eternal life of misery with him, etc. Those of them who are moved by pious desires to worship that good spirit, have not been taught to make their confessions and supplications directly to their God, as he taught the Jews and Christians to do. They have no idea of a personality of God, such as the Jews had, and which was manifested in the person of Jesus Christ, and are therefore at a loss to know how to make their praise, thanksgiving, and wants known to that God whom they believe is able and willing to grant their righteous requests, if they could make them known to him. They believe that he is omniscient, so far as to know what is transpiring everywhere. And to us who have been taught to pray directly to "Our Father who art in heaven," it may seem singular that the idea has not occurred to them to pray in the same way. Yet it evidently has not, or they would do so, as the more cheap and convenient, as well as the most acceptable manner of worship. They want and feel that they must have some object present to their natural vision to which they can address themselves in devotion. And believing that God, although unseen to them, will hear their prayers, when so directed for His ears, to an object they do see, and that He, knowing the honesty of their purposes, and the sincerity of their hearts, will be pleased graciously to accept their humble petitions as though He were in person present and they were made directly to Him, they bow before their images and address them, as *media* of communication with that Great Spirit, in whom they put their trust. What better could they do? On like principles their worship of created things may be accounted for.

But some one may point me to the hideous monster, Juggernaut, and inquire whether that idol is not made the ultimate object of religious worship? To such question, I should have to answer, that is an exceptional case. But I know of no sufficient evidence, that the degraded people who worship there, believe the image which they see is the great spirit whom they think presides there. There are strong grounds for suspicion that there is more villainy than ignorance about that temple. A great Christian nation may not be altogether free from fault in regard to the wickedness and cruelties practiced there.

The poor, ignorant, and deluded Hindoos, who are, if not encouraged, at least without due restraint, permitted to fall voluntarily before his ponderous wheels and gladly submit to be crushed to death, deserve pity rather than ridicule from their better informed fellow-men. Do they not? If they deserve the pity of men, will God forsake them? They are of His creatures.

There can be no dispute between enlightened and liberal minded Christians of this age, as to the party who is justly responsible for all the gross immorality, sin, and cruelties which are practiced there. He is the same arch enemy of Christ, and our lost race, that instigated and kindled the fire which consumed the bodies of the honorable and faithful, learned and god-like Latimer and Ridley. That was cruel, wicked, fiendish—very! Bad as was that monstrous deed, the Inquisition, which had been previously established for the INNOCENT and pious purpose (as it was said) of *extirpating* "*heretics*," puts the comparatively small matter of burning these two great and good men, in point of devilish cruelty, to the blush. All that was done in the name, and with the avowed object of promoting the interest of the Christian religion. The sacrifice of human life by Juggernaut amounts to nothing, when compared with that shed by the Inquisition.

These remarks are not made with a desire to disparage the claims of the Christian religion to the universal favor of the world. Far from it. They are rather submitted in shame and sorrow, and for the purpose of inducing my Christian brethren to review their own history, with a desire to encourage a better feeling and cordial co-operation of each and every branch of our, too much, divided family; and, at the same time, to impress upon the minds of others, as my own is affected by the remembrance of the erroneous opinions we have entertained, and the cruelties we have inflicted on each other, the necessity of a more charitable consideration of our heathen brethren.

It has been remarked already, that God supplies to each and all His responsible creatures, light and knowledge enough of themselves, and of the purpose for which they are here, to enable them to make a wise choice; and avail themselves of the pardon which is offered them, if they really desire to do so. In the absence of the direct communications which were made to the prophets, and by them to the Jews, various other modes are adopted by the Almighty to effect the same purpose.

God truly has, "at sundry times and in divers manners," communicated sacred truths to men, and just such as it was meet each should know, for the probationary purpose of our present being. Some think, that in the early ages of the world, the worship of angels was common. If so, it is more than likely that angel visits were frequent with other people besides the Jews; and they may have made known to the heathen world facts in relation to themselves, as fully and satisfactorily as they did to the Jews. No written account having been made, or, if made, preserved, of such spirit visits, we are left to conjecture alone concerning them. From the very fact of the universal prevalence, among all heathen people, of what we consider the superstitious notions of necromancy, or of holding converse with the spirits of the dead, we have proof conclusive, that they believe the souls of men survive their bodies, and, therefore, recognize the doctrine of a future state.

I am inclined to believe that one of the most common, efficient, and reliable methods adopted by the Almighty, in all ages and conditions of men, by which to instruct them concerning our spiritual nature and future interests, has been, generally, either entirely overlooked or not duly appreciated. That is, by *mental impression.*

The same thing, perhaps, or pretty nearly so, is intended by others when they speak of *intuition*, or *instinctive* teachings. The distinguishing feature between this and what we usually call *revelation* is, that the lessons which are taught by mental impressions are personal, and designed for the benefit of the individual so instructed; and that which is called revelation is intended for all, to whom the facts so revealed may be made known. It is the office of the Holy Spirit to teach by mental impression, and which is a sort of revelation. He communicates to and instructs all men who come into the world, as our Savior very distinctly taught. And therefore all men may be said, in some sense, to be inspired of God.

And it is not to be doubted for a moment, by any one who believes the Bible to have been written by the inspiration of God, that He visits, instructs, counsels, encourages, and warns all men of sin, righteousness, and of the judgment to come. This He does as a secret monitor within us, or as a friend whispering in the ear of friend. Families, communities, and nations, are made up of individuals. Where the mind of each is instructed by the same divine teacher, and in the same things, the impressions which were originally made on each, become the common belief of all. As God taught through inspired men, in figurative language, it is but natural to infer that he instructed those who had no more than the benefit of such mental impressions in the same way. The extent of information given each, and whether in the one way or the other, or by both together, it it easy for God to regulate, and apportion as desired; and so as to result in equal justice to all. This we can readily understand ourselves. Such has been, now is, and ever will be, His wise and merciful, as well as just and equal dealings with all men, and of every age and condition of the world; as we have sufficient evidence, and as due reverence requires that we should believe. Upon this hypothesis we can account for many of the apparently strange notions, which were and are entertained by heathen people. I will mention one only, and that in the way of illustration. They believe in a plurality of gods, and imagine that every great interest of man is presided over, and cared for, by a certain god, who has been assigned, by the great spirit, to that particular duty. Christians generally believe, with them, in one and but one great Creator, to whom all others are subordinate; but that he consists of three persons, the Father, Son and Holy Ghost. So that, for all practical purposes, their views are sufficiently near the same. And, as is no doubt true in many instances, the conceptions of neither may be precisely correct, yet both are sufficiently near the truth to effect the great purpose intended by the limited knowledge granted to each class. At the judgment, therefore, "every knee must bow and every tongue shall confess," that God has not only been just in all His dealings with us, but that He has been exceedingly merciful to all. And those who are finally lost will be constrained to praise God for His goodness, even to them. God's ways are not as our ways. We find ourselves often at a loss for means to carry into effect our best and most anxious desires. It is not so with Him.

A little reflection will suffice to satisfy any one, of a well-trained mind, that God could readily have effected all His benign intentions, of giving man a fair and favorable opportunity to repent, reform, and return to his allegiance, by means of such necessary instructions as He could readily give by mental impressions alone.

I, therefore, attach great importance to the result of the careful and laborious investigations of that great philosopher, Pythagoras, and, which was approved and adopted by his learned, and, in many instances, highly distinguished disciples, which was, that the human soul *was created in the beginning;* or, as it is usually expressed, "*pre-existed.*" I do so, not because I overestimate the value of the mere opinion of any man, or set of men, especially on a matter of such magnitude as this, but for this reason: God has, as has been mentioned above, of the many channels through which he communicates with men, adopted two as the most common and efficient; first, mental impressions; second, prophetic revelation. The former was evidently the principal one employed for the instruction of heathen, and the latter to enlighten, first, the Jews, and now Christians. The aggregate effect of such impressions made on the heathen mind, brought them to the conclusion that the soul of man is a "*pre-existent spirit.*" The result of all the Sacred Writings, as has been shown, proves the same awful truth. Here, then, we have the concurrent testimony, as far as the former extends, of mental impressions and the pen of Inspiration, in support of the hypothesis that the human soul is a pre-existent spirit—*a fallen angel.*

The Jews being the most highly favored people of God, and the mode of teaching by the instrumentality of inspired men, being the most permanent and satisfactory of the two, the prophecies were first intrusted to them, and then to the Christians. Heathens were left to other means of instruction, and which was mostly by mental impressions. And as the Jews originally were, and the Christians now are, by the providence of God, made the leading branch of the human family, they were and are the more fully instructed in all matters pertaining to the eternal future which awaits us. That has been the general rule by which divine light has been reflected upon the dark and mysterious way in which we are all traveling through this life. So it is in this important particular, the heathen are given to understand, not only that they are immortal, but that the living principle which animates the body is something more than a mere ideal or transitory rationality, which is incident to animal life, and that it was in a real state of existence from the foundation of the world, and was, therefore, a pre-existent spirit, and, furthermore, that it was of such as had, *by some means*, lost that favor of God, which it had previously enjoyed. All this has been recorded by the pen of Inspiration. And the Written Word goes one step further, and informs us by what means and under what circumstances we were cast off from the favor of God; and that this world was created, and the body of man "*formed*" and placed here, as the mere tenement of the soul, by Christ the Mediator, and for the benign purpose of making a reconciliation (as far as practicable) between an offended God and His erring creatures, with a view to the ultimate restoration of all who would accept his mediation to their primitive happy relations with God the Father.

To the attention of the inquirer, who may wish to prosecute the investigation of this subject further, I would recommend, with other terms of like import, a large class of words which have the Latin prefix *re* (again), and which are everywhere to be met with in the Sacred Writings. Many such terms and expressions are full of meaning.

The following are offered as examples: "*Return* unto the Lord."—Isa. 55: 7. "The *repairer* of the breach. The *restorer* of paths to dwell in."—Isa. 58: 12. "To make *reconciliation* for iniquity."—Dan. 9: 24; Heb. 2: 17. "I will *redeem* them from death."—Hos. 13: 14. "*Revive* as the corn."—Hos. 14: 7. "*Re*generation," as in Matt. 19: 28. "For the *remission* of sins that are past."—Rom. 3: 25. "When we were *enemies* we were *reconciled* to God."—Rom. 5: 10. "For ye were as sheep going astray; but are now *returned* unto the Shepherd and Bishop of your souls." —1 Pet. 2: 25. Heebless sinner, "Be ye *reconciled* to God." 2 Cor. 5: 20.

Men of all ages appear to have had a sort of intuition,

or perceptive impression, of which they are scarcely conscious themselves, of a previous existence, and in a better state than this, as well as of having incurred the displeasure of the Great Spirit who created them. Evidences of this fact are found alike in heathen mythology, and in a very large number of popular songs, sacred hymns, and favorite poems extant in our own time.

> "Good news from home, good news for me,
> Has come across the deep blue sea."

This beautiful and pathetic parlor song is relished as much by those who never were thirty miles from the place of their birth, as by others who have really crossed "the deep blue sea."

In any other view, the words and phrases, "prisoners," "captive exiles," "call home thy *banished* ones," "captive," and "captivity," in the following stanzas, are utterly unmeaning:

> "O let the *prisoner's* mournful cries,
> As incense in thy sight appear;
> Their humble wailings pierce the skies,
> If haply they may feel thee near.
>
> "The *captive exiles* make their moans,
> From sin impatient to be free;
> Call home, call home, thy *banished* ones,
> Lead *captive* there *captivity!*"
>
> "*Methodist Hymns*," *p.* 141.

As a specimen of the variety of evidences last referred to, I offer the following sublime extract, which was written by Hannah More:

> "The soul on earth is an immortal *guest*
> Compelled to starve at an unreal feast;
> A spark which *upward tends* by Nature's force;
> A stream *diverted* from its parent source;
> A drop dissevered from the boundless sea;
> A moment *parted from* Eternity;
> A *pilgrim* panting for the rest to come;
> An *exile* anxious for his *native Home.*"

CHAPTER XVIII.

The Same Subject Continued—Angel Visits Common Before the Advent of Messiah—The Holy Ghost Became the Medium of Communication after That—He Can Instruct us when we are Awake or Asleep—A Remarkable Dream—The Jews Taught by Prophecies—Heathen by Dreams and Mental Impressions—The Creatiani—Probable Origin of that Theory—Neither of the Popular Views on this Subject Sustained by the Bible—The Hypothesis of a Continued Creation of Human Souls Considered.

BEFORE passing away from the "*divers manners*" in which God speaks to His creature man, I desire to submit a few more reflections on that interesting subject.

In the early ages of the world, it appears to have been very common for God to send His angelic messengers, in the bodily form of man, to instruct individuals in things concerning their personal interest. This method of communication was, most likely, continued until Messiah came and informed his people that the Holy Ghost would, in future, give them all the information which might from time to time become necessary. Since then, we (of Christian countries, at least) have probably had no such angel visits as had Abraham, Isaac, and Jacob. We have a friend, who loves us better than a brother, who is always at hand; and of whom we may take counsel in all matters pertaining to our devotional duties and spiritual well-being, whenever we sufficiently feel the need of his help. He can interpret all Scripture, and will at all times instruct us as far as our necessities require.

He can visit us in our waking or sleeping hours, just as the nature of the kindly counsel, encouragement, or warning he may have for us requires, and so that, whether asleep or awake, we will be wholly unconscious of his divine presence.

I do not wish to be considered, as were the Athenians, "*in all things too superstitious.*" Nor can I consent to omit a sacred duty, for fear of personal injustice from erroneous opinions which others may form concerning myself.

I assure you, kind reader, that I have never seen a ghost, and that I entertain not the least fear, or hope that I ever will, while I look through these physical eyes. I have never been bewitched (in the popular sense of the term), nor have I any fear of witches, or of the devil himself, while Christ is my friend.

For a dream book, I feel no more respect than does the veriest atheist that Satan ever deceived. But, while all this is true, I can not say that God never visits men, or does not instruct them in dreams or visions of the night.

That God communicated to men information of great value in the olden time, in dreams, the sacred writers affirm too distinctly to admit of any doubt. And I know of no good reason why he should not do so yet.

While I doubt not that the vulgar notions of the value of dream books and dreams are based on ignorance and superstitious fear, I am well satisfied that God does sometimes instruct us in dreams, in matters of individual interest, at the present time.

Persons are sometimes said to dream that certain events transpire at places distant from them, and afterward to learn that their dreams were neither more nor less than precisely what did occur, including time, place, and every minute circumstance connected therewith.

We frequently hear also, or read, of dreams which excite fear or hope, as the case may be, and of subsequent occurrences so wonderful as to look very much like the dreams were sent by providence as premonitions of their approach. In some instances, too, such reports come so well authenticated as to command our serious consideration, if not to require implicit belief.

Some years since, the presiding judge of one of the superior court circuits of this State, and who is *Wrightly* esteemed as one of Georgia's most gifted sons, experienced one of the class first mentioned, and which is worth preserving in the most durable form. He was, and is, a man distinguished no less for his Christian humility than legal lore, and deserves the cognomen "*Christian lawyer.*"

At the time referred to, his custom was to preach the Gospel to the poor on Sabbath, and then preside in court during the week. He was then holding one of his distant courts, perhaps ninety to one hundred miles from home, and in a section of country which has not yet been penetrated by railroads; and had been absent from home about three weeks. When he left, his wife was complaining a little of feeling unwell, but was up and going about the house, and was not under medical treatment.

One night, wearied with his judicial labors, he slept soundly, but dreamed most distinctly, that sitting upon the bench where he usually sat, he looked out of the window at his back, and saw coming up over the hill in the distance a remarkably large gray horse, that he usually rode, with his servant Henry (then a slave) upon him; and that he rode up to the window near him and said: "Master, mistress is dead!" He awoke in much sorrow, and was troubled for some hours. But, on the next day, case after case had drawn his attention, and the dream, and its present effects, had passed from his mind. About 3 o'clock in the evening, turning casually, and casting his eye out of the window, he saw the gray horse and the boy just rising the hill, as he had seen so distinctly in his dream; and the boy went up to the window and delivered *precisely* the heart-rending message of which he had been notified in the visions of the preceding night: "*Master, mistress is dead!*"

The combined effect of that sad intelligence, and of the miraculous way in which it had first been communicated to him, was overwhelming. The judge was perfectly unmanned. He could not utter a word. No one else in the court room knew what had occurred. Suffused in tears, he walked down from his seat, passed through the *astonished* crowd that was in the court house at the time, and went to his room in the hotel. He there wrote a hurried note to the clerk, stating the cause, and ordering the court adjourned. His feelings were awful. The wife who had been the love, light, and life of his youth, and the pride of his early manhood, was gone! snatched suddenly away by the unrelenting hand of death, and in his absence, denying him so much as the melancholy pleasure of bathing her cold brow with his tears. Still he had the most extraordinary assurance that Christ was his friend. For none but a messenger from heaven could, at that time and place, have known, or so informed him, that his beloved wife had gone to the world of spirits, and that he was a widower and his children orphans. I would gladly give the name of the distinguished gentleman referred to, but knowing his modesty, I am unwilling to do so without his consent.

Having served as a member of the United States Congress before the war, he is well and favorably known to many persons in all the States, as he is to all who read the current history of the times in Georgia, and, therefore, more importance would be attached to that wonderful occurrence, if it were known on whose authority its verity rests. It was first related to me by the judge, soon after the death of his wife; and in that peculiar way in which none but a Christian man can talk under such trying circumstances, and in a manner in which he will only express himself to one whom he esteems as his personal friend and brother in Christ, who can sympathize with him in his bereavement, and appreciate his excitement. He left no more doubt on my mind, as to the truth of every word he said, than I would have entertained if it had all been my own painful experience.

I have reported this case with such care, for this good reason: If it stood alone, it would prove, to the satisfaction of all who admit that it is true, the position assumed, that God does, in this age, by His Holy Spirit, reveal to men facts which He desires they should know *in dreams.* One well-authenticated case of this sort is worth more than a thousand which rest upon mere rumor, and which we may suspect as being nothing more than the productions of the fruitful imaginations of as many superstitious simpletons.

The vague and discordant views of the pre-existence of the soul, which were entertained by heathen philosophers, and which were embraced by many of the Christian fathers, although not satisfactory or full, were yet sufficient to teach them that the soul was the older and most valuable part of man. They were, therefore, sufficiently informed of the necessity which rested upon them to take care of their future interest. To that extent, and no further, it appears to be, and to have been, the will of God to instruct all men, of every age and condition of life. And, as little as we may be inclined to believe it, we have no sufficient reason for believing that the lights which were shed upon the Jews, in the form of prophecies, were of any more practical value to individuals than were the teachings enjoyed by heathens, and which they received chiefly in the way of mental impressions and dreams. Prophetic revelation is the most valuable to our race, considered as one family; because it is durable in its nature, and was designed ultimately to be known to all nations.

The Jews being the representative member of our family, the prophecies were originally delivered to them. We should not, therefore, despise, or even lightly esteem the worth of the opinions of those great philosophers.

Better would it be for us, to weigh well their views and compare our own on kindred subjects with theirs. We know the Jews did sometimes err in the construction and application of the prophecies; otherwise they would all have accepted Jesus Christ as the Messiah. It is, therefore, possible that we may be wrong in some of our notions, and that the heathen may have been right in their views of the same subjects. Their Creator and teacher was ours also, and they were taught in the same school that we were, although in different text books. Some boys learn much faster in school than others, and understand more perfectly what they pass over. But, would it not be very remarkable, indeed, if two brothers should be sent to the same school, and that presided over by the same master, during all the portion of life which is allotted by the most wealthy, intelligent, and affectionate parents to the education of their children, and yet one of them should be always right and the other every time wrong, when they differ in opinion on any question whatever, and during their whole lives? We can not safely claim that sort of natural superiority over our heathen brethren, which such difference in scholastic success would require.

The hypothesis that the soul of each individual is created at the moment when the body is prepared for its reception, next claims our attention. In the absence of any authority in the Bible on which such a theory can rest, and as it would require the continued and most active work of creation to be constantly going on, in order to bring spirits into existence as fast as they are required, that each human body, when it comes into the world, may be animated by a living soul, it is difficult to imagine precisely how, or in what that notion originated. It may have grown out of the older theory of *pre-existence.* The fact that no reason was known why God should have created the souls of all men at the time Adam was created, or before, and as it was the prevailing opinion of that age, that the soul was created separately and distinct from the body, and would survive it, may have had great weight, at that time, in favor of the idea that each soul was created an entirely new creature when the body was born into the world. God could have so ordered. And it will be remembered that the views of the ancients were very vague and unsatisfactory as to when or where the souls of men were made, as well as to where and under what circumstances they are kept until sent to occupy the bodies allotted them.

The Pythagorian school had very conclusively established the fact, that man is possessed of an immortal spirit, and the Jewish Bible taught the same thing, and which was confirmed by the New Testament Scriptures. Yet, neither, as then understood, gave any clear or satisfactory account of the origin of that immortal spirit. Men were, therefore, left, to a great extent, at least, to conjecture as to when and where it was created.

The fact that the controversy about free will and predestination was in full blast at the time when the Christian world settled down on one or the other of the three old theories (as quoted from Dr. Knapp), may have had, and no doubt did have, much to do in adjusting the theories of Christian disputants of that age as to the origin of the soul. As has been mentioned already, some great men found it convenient, if not necessary, to change their front on the latter to sustain their dogmas as to free will and predestination. That was the great question of the age (and by the way, it has lost but too little of its interest yet), and, therefore, every other opinion was made bend to fit, or get clear out of the way of that. And to one who attaches as little importance to the quarrel about free will and predestination as I do, no feature of all the protracted, animated, and often bad tempered disputations which have been conducted since the introduction of Christianity, appears half so strange as that the great lights of the Church should, at any time, have attached more importance to that, or any kindred subject, than to that which should be, and ever should have been, the all-absorbing question, What is man? It occurs to my mind that the discussion of all questions as to the dealings of God with us, and as to whither we are going, are premature until we have first determined *whence* and what are we?

If we are perfectly satisfied as to the true origin and nature of our souls, we have a starting point from which to set out in the investigation of any and every other question, which may arise, as to the divine scheme for our probation, and as to our final destiny.

Suppose, for instance, reader, that you were satisfied, as I am, that we are of the fallen angels, and that the world was made for the temporary purpose of extending to each of us a fair trial, with a view to the pardon and restoration of all who really desire and prove worthy of such favor (with the light which is to be found in the Gospel, as to the plan and terms of pardon, and of the final disposition of those who are restored and those who are not), you would find but little difficulty in arriving at a satisfactory conclusion on any question of that sort.

It will be found much the most safe and speedy way to conduct all such investigations, to forget all we have ever read, or heard, outside of the Bible, on the subject under immediate consideration. The Sacred Writings offer much more reliable information, on any matter connected with the salvation of the soul, than the one-sided arguments of any uninspired man, how learned and honest soever he may be. And this is especially true as to the opinions of one whose mind is bent on one great dogma, and leans to that as the sunflower turns her virgin cheek to the lord of day, that she may receive the welcome kiss which comes from every genial ray of his from morn till night. Dr. Knapp says of the three old theories of the origin of the soul (that herein presented never having occurred to his giant and well-balanced mind): "The whole inquiry, therefore, with regard to the origin of the human soul, is exclusively philosophical; and scriptural authority can be adduced neither for nor against any theory which we may choose to adopt." I call attention to this remark here, for the purpose of showing why I do not attempt to reply to arguments drawn from the Scriptures, by their advocates, in support of each of the old theories. There are no such Scriptures on which to base argument.

He has investigated the whole subject of psychology more thoroughly than any writer after whom it has been my fortune to read, and I prefer to introduce him as a witness, to *prove* that neither of them is sustained by the Bible, than to offer my unsupported opinion to the same effect.

To undertake to prove that such is the fact, would involve a task no less than a commentary on the whole of that good Book; or, at least, that I should copy the whole of it here, and make constant pauses to say, that no such evidence is found here, or to ask, is it there? I beg pardon for saying further, also, that I have carefully read every chapter, verse, and word contained in that precious Volume, strictly with a view to this matter, and that I have been wholly unable to find anything therein contained, that can be considered as furnishing any valuable support to either the one or the other of them. And that I did so for the sole purpose of satisfying my own troubled soul on the very subject now under consideration, and before I ever conceived the thought of writing the first line about it for any other eye than my own.

I think, therefore, I may safely say that my views as to the origin of the human soul, are *not in* conflict with anything that is taught in the Scriptures. Whether they find sufficient *support* there, I have argued in a brief way, and leave others (who have the same interest in the question that I have) to form their own opinions and to act upon them when formed for themselves.

We are all to answer for our own works. If saved, it must be done of grace and through our faith. Our works are *directed* by our faith. If that be unfounded, our works are, therefore, not what they should be. They are to be tried as if by fire. If burned up we must suffer loss. If our souls be saved after our works are burned, it will be done on the score of our ignorance.

If we refuse to search out a great truth which is contained in the Bible, after having been notified that it is there, the plea of ignorance will not avail us. We are commanded to "*search the Scriptures.*" If we disobey that injunction, we are guilty of a voluntary breach of God's law. For the consequences of that disobedience we will each have to answer at the great day, who may stand indicted under that section of the divine code. We can not be too careful, therefore, of the opinions we form, or retain, as to the construction, and true intent and meaning of that law by which we are to be judged.

Do not misconceive me. It is not my wish to say that none can be saved but such as fully understand all that is contained in the Bible. Far from it! Under that rule the *last one of us would take our position on the left*, as I verily believe; and I am sure that I should be required to fall in line with the rest of the goats. For there is nothing more certain than that I do not understand some things therein written. All I intend by these remarks is, that we will be held accountable, according to the means given each to learn what God's law requires of us; and for the manner in which we discharge our duties, as well as for the improvement we may have made of our talents, as I have more fully explained already.

There being no scriptural evidence to support the theory of the *Creatiani*, let us see what foundation it has in reason.

If there were no occupants already in existence who had no need of this world, why was it made so imperfect, perishable, and changeable as it is? Or, why make it at all? *Cui bono?*

If there were a large number of poor outcast angels in being at that time, under circumstances calculated to excite the pity of their Creator, and He desired to give them a brief trial midway between heaven and hell, a temporary establishment like this was a good idea, and is a capital place for such purpose. But some one may say to me, you do not understand the providence of God in relation to our present imperfect state of existence. He has placed us here for growth and improvement, that we may be made fit to live in a higher, more perfect, and happy state hereafter. Well, He could have done so, I admit. But it is said that God is not deficient either in wisdom or power, and if that be true, and you are right, my friend, He has put himself to so much unnecessary care by creating us at all.

If he had a wish to bring into existence more wise, holy, and good creatures, for any purpose whatever, it would have been quite as convenient for Him to have created them at once in that state of perfection to which he wished they should finally attain. Would it not? Then, why did He not so make us.

We have no evidence that the wise and holy angelic creatures, who now inhabit the upper regions, were originally as ignorant and wicked as we are. If God made them better than we, and if we were never better than we are now, why were we made so imperfect? Has God lost any of that skill which He once had? Who will say He has? Or, will it be said that He could have made a better job of this, but preferred to put us in our present shape, and let us grow better? *Experimenting, then, was He?* If that be so, there is no hazard of the truth in saying, that if he desired us to grow up to wisdom and perfection, and so hereafter fill a better and more exalted position than our present one, He will never make such another *experiment.* In that case, a more signal failure, on the part of one of His most unskillful human creatures, can scarcely be imagined. For, if any reliance is to be placed on biblical affirmation, or the most perfect dictates of natural reason, based on daily observation, an enormous majority of us grow worse instead of better in this life, and when we leave we will take the *downward train*, and not that which runs on an *up grade*, in like greater numbers.

Or, to say that He created us with the desire of populating an unoccupied and vacant region of hell with a race which was well adapted to that use, will not relieve the subject of any part of the embarrassment which surrounds it in the first view.

The same objection applies to this hypothesis as to the other, and another also which is much worse. If He designed us for that region, why not put us there at first? Why deceive us with false hopes of heaven, if to hell we were doomed when created?

But it is said some will be saved, and others lost. Then, why create any but those whom He intended to save? The salvation of a few will be but poor comfort to those who are lost. Their condition will be just as bad as if no others had been made. Therefore, none of the objections which apply to that theory, if all be lost, lose any of their force, if any are so unfortunate, so far as they are concerned. If there be cruelty in creating a whole race for no other purpose than to witness their torments in hell, it would be cruel to make one poor immortal soul for that purpose.

These suggestions are not made, my Christian friends, in any spirit of irreverence for that almighty, all-wise, and exceedingly merciful God, whom we so highly venerate, and *should* so dearly love.

They are submitted with full confidence that He who observes, with an all-seeing eye, every black mark I am making on this paper, fully comprehends and at the same time approves the pure motives which direct this pen. I charge not my God with imperfection, or with that want of ample power or wisdom, which the thought that he is experimenting necessarily implies. Far, indeed, be it from me to charge Him with taking upon himself the office of the deceiver. That is the business of the common enemy of God and man. And, above all other things, would I dread to accuse Him of *cruelty* to His own creatures! The very thought of such fiendish irreverence should, and probably would, shock the moral sense of the devil!

No, reader, I have no such taste. My sole object in adopting this line of argument is to expose, in the best way I can, the gross errors on which the theory now under review is founded; and to point out some of the absurd, not to say ridiculous conclusions, which must necessarily present themselves on a critical investigation of its claims to our confidence. This is done, also, with the humble hope that good may be done in this way, by inducing great and good men, as well as the less favored, to examine for themselves the sandy foundation on which their whole religious creed rests.

I hope this explanation will be accepted as a sufficient apology (so far, at least, as intention is concerned) for other apparently light, quaint, waggish, or irreverent remarks which may have been, or may further on be, found in this imperfect work. That some of a more grave and dignified cast of mind than I possess, will take exception to certain forms of expression and illustration indulged by me, I have no doubt. All I ask of such good friends is, that they believe *I aim well*, even if constrained to say that such things look odd in a work on such a serious subject.

I admit that I am somewhat "*a man o' the world*," as Sam. Weller would say. For me to put on the form of dignity and gravity, which is natural with some men, would be arrant hypocrisy; a thing which God hates. But, *verbum sat sapienti*, I must proceed.

If we never existed in a different capacity, but are newly created beings, why did God make us so wicked? Or, if contaminated by Satan since we came into life, why did God suffer him to spoil His perfect work so completely and so soon?

Satan is a creature of His, and is as fully subject to His power as we are. If God makes all His creatures pure and good, and we are as first made, who made Caligula, John A. Murrell, and some of our contemporaries, such as we all wot of?

If the soul is made as simple, even unconscious as is that of the young infant, it can properly be considered as but the cion from which the tree grows; if that be pure and holy, the fruit must be so too, or it was error to say: "A good tree can not bring forth evil fruit."—Matt. 7: 18. Some, however, admit the fruit to be sometimes a little sour which we bear in this life, but it is said there is a *purgatory* to which some of us are sent, after leaving this world, for a spell, and where all that is cured, and we then come out all right. If so, that is a much better place for the preparation of souls for heaven than this. Would it not, therefore, have been best to have sent us all to *purgatory* at first? This work of creating new creatures, according to that hypothesis, has been going on a great while, and with like bad success all the time. If a mere experiment when first commenced, is it not most reasonable to believe that God would have discovered that it was not working well very soon, and tried some other plan? Would He not have been more likely to have done so, than to have persisted in a work, which cost the life of His Son to repair *a part* of the damage so done?

My Christian friend, allow me, if you have suffered yourself thus far to sleep soundly under a fabric so rickety, as such faith certainly is, to urge you to awake, arouse yourself to the sensibility of one just out of a death-like slumber, and examine the old castle in which you and your fathers have resided so long, without ever taking care to examine the foundation on which it stands.

God is the author of human reason. He has endowed us with a little of that God-like faculty which He possesses in perfection. He can not err. Nor can He be disappointed in the working of any of His plans. If we hold to any opinion, on any subject whatever, which is involved in so much inconsistency, even when examined before the light of human reason, we should know that we are wrong, and look in some other direction for the truth.

CHAPTER XIX.

The Propagation of the Soul—Unphilosophical—Not within the Natural Course of Reproduction—Inconsistencies Encountered by Her Advocates—Phrenology Introduced—Physiognomy but an Art—Analogies between Men and Other Animals—Different Characteristics Observable in Families Accounted for—Various Orders of Angels and Devils—Regular Gradations of all Classes of Creatures—For Each Spirit a Body Expressly Provided—Dissimilarities in the Same Family—The Skull Accommodates Itself to the Brain—Native Depravity.

THE next and last of the old theories, as presented in the second chapter, is, "The hypothesis of the *propagation of the soul.*" That is, that the *souls and bodies* of all children are, together and alike, propagated from their parents.

The first great, and, as I think, self-sufficient objection to this hypothesis is, that it is perfectly unphilosophical and unreasonable. How it is that immortal spirits can be produced by mortal bodies, no man, whether now living or dead, has ever yet been able to answer, with any tolerable degree of satisfaction. The best reply which its advocates have made, or probably ever can make, to this stubborn difficulty in their way is, that nothing is impossible with God. That is true. But many things are so with man; and to create, or bring into being a spirit which had never existed before, and yet shall live forever, is one of the many things that man can not do.

The reader will perceive that this is not within the natural course of reproduction, which pervades both vegetable and animal life. The acorn falls to the ground, sprouts, springs up, grows, and in due time becomes an oak, which, in turn, bears seed and dies. The hen lays her eggs, sits, and hatches her brood; they grow up to maturity, do likewise, and pass away. Man (as a mere animal) is born in the world an infant, grows into the full vigor of middle age, propagates, dies, and is gone. In each instance, a perfect circle is formed, in which the round of life is run. So it is, or appears to be, with all animate creatures in this world.

But, if the soul is propagated as is the body, and when the body dies it flies away into eternal life, there is an instance in which the laws of nature not only deviate from the regular course, but become mysteriously deceptive. If that be so, we have not only all been wrong in considering the laws of nature uniform, but the writer, with many others, has been laboring under three other errors not before discovered: 1. In believing that man had no creative power, and that God only could create. 2. That no power could make anything superior to itself. And, 3. That nothing which could be done at all, would be impossible with God. For, if that be true, man can, as an animal, create, or bring into being, an eternal spirit, and which is beyond all comparison of more value and superior to him who created it, but God can not make a greater than Himself.

To this, it may be replied that the production of the soul is not in virtue of any inherent power of man, but that God, of his almighty power, causes the soul to come into being with the body. That is possible. But, if it is in that sense only that the soul is propagated with the body, these two difficulties get in the way of the advocates of this theory: first, the soul is just as much a new creature of God, as if created as is supposed by the *Creatiani;* and worse still, in that case God creates through the instrumentality of man, as his agent and proxy.

Of that supposed mode of creation, two remarks may well be made: 1. That it is exceedingly unlikely that God would employ as corrupt and unreliable an agent as man is known to be, in a matter so important as that of creating immortal spirits, which are to live forever in heaven with him (and as part of that celestial band of minstrels who are to sing His praises forever), or be cast into hell with the devil and his angels; and, 2. That if the souls of men are created by God, as new creatures, in any way He may choose to adopt, we would have the right to expect that they would be pure, as the other spiritual creatures of His power originally were, because they would be of God's work, in such case, as much as if created directly by Him, (they being) the fruit of his creative tree, and, therefore, would be good fruit. For "a good tree can not bring forth evil fruit."

Dr. Knapp, in reference to the Protestant school, of which he was one, says: "The reason why this theory is so much preferred by theologians is, that it affords the easiest solution of the doctrine of native depravity." In a man of his fairness, who had probably not looked beyond the old theories for a solution of the mysteries which surround the whole subject, as viewed in the light of either one, or all of them together, such a remark should be readily excused. For he, further on, also says: "This hypothesis is not, however, free from objections; and it is very difficult to reconcile it with some philosophical opinions which are universally received." And again: "And if the metaphysical theory of the entire simplicity of the human soul be admitted, the whole subject remains involved in total darkness."

It would appear remarkable that a theological school, which insisted with so much zeal and perseverance, as the one to which Dr. Knapp refers has, upon their favorite dogmas of total depravity and predestination, should be so easily satisfied with their faith, as to the origin and nature of their own souls, as to allow the mere fact that any particular theory "*affords the easiest solution of the doctrine of native depravity*," to have such weight as to become their controlling reason for adopting one which is so unsatisfactory, of the soul. The more singular will this fact look, if we take the care to notice the unfavorable light in which it exhibits their other pet—*predestination*. To imagine a doctrine, less respectful to our Creator, would be difficult, indeed, than it would be to charge Him with allowing our progenitors, after their fall, to bring into being a race so numerous as ours, and which never was in existence before, a large majority of which He had doomed to damnation in hell, before the first one had been born into the world. Monstrous! Is it not?

This, however, is but another instance, showing the wonderful inconsistencies into which the greatest and best men often suffer themselves to run in support of a pet idea. And whether, in this case, they have or have not succeeded in establishing their dogma of total depravity, they certainly have successfully illustrated the no less valuable biblical doctrine of man's *fallibility*.

In the absence of scriptural authority to sustain a hypothesis which was supposed to serve a purpose which was so desirable, in consequence of its convenience and utility, its advocates appealed to such facts as that "the natural disposition of children not unfrequently resembles that of their parents; and the mental excellencies and imperfections of parents are inherited nearly as often by their children as any bodily attributes." Again: "The powers of the soul, like those of the body, are at first weak, and attain their full development and perfection only by slow degrees."—*Knapp*.

The circumstance that the soul like the body attains maturity slowly, and as does the body, has already been accounted for, as I hope, satisfactorily. No fair inference can be drawn, in favor of that hypothesis, from any resemblance which the disposition of children may bear toward that of their parents, or from any apparent mental excellencies or imperfections which children are supposed to inherit from their parents.

It must be remembered that man is a compound being. He is as fully *animal*, and a more perfect one than the horse which he rides, or the dog with which he hunts, *and something more.*

The science of phrenology proves this clearly. But it may be said by some, that another of my witnesses needs sustaining. I can not pause long to do so, and would not say a word for that purpose but that the cause of scientific truth, in my judgment, requires it. I will do no more, however, in that way, here, than offer a little of my own experience and observation on that subject. When quite a young man, curiosity, at first, excited with me a desire to know something of that which some called a science, but others then, as now, ridiculed as all nonsense. I procured a copy of what was then considered one of their most perfect and reliable text-books, and read it carefully, as I could find leisure hours which could be employed in that way. I soon became satisfied that the observations and discoveries on which the whole structure rested were the fruits of the most indefatigable labors of practical scientific men, and learned to respect their opinions. By the time I had gone through the volume, I was convinced that whether phrenology, at that time, deserved the name of *a science* or not, that enough of leading facts had been discovered, and observations made on them, to warrant the belief that, at some time, its friends would exalt it to the proud eminence of a place beside the most sublime and beneficial branches of natural science. Although I never so much as tried to locate all the organs in the cranium myself, and never saw the naked human brain, I soon found that I could easily form a very reliable opinion of the more prominent natural proclivities and comparative mental capacities of men, or other animals, simply by looking at them, and observing the size, shape, and relative proportions of each section of the head, and the general contour of the head and face together.

While engaged in that study, I found it a very fruitful source of pleasure, and profit also, on all suitable occasions to make such observations of persons with whom I was well acquainted, but without their suspecting it, of course; and every such test went to sustain the theory on which the science was based.

About the time my interest in that direction was at the highest point, I had occasion to visit and remain a night with a friend in the country, who kept a large pack of hounds, and of which he was very fond. During the evening, the conversation turned to the subject of phrenology. He remarked he would like to have me inspect the heads of his dogs, and let him see if there was probably any truth in it. I cheerfully assented, and was pleased with such favorable opportunity of applying my usual tests to dumb brutes; for he knew them all well, having hunted with each one from the time it was large enough to be taken to the woods, and I had never seen or heard anything of the qualities of either one of them. The next morning we were in the back yard betimes, with all the hounds sporting around us, whining, yelping, or barking, eager for a chase. I observed the head, eyes, nostrils, etc., of each without touching either, and gave my opinions as to their good and bad qualities, and in what particulars each would fall behind, or excel another severally, as so hastily formed. The result was that he became *a believer*, and my own faith was greatly confirmed in the truth of phrenology; for he said I had not failed, in any one instance, to give the relative capacities and peculiar qualities of each and every one of them.

I soon became so well satisfied, both as to the truth and practical utility of that science, that (although I have not, so far as I now remember, read a page on the subject since I concluded the investigation I then gave it), I have availed myself of her valuable lessons in business transactions ever since. And, from that time forward, I never bought a slave, hired a white man, for any important service or considerable length of time, accepted a partner in business, or so much as purchased a horse, or mule, without first looking to his external phrenological developments. And, though strange it may seem, it is no less true, that I have never yet been deceived as to the general qualities, or capabilities of any one I have selected from then till now, and whether man or beast. It is true that I have sometimes found it necessary, because I could do no better at the time, to purchase servants, or stock, or to hire servants possessing bad qualities, but I always had the advantage of knowing wherein their faults or deficiencies lay, and was thereby enabled to guard against damage from them. Whether it has been on account of my very partial acquaintance with phrenological laws, as the chief means under Providence, or not, I will not say, but it is true, that from then until now, I have never sustained any considerable harm, loss, or detriment from either horse, mule, slave, servant, employe, or business partner.

Some may say and insist, that all such indications are but the teachings of the time-honored and universally admitted science of physiognomy. That is all error. The few facts, which are observable under the rules of physiognomy, are but so many indices or pointers to the occult but divine science of phrenology, which lies concealed within. Physiognomy is but an art, and deserves not to be classed with the sciences. No sufficient philosophical reasons can be assigned for the truth of the few rules known to that art, without the aid of the theretofore hidden treasures which were brought to light by the phrenologist.

It may be thought that I have gone further out of my way, than prudence would dictate, to get the unenviable privilege of indorsing for a friend, whose solvency is doubted by many who should know her resources as well, or better, than I do. To such intimation I should say: 1. That I do not undertake to defend all the absurd, and sometimes ridiculous claims which shallow pretenders have, or may, set up for phrenology. I propose simply to give the cause of natural science the benefit of my humble testimony (whatever that may be), to the claims of one of the most interesting and valuable of the whole sisterhood, upon the respect and confidence of a discerning public opinion. 2. That the criticisms of such persons, as have learned to appreciate, as of any great value, nothing but his double-barrel shot gun and pointer dog, or the graces of her toilet, or other like worthy objects of admiration, have never had any hindering terrors for me. And that I have never yet met with any one, who has given the subject of phrenology that attention which was necessary to have enabled him to form any valuable opinion of her claims to public confidence, who had not been as well satisfied as I am, that the valuable discoveries and observations on which the science is founded are sufficient to sustain her leading friends, in all they have claimed for her.

It is now so generally conceded that the brain is the seat of the intellect, the mind, the soul of man, that I do not think it necessary to do more than assume that as true.

Phrenology proves that the human cranium contains all the parts or organs of the brain, which exist in the head of any other animal, and others also, which are used by the mind of man in the exercise of his reasoning powers, and which are peculiar to himself, in addition thereto. These organs are located in the upper frontal part of the skull, and give the head of man that prominent oval form, which that of no other animal has. All the other organs of sense (which amount to some thirty odd) are common to all animals of a higher order. The presence of these organs, in the heads of such animals, indicates that they possess all the senses, of which each, in man, is the organ; and observation proves that they do enjoy all such intellectual powers. These, I repeat, embrace all the mental powers of man, except that of reason. To illustrate the difference between the nature of the intellectual powers of men and brutes, take an apple and show it to a monkey, and let him see you toss it up over his head; he knows it will fall back as well as you do, but he has no conception of the laws of gravitation in obedience to which it returns.

A horse knows, as well as his owner, that day will succeed the night, and that night will next follow day; but he has no knowledge of *the reason why* it is so. The oxen that draw the wagon know that the hind wheels never overtake the fore ones, yet they never trouble themselves to inquire *why* they do not. Other animals, however, have, and in different degrees, just like men, nearly all the powers of perception, natural propensities, and sentiments which he enjoys; such as a knowledge of size, form, color, locality, etc., amativeness, philoprogenitiveness, secretiveness, combativeness, destructiveness, and others; and benevolence, firmness, cautiousness, and other sentiments. So that, on a careful examination, it will be found that the differences between the intellectual powers of man and beast are but few; and, to speak in general terms, we may say there is but one difference between them, in that regard, which is capable of being observed by another. And that is the power of tracing from effect back to cause, and from cause to effect, and the faculty of reasoning from comparison, analogy, etc.

Man being superior to other animals, in every respect, possesses all these qualities in a far higher degree of perfection. But, as between each other, there are as many points of difference between other animals as between men, with that one exception.

Now, observe, man is a perfect animal, and he is man also. And there is but one intellectual difference which is susceptible of observation between men and other animals. Man, therefore, and other animals alike, possess physical bodies, and intellectual capacities; different in degree but the same in number, with but one exception.

Brute animals of the same families are often as much unlike as men are. They as frequently inherit good or bad qualities from their parents as do children. Do they not? Take horses and dogs for illustration. Do not colts and puppies, from the same parents, respectively, differ in their capacities, tempers, and general proclivities, as often and as materially as do children? My observation has been that they do.

All the resemblances and differences, therefore, but one, which are found to exist between children of the same parents, are referable to, and fully accounted for, on the score of their animal nature. The only one left, as not so referable, is that of the diversities of disposition which are observable in children in relation to piety or wickedness, and which are peculiar to man. A little reflection, it is conceived, will suffice to relieve the mind of every one from all doubt and embarrassment on that account.

First, I remark, the secret thoughts of the soul of one can not be known to another. It is for this good reason that we are commanded: "Judge not lest ye be judged." We are incompetent to understand the internal desires, workings, or conflicts, which may be going on within or upon the mind of another, as a rational and accountable creature; and hence, the opinions we may form of them are wholly unworthy of reliance, and we are, therefore, required to suppress them. It is only permitted us to judge of a tree by its fruit. A good tree will produce good fruit, and a bad tree evil fruit. But we can form no just or valid opinion of what a man or boy is to-day by what he was yesterday. From the time the human soul has advanced far enough to know right from wrong, he is subjected to the counter influences of the corrupting temptations and deceitful arts of Satan, and at the same time is visited and counseled, warned and encouraged, by the Holy Spirit, and may, at any moment, yield to the control, for the present at least, of either.

One of a pair of twin brothers may, therefore, from the very first of such visitations, incline to the one, and at the same time his brother may lean to the other of such adverse influences; and thereby they may become, at an early age, as diverse from each other, in that respect, as day is from night.

And this may be the case whether the soul pre-existed, was created apart from the body, but when it was born, or was produced with it. No inference of any value can, therefore, be drawn from that source for or against either hypothesis.

The reasons on which the truth of these remarks rest, apply with equal force to all other phenomena of resemblance or the contrary, which are observed between members of the same families. But again, it should be remembered that angels and devils are as dissimilar as men, and far more so.

This proposition is sustained by the concurrent evidences of heathen philosophy, the Sacred Scriptures, and the testimony of the best thinkers of our own age, and whether Christian or not. The heathen philosophers, and those of our contemporaries also, proceed on the supposition confirmed by so many experiments and observations, that there is, in nature, a general connection or chain by which all creatures are most closely united together; that individuals of each class of beings border upon and run into each other, so that there is no break in the descending scale from the highest to the lowest.

The Old Testament writers speak frequently of *Cherubim* and Seraphim, as in Gen. 3: 24, and Isa. 6: 2. And in the New Testament, such expressions often occur, as: "Far above all principality, and power, and might, and dominion, and every name that is named, not only in this world, but also in that which is to come."—Eph. 1: 21; Col. 1: 16; Rom. 8: 38; 1 Pet. 3: 22.

From all which we are bound to believe that there are different classes of angels. The Scriptures as plainly teach that Satan was an angel of high order, and far above others that were seduced by and cast out with him. And, if the regular descending scale prevails with them, as we have every reason to believe it does, the followers of Satan consist of every order and degree below him, and even down to the most ignorant of the wild African races, which are scarcely distinguishable from some of the monkey tribes.

Here we have a satisfactory solution of all the mysteries which have hitherto prevailed, as to why it is that such wonderful differences exist between the capacities of various races of men, as well as between individuals of the same race and family.

St. Paul distinctly says, that God giveth "*to every seed his own body.*"—1 Cor. 15 : 38. From this pregnant remark of his, and many others of like import, already but elsewhere referred to, when considered in connection with His uniform economy of preserving perfect symmetry and harmony in all His works, we may safely conclude that God sends the spirits, for whom a probationary term has been provided, into the world in such order, that each class at all times, and in every age of the world, shall be represented in due proportion. And that, as a general rule, He sends those of similar capacities and inclinations into the same countries and families.

And so wisely and perfectly are all His providences ordered, that arrangements were made "before the foundation of the world," for the production of the body, intended for each, at the proper time, and of the family, and under all the circumstances best adapted to the accomplishment of all the divine purposes assigned to and for each and every one. And in this view we can perceive why each should, and how he can have "*his own body.*"

The physical body being the offspring of the parents, produced strictly pursuant to natural laws, would be expected to resemble that of one or the other of the parents, and in some respects bear a resemblance to both. That children of the same family should physically be very much alike, is no less reasonable. The body being the tenement of the soul while here, and the brain the machinery through the instrumentality of which it accomplishes all the purposes of its earthly destiny, and as those pertaining to each family are usually very much alike, it is equally reasonable to suppose that the tenants and operators to which each is given would be as much alike; for, if so, their necessities would be the same.

It sometimes *happens* (as we erroneously suppose) that children of the same parents resemble each other but little, either in body or mind; some proving far above, and others as much below the average family standard. Such exceptional instances are everywhere to be met with, not only among men, but inferior animals, and it is no less common in the vegetable kingdom. No conclusion, of any worth, can be drawn from such extraordinary cases in favor of the theory of the propagation of the soul. But, if it were deemed necessary, an argument could be made on that phenomenon alone, in favor of pre-existence, which would be found hard to answer. If the soul existed before the body, and the body was made for its habitation, there is nothing at all mysterious in the circumstance of souls, of entirely distinct orders, being furnished with bodies from the same family. All that is necessary to adapt a body to the use of one of the first class of lost spirits (as well as for the lowest) is that the cranium should be large enough and sufficiently well proportioned to accommodate such occupant with the instruments and facilities required for his greater reasoning operations; and, as is known to all who have observed, with any considerable care, the skull, in its growth, will accommodate itself very much to the size and form which the brain is, at the same time, assuming.

From this fact arises one of the chief advantages of an active early education. The brain being, in such cases, kept actively at work, will grow larger and in better proportion, and thereby become more healthy and vigorous also; precisely as is the case with the body, which has been brought up to habits of industry and appropriate exercise.

The detriment which one of the favorite notions of the special advocates of total depravity and predestination received, by adopting the propagation doctrine, was very inadequately compensated by what little benefit the other received from it.

It is true that their view of the origin of the soul was more consistent with that of the depravity of our nature, as observation must and does teach, than was that of their most troublesome opponents, yet it fell far short of coming up to anything approaching a full or satisfactory solution of their problem.

The hypothesis that our souls were fallen angels, and have long since been properly designated as *devils*, is the only one which has yet been presented to our consideration which does, or can, account for the fiendish wickedness of human nature. And that can only do so by making large allowances for the downward road we have been traveling for the last six thousand years, under the lead of Satan, and by associating with devils only.

None, comparable to many who have inscribed their names but midway up the scroll of infamy in this world, could have been tolerated in heaven for a single moment, as they were up to the time when they were expelled. So that, as has been remarked above, they must have become incomparably worse since they were cast out hence, than they then were.

"The heart is deceitful above all things and DESPERATELY WICKED; *who can know it?*"—*Jeremiah.*

CHAPTER XX.

AN APPEAL TO THE ISRAELITES.—*Apology—Preservers of the Prophecies, and Light to Christianity—Friendly Relations Commended—Will the Jews be Restored to Palestine?—Who are the Israel of God?—Abraham had Eight, or More Sons—Converted Jews Identified with Christians—Who are Not of the Seed of Abraham?—Israel to be Called by a New Name—Ezekiel's Vision of the Dry Bones—The Two Sticks—The Corn—Solomon's Temple—Lost and Driven Away—The First and the Last—Captivity in Egypt—The Ark—Christ both Ben-Ephraim and Ben-David—Michael and Messiah—Purgatory—Saul of Tarsus—Conclusion.*

MY DEAR HEBREW FRIENDS: I want to submit to your consideration, a few suggestions, but fear you will not appreciate my motives. My object is not to offend you, but if possible to gain your willing and unbiased audience for a few brief moments.

Do not turn away, saying, I have not asked your counsel. I know you have not. And I also know the estimation in which voluntary advice is usually held.

I do not propose to address you as those who are unable to read or think for themselves, and much less because I consider you without competent theological advisers of your own. You can boast much of the best talent and most profound learning from the days of Abraham to the present time. Nor do I pretend to any means of acquiring biblical lore superior to your own. To your fathers were the written oracles of God first committed, and you have preserved them with a fidelity worthy of all praise.

Your Bible is the best evidence of the truth of the Christian religion now in existence. For near two thousand years you have served as torch-bearers to the Christian world.

While you reject the meek and lowly Jesus of Nazareth, and disown him as the promised Messiah, you testify to the genuineness and verity of the Scriptures on which Christians build their faith; and your evidence is received and valued by others as the voluntary admissions of an honest party litigant against his own cause. Without the prophecies which you have so faithfully and carefully preserved, the preaching of the apostles would have been all in vain, and deprived of that divine support, the whole fabric of Christianity would yet tumble and fall to the ground.

Do you not perceive that wherever you have carried your Bible, and the Gospel has followed it, all who investigate the subject but yourselves, become Christians? I do not wish you to consider me as impertinent. No such thing, I assure you, is intended. So far from that, it is with diffidence, hard to overcome, that I get my own consent to address you a solitary line, even in the way of the most delicate intimation on a subject with which you are so familiar, and with regard to which your minds are so firmly settled. Insisting, then, that you do not charge me with vanity, or any impure motive, I beg of you a brief but impartial hearing.

Remember, we are all imperfect and liable to err, you may know incomparably more than I do, and yet it is possible that *one idea* may have occurred to my mind that has not to yours. Personally, I have no interest in your faith. Should I, through the tender mercies of God, get to a better world after this life, I will not need your assistance to render me happy; and if I go to hell, it will be a matter of little consequence to me where you are. While we are together here, however, we have a common interest in cultivating and preserving the most friendly relations.

We should not only as friends, but *as brothers*, consult and advise with each other, frankly and freely, about our great and eternal salvation. We have all set out to wander, as best we can, through the wilderness of this world, and each has the same interest to find a safe passage over the Jordan of death. If you think you are on a more direct or safe route than I am, you should so inform me, and invite me to come and go with you; and I am under the same obligation to you. It is in this view that I venture to suggest a few thoughts, for your own serious reflection, as to some difficulties which *I think* lie in your way. And I would, with great pleasure, hear any remarks you may desire to make on the same important subject, in the same cordial friendship.

I am not one of those who can not respect or esteem a fellow-man because of a difference of opinion on any question whatever. The name *Jew* is as agreeable to my ear as any other, except that of *Christian.* And I love the kind-hearted, affable, and socially inclined Israelite, as well as any other man, who is not a consistent, *practical* Christian. The humble hope which I feel, that what I wish to say may, under the kind providence of that merciful God whom we all profess to adore, prove a blessing to some of my associates in crime, and fellow prisoners in this world, is the sole cause of my volunteering to say a word to you as a distinct family. And with these apologetic remarks, I proceed to the task before me.

In the first place, I desire you to answer *yourselves* this question, is it true that wherever we have carried our Bible, and the Gospel has followed it, that everybody who has investigated the subject, but ourselves have become Christians? This interrogatory, as you will perceive, is based on the preceding remarks about *torch-bearing*, and is designed to invite you to a retrospective view of the effect produced by the *law, prophets, and Gospel* together, on those who feel no national interest in the family quarrel in relation to the "Babe of Bethlehem."

Is it not possible, my dear Hebrew friend, that you are in error as to the promises relative to the return of your people to Palestine? I know it is generally believed alike by Jews and Christians, that you, as a nation, will at some future period return to and again occupy the holy land, before the great and final judgment. It is due to you, as my dying fellow-men, that I should, in all candor and frankness, say, that *I do not so understand the prophets.*

I must, therefore, in the most respectful and affectionate possible way, suggest to you the propriety of reviewing those prophecies, in the light of the views submitted in the preceding chapters of this work, as to the origin, nature, and value of the human soul, as well as of those here offered, especially to yourselves.

The first important inquiry which arises in this connection is, who are intended by the "*Israel*" which is to be restored?

I do not propose to argue this question, further than to throw out such intimations as, I trust, may direct your attention to a line of investigation, which, I think, may prove of some value. Your ability to discuss this, or any other scriptural truth, for yourselves I fully recognize.

The promises on which that belief rests were made to Abraham, and through him to his seed. They were renewed to Jacob, whose name was changed to *Israel*, and were confirmed by the prophets, who most frequently use the general name, or term, "*Israel.*"

It should be remembered that Abraham had at least eight sons, and daughters also, but of the latter we are not informed how many. That the Messiah was to come of the family of Isaac is very clear. But there is no evidence that any of the seed of Abraham were to be denied a full share of all the spiritual blessings which the promised Messiah should bring upon any branch of his family. Indeed, these promises extend to all nations: "*And in thy seed shall* ALL *the* NATIONS *of the earth be* BLESSED."—Gen. 22: 18. See also Ib. 12: 3; 18: 18; 26: 4.

The present Hebrew family can include but a very small fractional part of the seed of Abraham, who were embraced in those divine promises, as must appear to every unbiased mind. When Jesus of Nazareth was proclaimed the Christ, the expected Messiah, many Jews, of his day, believed on him. *All* who are *now* so called, *reject him.*

Think of that! After the crucifixion, and under the preaching of his immediate disciples, a vast number were soon converted to faith in him. The eloquent and indomitable Saul of Tarsus, who at an early period avowed his faith in Jesus as the true Messiah, with others of less distinction, and within a few years preached the Gospel of Christ throughout all the chief cities and countries into which your people had fled, from the political sufferings which they endured at home, and a very large number were, by that means also, converted to the Christian faith, both of Jews and heathen nations, as is well known.

Observe, now, that the disciples of Jesus (and who were first at Antioch, and afterward everywhere, called "*Christians*") were cruelly persecuted, and often severely punished, alike by such Jews and Gentiles as disbelieved the preaching of Christ.

It became necessary, therefore, as well as more agreeable to their feelings, for all who professed the Christian religion to associate chiefly with each other. With them the barrier which prevented the intermarriage of Jews with Gentiles was broken down. And, as a matter of course, the children of Christians, whether of Jew or Gentile parentage, married together, at least in a very large majority of cases. That custom has continued down to the present time. And when an Israelite is converted to the Christian faith, he or she becomes attached to, associates with, and marries, if at all, in Christian families, now as well as then. And, in this way, the Hebrews, as a sect, have been relatively diminishing from the days of Jesus Christ to the present moment. If this be not true, then, what has become of all the Christian Jews and their descendants?

The blood of Abraham, Isaac, and Jacob, as well as that of Judah also, has become so completely intermixed and mingled with that of Gentiles (and of *other Gentiles*, as I might say, for the descendants of all Abraham's children but those of Isaac, have been by them called Gentiles all the time), that it can not now be identified, except the small proportion of it which is found in the veins of the comparatively few who are now called Israelites. And that amounts to but little more than does a drop in a glass of water.

Bear in mind, the promises were to Abraham and *his seed.* Now, who are the *seed* of Abraham in 1870? Or, it might rather be asked, who are not of *his seed?* It is by no means probable that any considerable number of the natives of Europe, Asia, or America of this age (except those of African extraction), do not partake more or less of that patriarch's blood.

May not all the prophecies, from which the opinion has been drawn, that your people, as a nation, shall return to repossess, rebuild, and again dwell in Jerusalem and the holy land, refer to the redeemed of the Lord—the promised Messiah? And, may not the term "*Israel*" apply to the believers in, followers of, and the restored by Christ?

Your attention is earnestly invited, in this connection, to the following Scriptures: "And the Gentiles shall see thy righteousness, and all kings thy glory: and thou shalt be called by A NEW NAME, which the mouth of the LORD shall name."—Isa. 62: 2. "And ye shall leave your name for a curse unto my chosen: for the Lord GOD shall slay thee, and call his servants by ANOTHER NAME."—Ib. 65: 15. May not "*Israel*" be "*your name,*" which is to be left; and "*Christian,*" the "*new name,*" by which those who are "his servants"—"shalt be called?" Of whom is it here said, "the Lord God shall slay thee?"

"And the Redeemer shall come to Zion, and unto them that turn from transgression in Jacob, saith the LORD."—Isa. 59; 20; and 1: 27. "And the ransomed of the LORD shall return, and come to Zion with songs and everlasting joy upon their heads: they shall obtain joy and gladness, and sorrow and sighing shall flee away."—Isa. 35: 10; and 52: 7 to 10; 60: 14 to 22; 65: 8, 9; Jer. 3: 17; 50: 4, 5; Ezek. 36: 26; Hos. 1: 4, 5; Ib. 3: 5.

From these Scriptures does it not look very much like the "*Israel*" which is to "*return and come to Zion,*" are to be those who are "ransomed of the LORD, by the Redeemer (or Messiah) who was to come?

"For, behold, I create new heavens and a new earth:

and the former shall not be remembered, nor come into mind."—Isa. 65: 17. "Behold, O my people, I will open your graves, and cause you to come up out of your graves, and bring you into the land of Israel. And ye shall know that I *am* the LORD, when I have opened your graves, O my people, and brought you up out of your graves, and shall put my spirit in you, and ye shall live, and I shall place you in your own land: then shall ye know that I the LORD have spoken *it*, and performed *it*, saith the LORD." —Ezek. 37: 12, 13, 14. Does it not appear from this, that those, or at least some of them, who are to be brought back, or return "*into the land of Israel*," are first to pass through their graves? And does not this view accord far better, also, with the signs of the times?

God can do all things, but would it not require a wonderful intervention of miraculous power to restore your people, as a nation, back to Palestine? Suppose the country abandoned by its present and all other inhabitants, and your people should be invited to return by another Cyrus, would they accept the invitation? Would not a large majority now, as when called from Babylon and elsewhere, to return to Jerusalem, rebuild the city and temple, and reside again in the holy land, prefer their present places of residence and business pursuits, and therefore decline going? Is it not, indeed, beyond all human probability, that the Hebrews ever will, in this life, be restored to that country, and occupy and control it, as in the time of King David?

Before passing away from this remarkable chapter of Ezekiel, I beg leave to call your attention to two other revelations which are therein allegorically made, and so illustrated:

"The hand of the LORD was upon me, and carried me out in the spirit of the LORD, and set me down in the midst of the valley which *was* full of bones, and caused me to pass by them round about: and, behold, *there were* very many in the open valley; and, lo, *they were* very dry. And he said unto me, Son of man, can these bones live? And I answered, O Lord GOD, thou knowest. Again he said unto me, Prophesy upon these bones, and say unto them, O ye dry bones, hear the word of the LORD. Thus saith the Lord GOD unto these bones; Behold, I will cause breath to enter into you, and ye shall live: and I will lay sinews upon you, and will bring up flesh upon you, and cover you with skin, and put breath in you, and ye shall live; and ye shall know that I *am* the LORD. So I prophesied as I was commanded: and as I prophesied, there was a noise, and behold a shaking, and the bones came together, bone to his bone. And when I beheld, lo, the sinews and the flesh came up upon them, and the skin covered them above; but *there was* no breath in them. Then said he unto me, Prophesy unto the wind, prophesy, son of man, and say to the wind, Thus saith the Lord GOD; Come from the four winds, O breath, and breathe upon these slain, that they may live. So I prophesied as he commanded me, and the breath came into them, and they lived, and stood up upon their feet, an exceeding great army.

"Then he said unto me, Son of man, these bones are the whole house of Israel: behold, they say, Our bones are dried, and our hope is lost; WE ARE CUT OFF FOR OUR PARTS. Therefore prophesy and say unto them, Thus saith the Lord GOD; Behold, O my people, I will open your graves, and cause you to come up out of your graves, and bring you into the land of Israel. And ye shall know that I *am* the LORD, when I have opened your graves, O my people, and brought you up out of your graves, and shall put my spirit in you, and ye shall live, and I shall place you in your own land: then shall ye know that I the LORD have spoken *it*, and performed *it*, saith the LORD."—Ezek. 37: 1–14.

On this Scripture the views which follow are respectfully submitted for your investigation, and approval or rejection, as they may affect the mind of each. That the dry bones (for lo, they were very dry) represent the souls of men, as they were in exile, and before entering this world, as the "*breath of life*," the animating spirits of men. There were "*very many*" of them; and there are, also, many who have, do, or will live in this world, in hope to live again.

The body of Eve was made of a bone. *Dry bones* are a fit emblem, as found used here. When the bones came together, bone to his bone, and the sinews and flesh came upon, and skin covered them, they were just in the condition in which the body of Adam was before "*the breath of life*" was "*breathed* into him."—Gen. 2 : 7. And they were animated *in the same way;* "Thus saith the Lord GOD; Come from the four winds, O BREATH, and breathe upon these slain, that they may live." "And the BREATH CAME INTO THEM, and they lived, and stood up upon their feet, an exceeding great army."

Now, note the first part of the eleventh verse: "Then said he unto me, Son of man, *these bones are the whole house of Israel.*" Observe, again, these were they whose graves are to be opened, and who are to be brought up "*out of their graves,*" and "*into the land of Israel.*"

The other prophecy referred to, is that which is illustrated by the figure of the two sticks:

"And the word of the LORD came again unto me, saying, Moreover, thou son of man, take thee one stick, and write upon it, For Judah, and for the children of Israel his companions: then take another stick, and write upon it, For Joseph, the stick of Ephraim, and *for* all the house of Israel his companions: And join them one to another into one stick; and they shall become one in thine hand.

"And when the children of thy people shall speak unto thee, saying, Wilt thou not shew us what thou *meanest* by these? Say unto them, Thus saith the Lord GOD; Behold, I will take the stick of Joseph, which *is* in the hand of Ephraim, and the tribes of Israel his fellows, and will put them with him, *even* with the stick of Judah, and make them one stick, and they shall be one in mine hand.

"And the sticks whereon thou writest shall be in thine hand before their eyes. And say unto them, Thus saith the Lord GOD; Behold, I will take the children of Israel from among the heathen, whither they be gone, and will gather them on every side, and bring them into their own land: And I will make them one nation in the land upon the mountains of Israel; and one king shall be king to them all: and they shall be no more two nations, neither shall they be divided into two kingdoms any more at all:

Neither shall they defile themselves any more with their idols, nor with their detestable things, nor with any of their transgressions: but I will save them out of all their dwelling places, wherein they have sinned, and will cleanse them: so shall they be my people, and I will be their God. And David my servant *shall be* king over them; and they all shall have one shepherd: they shall also walk in my judgments, and observe my statutes, and do them. And they shall dwell in the land that I have given unto Jacob my servant, wherein your fathers have dwelt; and they shall dwell therein, *even* they, and their children, and their children's children forever: and my servant David *shall be* their prince forever. Moreover, I will make a covenant of peace with them; it shall be an everlasting covenant with them: and I will place them, and multiply them, and set my sanctuary in the midst of them for ever more. My tabernacle also shall be with them: yea, I will be their God, and they shall be my people. And the heathen shall know that I the LORD do sanctify Israel, when my sanctuary shall be in the midst of them for ever more."—Ezek. 37: 15 to 28.

One of the same great events is represented, although in a very different form, by the "*two sticks*," as by the "*dry bones*." To a correct understanding of the "two sticks," it is necessary that we consider it in connection with other Scriptures. Such, for instance, as those quoted above, about the *change of names*, and as the following from Hosea: "Yet the number of the children of Israel shall be as the sand of the sea, which can not be measured nor numbered; and it shall come to pass, *that* in the place wherein it was said unto them, Ye *are* not my people, *there* it shall be said unto them, *Ye are* the sons of the living God."—1: 10. "And I will sow HER unto me in the earth; and I will have mercy upon her that had not obtained mercy; and I will say to *them which were* not my people, Thou *art* my people; and they shall say, Thou *art* my God."—2: 23.

The term "*Israel*" must be construed to cover all the redeemed of the earth, of whatever name or race they may have been. It was of the tribe of Judah and seed of David, that the Messiah was to come. In the figure of the "two sticks," therefore, that of Judah should represent all the redeemed through the mediation of the Savior. Now, to get at the meaning of the two sticks, let that, "For Judah, and for the children of Israel his companions," stand for *all Israel*, as to be *restored;* and that "For Joseph, the stick of Ephraim, and *for* all the house of Israel his companions," represent that part of all the children of Israel, who are to be taken *"from among the heathen whither they have gone;"* and let the term "*heathen*" indicate all, both Jew and Gentile, who finally refuse to return to God, but prefer the lead of Satan and the way of sin. In this way we can readily perceive how the stick of Joseph "and the tribes of Israel his (Ephraim's) fellows," can be put "with the stick of Judah and they become ONE STICK. And they shall be one in mine hand," saith the Lord.

And in this way we can understand all other remarks which are found there, such as of their *purity*, dwelling there *forever*, David being "their *prince* forever," "one shepherd," God's tabernacle being with them, etc.

To God's Israel many precious promises are made by the prophets. Further on, in Hosea, he says: "I will be as the dew unto Israel: he shall grow as the lily, and cast forth his roots as Lebanon." "They that dwell under his shadow shall return; they shall revive *as* the corn, and grow as the vine," etc. Who *is* wise, and he shall understand these *things?* prudent, and he shall know them? for the ways of the LORD *are* right, and the just shall walk in them: but the transgressors shall fall therein." —Hos. 14: 5, 7, 9.

These promises to his servants are everywhere intermixed with warnings and threatenings to the impenitent and wayward, as in that chapter of Hosea.

"*They shall revive as the corn.*" This evidently has reference to the soul, in its fallen state, being prepared to live again, by entering the body, as the life of the corn is reproduced through the instrumentality of the stalk. And which was more fully explained, in commenting on Mark 4, and 1 Cor. 15, in the twelfth chapter.

Such figurative allusions are abundant, both in the Old and New Testament Scriptures. And for the benefit of my Hebrew friends, who have not been taught to confide in the latter (and from which most of the evidences in support of the theory of the soul, which is herein presented, have been drawn), as I, and most readers of this age, have been, I will suggest, for their investigation and application, a few more from the Old Testament.

The temple, as originally built by King Solomon, the materials of which it was composed, and the manner in which they were prepared, is a perfect emblem of the Israel of God (some of whom, in this life, were to worship there), when restored to his favor. Each piece of timber and every stone, which went into the building, existed before it was applied to that divine use; and in a rough or crude state, wholly unfit as it then was, for the noble purpose to which it was destined. And it was all prepared before it was brought even to the place where the edifice was to be erected. "And the house, when it was in building, was built of stone made ready before it was brought thither; so that there was neither hammer nor ax, *nor* any tool of iron heard in the house, while it was in building." The rough ashlar was taken from the rude quarry where it was found, and carefully squared and dressed, ready for the builder's use, before it was taken to the place of the building. See 1 Kings 5: and 6.

"I will seek that which was lost, and bring again that which was driven away, and will bind up *that which was* broken, and will strengthen that which was sick: but I will destroy the fat and the strong; I will feed them with judgment."—Ezek. 34: 16.

What are we to understand by the double figure, *I will seek that which was lost, and bring again that which was* DRIVEN *away?* Do not err so far as to construe the terms *lost* and *driven away* as applicable to events all occurring in this life. For if it were so, all who die while *lost* or *driven away* from their friends, home, or country, could not be found, or brought back again. To all that vast number such promises would be altogether deceptive. But God will not deceive his people who put their trust in him, and keep his commandments:

"Thus saith the LORD the King of Israel, and his Redeemer the LORD of hosts; I *am* the first, and I *am* the last; and beside me *there is* no God."—Isa. 44: 6; 41: 4; 48: 12. What is meant by such expressions and which occur so frequently as, "*I am the first and I am the last?*" In Rev. 22: 13, the same thing is expressed, but more fully illustrated: "I am Alpha and Omega, the beginning and the end, the first and the last." Alpha and Omega, being the beginning and the end, "the first and the last" letters of the Greek alphabet, having preceded the words "*the first and the last,*" in this quotation, although they do not vary the meaning, yet they indicate more clearly what is intended. If Jesus Christ made the world and the body of man, as I have insisted that he did, he was here *first*, that is, before any of us, *as men;* and should he return as judge of the living and dead, as it is insisted that he will, at the end of time, then he will have been the *last* to come. All who were to have been sent here for probation will, of course, have come into the world as man, before that awful event; and hence he will have proven himself to be, and to have been, "*the first and the last.*"

The captivity of Israel in Egypt, their miraculous deliverance, their travel through the wilderness, and entry into the promised land, furnishes another and a striking illustration of the captivity of our spirits, the probation extended in this world, and of the preservation and final restoration of the faithful to the heavenly Canaan; and of the punishment also of those who reject salvation on the terms prescribed. "Ye have sold yourselves for nought; and ye shall be redeemed without money."—Isa. 52: 3. In your application of this, let Moses stand as the vicar of Messiah.

You can draw another perfect picture, and of the same fearful events, from the designs of the divine Artist, which may be found in the account given of the condition of man at the time—the building of the ark—the preservation of Noah and his family, and of the destruction produced by the deluge. The painting of this, I must also leave for the easel and pencil of the skillful reader, and pass on.

Permit me, in conclusion, my Hebrew friend, and most affectionately, to urge upon you the propriety of reviewing your prophecies which relate to the Messiah. And, when doing so, that you keep before your mind these questions: May it not so turn out that Jesus Christ comes fully up to your ideality, both as to Ben-Ephraim and Ben-David? And can not all the prophecies, on which the expectation of each is based, be fulfilled by the second advent of Jesus Christ as Ben-David?

"Rejoice greatly, O daughter of Zion; shout, O daughter of Jerusalem: behold, thy King cometh unto thee: he *is* just, and having salvation; LOWLY, AND RIDING UPON AN ASS, *and upon a colt, the foal of an ass.*"—Zech. 9: 9. "For unto us a child is born, unto us a son is given: and the government shall be upon his shoulder: and his name shall be called Wonderful, Counsellor, The mighty God, The everlasting Father, The Prince of Peace."—Isa. 9: 6.

Both of these prophecies (and many others similar to each) apply to the promised Messiah, as all who believe the prophets admit; and yet it is not easy to conceive of forms of speech, which would have been better qualified to produce opposite expectations, in some respects, of that Messiah, when he should come. I must insist, however, that these prophecies apply to one and the same individual.

They must be reconciled on some reasonable hypothesis, or rejected. If either be false, we can trust neither, unless we can find wherein the error lies: and it is now, most likely, too late to do that, if there were any.

Let us try, therefore, to harmonize these two classes of descriptions. Jesus of Nazareth filled, quite well, the idea of Messiah, as indicated in Zechariah. He was so poor that he had "not where to lay his head."—Matt. 8: 20. In Dan. 7: 13, 14, we read: "I saw in the night visions, and, behold, *one* like the Son of man came with the clouds of heaven, and came to the Ancient of days, and they brought him near before him. And there was given him dominion, and glory, and a kingdom, that all people, nations, and languages, should serve him: his dominion *is* an everlasting dominion, which shall not pass away, and his kingdom *that* which shall not be destroyed." Now, suppose Jesus Christ should return to earth in all the pomp, power, and glory which was revealed to Daniel, to sit in judgment and receive that everlasting kingdom, would he not fill the highest expectation which the quotation above from Isaiah, or any other such description, has or could have excited?

This view of their meaning removes all seeming discrepancy between those prophecies. And just in that way, I confidently believe, the class first referred to have, and the other will, in due time, be fulfilled, *in letter* and *in spirit.*

As you are aware, some of your most learned Rabbins have held, that the Michael of Daniel was to be the Messiah. In that we agree. And from this point, it is by no means difficult for us to concur, also, in the opinion that he will return to earth as the final Judge and Restorer of the lost but repenting spirits; provided that you agree with me, that we are of the fallen angels who were cast out with Satan from heaven. And this, I feel very sure, all will do who give the subject that careful investigation which its magnitude demands.

Hoping you will pardon me for so doing, I will also suggest, as a matter worth the most anxious examination, that the notion which has prevailed so long, and with so many pagans, Jews, and Christians, that there is a "*Purgatory*," or place of purgation and preparation to which the departed spirits of men will be sent, and where they will or may be fitted for heaven and happiness, may be wholly unfounded in fact, and a most dangerous delusion.

How such an idea, which is so poorly sustained by the written Word of God, or natural reason, ever became so prevalent, is, to my mind, wonderful. It can, as I humbly conceive, only be accounted for on the supposition that our arch deceiver has succeeded in causing so many to misapply the mental impressions which have been made by the Holy Spirit of God upon men of all ages, that we are in a fallen and sinful condition in this life, and that our spirits must be cleansed and purified before we can be restored to the divine favor. On the hypothesis that we are in a primitive state of existence, such deception could, by the ingenuity of Satan, readily be produced. But if we are of those lost spirits, we are now passing through that "*Purgatory*," or place and condition where, and in which, the necessary purification must be made, if anywhere effected. This great truth is so apparent, in this view of our being, as to strike the mind of every one with a force which can not be resisted.

The idea, and which is so natural, that eternal punishment, for the sins of this life, is utterly unreasonable, has, as it is most likely, contributed very much also, to the support of the doctrine of "*Purgatory*," and likewise to that of *Universal Salvation*.

The Apostle Paul was an unbelieving Pharisee, of distinguished learning and ability. He *said* he had a vision while engaged in the persecution of Christians, and which satisfied him that he was wrong and they were right. If he was honest in what he said on that subject, his opinions should have great weight, at least, with his own family relations, even down to the present, and, in fact, to all future generations.

What possible motive could he have had for adopting the Christian faith, if he was not honest in his professions? He thereby lost the pleasures, wealth, and honors of this life; and, if a false pretender, he could have entertained no fond hopes of the future. Are not, therefore, his views of the interpretation of the Old Testament prophecies, as to the Israel of God, worth so much as your careful reading? I beg of you to give them your serious consideration. And especially would I commend to your examination, the third and fourth chapters of his letter to the Galatians. If he is right, you will never be restored to

Palestine, or see the New Jerusalem, unless you go by the way of faith in Christ Jesus our Lord.

Oh that the Holy Spirit of the great Creator, may guide the footsteps of the reader and writer of this unsought and imperfect address, in the way of truth, peace, and love which leads to that celestial city—the glorious home prepared for Israel restored.

CHAPTER XXI.

Conclusion—Divinity of Jesus Christ—The War Which was Begun in Heaven is Progressing on Earth—Infants Saved and Why—God can not Fail of His Purposes—The Aggregate Quantum of Happiness not Diminished by the Fall of Satan—A Few Remarks on Religious Creeds—The Evangelical Alliance—Reunion in Heaven.

AND now, indulgent reader, we are nearing the point of our present parting. With a few more suggestions, on as many interesting topics, I must bring these labors to a close.

There is much error in the Christian world as to the human and divine nature of our Blessed Redeemer, and which affects the doctrine of the Holy Trinity. I understand the Scriptures to teach that Christ was, and is, God, and not man; that he was not a man in any sense. His body, although very much like those of men, was produced miraculously, and not as were ours.

To talk about the *humanity* of Christ, in a spiritual sense, is at once idle and irreverent. A moment's reflection ought to convince any one, who can couple two ideas together, that nothing is more unnatural, or unreasonable, than that he could have possessed *a human soul.* Pursuant to any psychological theory which was ever presented, he could have had none. He had, however, all the physical senses, and could see, feel, taste, smell, and hear, probably, better than we can. His body required food, drink, and rest as ours. It is most likely that his head was furnished with all the organs of sense, which exist in those of men; but his superior reasoning powers were, in proportion, so far above those of men, that they kept his purely sensual organs quite as dormant as they keep the reasoning faculties in the heads of some people.

With reference to the great mission on which he was sent, he was one with the Father. Their relations, while he was here, were such as that he could pray to the Father, and his prayers were heard, and he was glorified by the Father as, and very likely more than, before he came into the world.

The relative positions which the Father and Son occupy toward each other, are wisely concealed from the curious eye of sinful man, while in this world; and we should not desire to know more of those sacred mysteries than has been revealed. Enough light has been so given, however, to enable us to learn all that it is material we should know of the Father, the Son, and ourselves, to profit by the merciful privileges, which are, in this world, extended to each of us.

We are informed, 1. That the "*Michael*" of that "WAR IN HEAVEN," Jesus of Nazareth, and Messiah are one. 2. That the war, which Satan so ingloriously waged in heaven above, has been transferred to earth, and is now being prosecuted by Christ below. The captains are the same, but the opposing hosts are not. When peace was restored in heaven, Christ, sympathizing with those who had been deceived and betrayed into sin and rebellion by Satan, followed us here; and having himself expiated our crimes, and purchased pardon for all our iniquities, now invites all who repent of their sins and ingratitude to God their Maker, and desire restoration of their allegiance to Him, to come, receive full and free pardon for the past, and enlist under the banner of the Cross, and fight with him and his the more glorious battles of righteousness, truth, and love. And that a few, who have magnanimously come forward, confessed their error, and received pardon, have been organized into a little army, and which, although comparatively small and impotent of itself, yet, when faithful to their Chief and confiding in his might, they are always victorious over Satan and all the deluded hosts which still adhere to him. 3. And that this warfare will continue until all shall have had an opportunity to repent and turn again to the love of God; when Christ will return, in person, as the judge of quick and dead, and stern avenger of the unrepented wrongs to God the Father and His unsuspecting creatures. And then He will bring to certain and speedy destruction all the remaining works of the devil.

SALVATION OF INFANTS.

It may be well enough to state my views of the future of those who die before they are capable of repenting for original sin, any more than of committing crime in this life.

As has been said already, the probabilities are that some were more and others less involved in the guilt of rebellion in heaven. Some also may have become so penitent, immediately after they witnessed the painful result of their misguided conduct in that affair (whatever it was), and remained so ever since, that God requires no more of them than a momentary death, or, at most, a very brief stay in this sinful world, to entitle them to restoration to the divine favor. And of such are the spirits of those who are removed from earth to heaven before they become contaminated by the wiles of Satan. That is done as a special favor to them, and the departure of such is often used as a means, in the hands of a merciful Savior, to awaken their parents and other near relatives, and bring them also to repentance, faith, and salvation.

Less can not be required of any; for God has said, and often repeated, in different forms: "The soul that sinneth IT shall die." (Not *he* or *she*, but IT, *shall die*). Ezek. 18: 4, 20. God will not suffer sin to go unpunished, in some way, but as the sting of repentance and remorse of conscience of one in this life, who intends well, will be sufficient to secure pardon, so it is reasonable to suppose that on those whose criminality was less, in a previously committed sin, a less punishment would be inflicted and pardon more certainly secured.

I understand the covenant relations which exist between the Father, Son, and ourselves to be, in substance, this: The atonement which Jesus Christ made on the cross was the price paid by him for the privilege of extending pardon to all who repent and come to him pursuant to that plan of redemption. Sin had been committed and death was the penalty. But under that covenant Christ procured the privilege of dying a vicarious death for us all; and, in virtue thereof, purchased a commutation of the punishment of eternal death in hell (to which we then stood exposed), to the mere formal, or figurative death, which all must die to come into this state of existence; where mercy may be sought by all and pardon found, on the terms prescribed, and nothing less is required of any. To those, however, who have fully repented already, and sufficiently suffered, an unconditional release may be, and is, extended by the Son while infants. But all others must be held to answer at the judgment, when he "will render to every man according to his deeds."—Rom. 2: 6; Rev. 20: 12, 13, and 22: 12.

GOD'S PROVIDENCES EVER SUCCESSFUL.

It may be objected to the hypothesis, that men have existed as pure and happy angels of heaven—apostatized—been cast out thence, become devils, deserving eternal punishment, and, by a celestial agreement, that penalty was commuted, a respite granted, and a pardon offered—that it involves a supposed change of the divine purpose, or even a failure of success in the providence of God. In one sense, it may be said that He does change His plans and providences; and in another, that He does not. That He should always so shape His providences and dealings with His creatures as to do exact and even-handed justice, and in equal mercy to all, and in every contingency, is but reasonable and right, and that He does so, should be conceded at once.

If, then, angels and men are not controlled in their conduct as slaves, but are permitted, in many particulars, to do as they please; and some discharge faithfully all the duties required of them, and others rebel against His laws, and set up for themselves, and elect to follow the counsel of a creature, in omitting duties and violating commands of the Creator, it becomes necessary that He should change His dealings with them also. For, were God to treat all alike, the obedient and recusant, He would have to punish the innocent with the guilty, or suffer the guilty to pass unwhipped of justice entirely.

It is repeatedly said by the sacred writers, that God "*repented;*" as in Gen. 6: 6, "And it repented the LORD that he had made man on the earth." Again, in Exodus 32: 14, "And the LORD repented of the evil which he thought to do unto his people." We are not to understand from such Scriptures that God is fickle, as are men; and that He becomes sorry for that which He has done, as we should do in many instances. Nothing more was intended by such expressions, than to say, that God had, or intended to change the course of his dealings with men on account of something done amiss, or of some duty left undone, and repented by them.

This will clearly appear by reference to Jonah 3: 10. "And God saw their works, that they turned from their evil way; and God repented of the evil, that he had said that he would do unto them; and he did *it* not." Such changes in His dealings with men, according to the conduct of each, is part and parcel of His laws, included in the Divine Code, and are not, therefore, *changes* of His providences, or so much as exceptional cases. See on this subject Ezek. 18. That chapter will (if read with practical common sense, as an article in the morning's paper is read), prove full and satisfactory on this question.

By so shaping His providences as to provide for and meet every contingency which may arise, His infinite wisdom is manifested, and no lack of that firmness of purpose is betrayed, of which mention is made (in Heb. 6: 17, 18), as never observed in Him. Certainly no insinuation against His almighty power is contained in the evidence referred to, of the adaptation of His providences to meet all cases. For it can not be less difficult to manipulate machinery after it is put in motion, so as to cause it to do the work desired, than it would be just to let it run at random, and spoil everything within its reach and power.

I do not think any argument necessary to prove the omnipotence of God. That is so fully sustained, both by revelation and daily observation, that I am willing to let the matter rest where it now stands.

No failure in the success of any one of His wise and beneficent schemes can fairly be inferred from the circumstance of a part of His holy angels having violated His righteous laws, and gone so far into sin as to require their removal from the presence and association of those who remained steadfast. It is hazardous for erring man to essay any great penetration into the thick darkness that conceals from us many of the divine secrets, which are connected with the wonderful providences of an All-wise God. It may not, however, be considered presumptuous to make a suggestion as to a probable reason why the Almighty permitted the devil to deceive some of the angelic creatures, which were originally made holy and good, into sin and rebellion.

That God could have restrained Satan and all his dupes from doing that, whatever it was, for which he and they have been, and are to be, severely punished, there need be no doubt, and will be none with those who admit the truth of the Bible. He did not, however, and for some good reason, as we must believe, see fit to do so. Then the question arises, why did He not interfere to prevent the serious consequences of his and their conduct?

Good and sufficient causes may have existed, and of which we can form no sort of conception, why He did not interfere. But one reason occurs to my mind, why He allowed Satan, and all who associated and co-operated with him, to pursue just such course as each might prefer in the matter, and then held all parties, of every grade of capacity and social position, to strict account for whatever part each may have taken therein.

Let us first notice the effect that the contrary course would have had. To have prevented Satan, for instance, from doing that which he desired to do, would have been inconsistent with that freedom of will, which must be enjoyed by every rational creature, to render him happy.

If not free, he was a slave; and if a slave, and possessed of any very high order of intelligence, as he assuredly was, and yet is, he would have been miserable. He could only be happy as long as he was free to act upon his own judgment, and pursue the dictates of his own will. God, therefore, saw fit to allow him to enjoy his unrestrained liberty, and to act in that way which pleased him most, as long as his conduct consisted with the peace and contentment of others who loved Him and kept His commandments. But when the time came that the quiet and happiness of others were seriously interrupted by the course which Satan and his followers were pursuing, he and they were driven out of heaven, and sent to a place of safety, until they shall be finally disposed of; and where they could hinder the joys of none but themselves.

Of course, God foresaw what the result of giving His holy angels the liberty of doing as they pleased would be, when He made them. And as He could have made them either so perfect as to be infallible, or have restrained their conduct as He pleased, but did neither, we must conclude that He had some good reason for leaving them both fallible and free. We may, therefore, safely infer, that such state of being is more conducive to the happiness of His creatures than any other; and that, too, when we estimate the consequences of our fall.

It may be, and the presumption therefore is, that the aggregate amount of happiness enjoyed by His rational creatures, after making due allowance for the miseries suffered by Satan and his adherents, is greater than it would have been, if God had ordered His providences in any other way. Is not fallibility incident to freedom of the will?

The loss of Satan, and of those who have or may elect to remain with him, may prove such wholesome warning to others as to prevent, during all eternity, another revolt from the just and liberal rules prescribed for the government of all the heavenly hosts. The most perfect freedom of will may, in all probability, be enjoyed by all others with entire safety. Those who finally may be redeemed on earth, and restored to their former relations with those they left in heaven, having the privilege to mix and mingle freely with them (as it is most likely will be the case), must exercise a wonderfully healthy influence on others, who have had no experience of the hardships of a sinner's career.

There would be no risk in becoming the surety of any one of us, who may be so fortunate as to make our way back to that fair and happy land, that we will keep the peace ever thereafter. Should any of the redeemed of earth ever witness another WAR IN HEAVEN, it will be only in the capacity of spectators. And the happiness of the whole celestial family will probably be highly intensified by the contrast of their condition with that of those miserable lost creatures, who will ever stand as living witnesses to the vengeance of an angry God, and of the folly and danger of worshiping a creature rather than the Creater.

If these views be correct, the very rebellion of Satan will redound to the glory of God, and increase the quantum of happiness enjoyed by His creatures. The wisdom of His laws will have been put to the test, and thereby proven to the satisfaction of all His rational creatures, Satan included, to have been the very best that could have been devised, and perfect in every particular.

A FEW REMARKS ABOUT CREEDS.

Before the death of the apostles, a disposition was manifested, by a few professed Christians, to pervert the gospel of Christ, and require more of his disciples than he had done, or authorized others to do. And soon after they had been called home, some undertook to construe the Scriptures for others, and to direct and control their religious exercises by the penalty of ostracism from the fellowship of Christians, if nothing more.

Finding that they, who assumed the right to think for their brethren, differed between themselves in divers particulars, it became necessary for them to meet in council and adopt a uniform system of faith and practice.

And I pause right here to say, once for all, that in making the following strictures on human creeds in general, I do not wish to be understood as intending to cast the least unkind or unfavorable reflection on the motives of the great and good men, who have, from time to time, or on any particular occasion, participated in that unfortunate business, and which has resulted so disastrously. Far from it. That they, in many cases at least, were prompted by the best of motives, I entertain not the slightest doubt.

The ever to be lamented participation of the best of men in that employment, is but another evidence of the fallibility of our nature; and that our Savior was right, when he said that Satan "deceiveth the whole world." He is able, willing, and always ready to deceive and mislead any of us, if unprotected for the moment by the preventing grace of Almighty God.

That the earlier reformers of the Church should have attempted to combat the Church creed, as they found it by others less objectionable, is quite natural. Great revolutions are always progressive. The idea of resisting all human creeds of religion, as unauthorized and dangerous, did not, perhaps, occur to them; or if it did, they may have wisely considered it impracticable to do so at that time. But it does seem that the Christian world, at this age, is sufficiently enlightened to listen patiently to an invitation to come back to the Gospel creed, and reject every other, as a rule either of faith or practice. If Christians ever meet in harmony again in this world, it must be on that broad platform.

But to return. Of such councils, it is usually agreed that eight Eastern and nine Western have already been held, and the tenth is now (June, 1870),in session at Rome, which deserves the name of Ecumenical, or general, and many more that are considered as merely provincial, or occasional.

In these general councils, the majority rule; and the minority in each had, and have, nothing less to do than remold their faith, and conform in practice to the behests of other men, or submit to the anathemas of the Church and all other consequent persecutions. It soon became necessary to invoke the aid of the civil authorities to enforce obedience to Church decrees. And when the ecclesiastical authorities were not obeyed, force was resorted to.

The most severe penalties were inflicted, also, to compel rational men and women to *believe* with the majority, and to adopt the *manner and form* in which they should worship that God to whom they were each accountable, which were prescribed by others.

Individual punishment having proven insufficient in some instances, wars, the most devastating, bloody, and cruel, that have ever afflicted or disgraced humanity, were waged and prosecuted for the *pious purpose* of exterminating heresies and heretics together. These were of the first fruits of *human creeds.* That prescribed by the meek and lowly Jesus was based on *faith, hope, and love.* What a contrast! As other works of Christ compare with those of Satan, so do the effects of the divine and human creeds. Then, whose children are the latter?

In modern times, and in countries where *heresies* are tolerated, and *heretics* are suffered to go at large, through the intervention of the temporal powers, death penalties are, of course, withheld; but we yet have our creed factories in full and successful operation, where creeds are fitted up by the gross; and to some one or another of which all Christians, or nearly so, must conform, or suffer the pains and penalties of excommunication from the Church. And to many of the more humble and devoted followers of Christ, and who are, therefore, the most beloved of him, the agonizing pains of ostracism from the society of, and communion with his people, are but little preferable to the *guillotine.*

By such means, to say nothing of the vast number of innocent but helpless women and children who have been cruelly butchered, the world has lost the light, and the Church been deprived the blessing of hundreds and thousands of the greatest and best men who have been sent to earth; and the Church has also been divided and subdivided, from time to time, into a number which it would now be difficult to count.

Has more good or evil accrued to the cause of Christ by these instrumentalities, all weighed together? My Catholic, my Protestant brother, answer this question to your own heart and conscience, as you expect to answer it before Him, who will sit in judgment over all at the great day!

Christ is the friend of his Church and Satan her enemy. If, therefore, the Church has been benefited by the adoption and enforcement of creeds and confessions of faith, more than she has been injured thereby, it is fair to conclude that the Holy Spirit dictated them, and that they are Christ's creeds and confessions. On the contrary, if the Church has been more injured than benefited by them, it is equally fair to believe that they were dictated by the evil spirit, and that they are Satan's creeds and confessions. Is not this good logic? It appears to have the ring of pure metal. Inasmuch, therefore, as I believe that infinitely more harm than good has accrued to the Christian Church, in consequence of the production, promulgation, and enforcement of so-called religious creeds and confessions of faith, of course I, and others who concur with me in this opinion, must believe that they were and are the handiwork of him whose purposes they have best served.

In fact, after a careful review and critical observation of the effects of the creed system, for more than twenty years, and as a mere "*looker-on in Venice,*" I have formed a well-settled opinion against the whole policy which gave them birth. And I confidently believe that each and every creed and confession of faith, which has been produced since the apostolic age, either with a view to their enforcement on others against their free will and consent, or to their becoming a test of Christian fellowship, has been, was, and is, *a legitimate child of the devil!*

I know this will be considered by many as a bold and rash avowal. It is not made to flatter the vanity of men, or with any expectation of making to myself friends thereby. But it is offered in faith and humility, and as but a reasonable sacrifice upon the altar of truth.

Some one may ask me, have you no confession in your Church? I answer, yes, Then, why do you not abandon it? Because, it is Christ's Church; and if I be a Christian, I have a better right there than a mere *imp* of his enemy. The creed is but *a child* of the devil, and if nothing worse were there, I should love the venerable old edifice much better than I do; but every time the doors are opened for the worship of God, in goes the devil *himself*. And if I can feel safe where he is, I need not run off because one of his children is there.

Human creeds were the engines by which the serpent "cast out of his mouth" the waters of persecution "as a flood" upon the Church, in the earlier Christian ages. And after "the earth" (the civil authorities) came to the help of the "woman" (the Church), and "opened her mouth, and swallowed up the flood" (by tolerating enactments), he has, by the same efficient means, succeeded, up to the present hour, in splitting up and keeping the Church divided into opposing sects, squads, and squadrons, sufficient to paralyze, and destroy by far the greater portion of her influence and power to do good.—See Rev. 12: 15, 16.

Satan has so managed as to keep many of our most gifted and chivalrous champions, and their respective commands, bravely fighting against each other; just as so many shepherds, who, being sent to mind the flock, stop on the way-side to wrangle and fight about some imaginary grievance of their own, while the wolves attack and devour the sheep. Suppose the Christian Church had been allowed to remain on the creed whereon she was placed by Christ and his apostles, and all Christians had rallied around it, as it was, and the whole family had loved each other, as therein commanded, who can imagine what her proud position would now have been! Would it be too much to say, that, long ere this, Satan and his hosts would have been driven off the battlefield, and the blood bought banner of the Cross have waved in triumph over every land and every sea? And that all men, of whatever nation, tribe, or complexion, would have been brought to know the true and living God, and to confess His Christ, the only but sure hope of salvation?

Should not every Christian loathe, hate, and abominate all earthly creeds, for the wrongs they have done our fallen and miserable race, and the self-denying cause of our blessed Redeemer? They are all wrong! It matters not though every one and each paragraph, sentence, and word contained in either were true (but that is impossible), they would be, nevertheless, awfully wrong! O, that I were their librarian, and had the first, last, and every other copy of each and every creed or confession, as of Christian faith, which uninspired man or men, have ever yet advised, composed, written, printed, published, and imposed on the conscience of man, woman, or child, whether Christian, Pagan, or Mohammedan, safely and securely housed within walls, roof, and floor of the largest, richest and best pine logs that ever grew on lower Georgia's soil; with shelving ample, and of the same material, to accommodate all, allowing each good breathing room. Then, before I sleep, we would have *one grand bonfire,* and which would reflect more light on the ladder Jacob saw, than they have ever shed on this dark world.

Nothing better can be said for such creeds, than that they contain the substance of the Bible doctrines in a more plain, concise, and simple form, and so expressed as to be easily understood by the less informed of our people. If that were true, they would all stand exposed to another objection still, and which of itself should, and if rightly considered, would prove sufficient to destroy the last gleam of respect for them, on the part of the best friend of either who loves the Savior more.

Jesus Christ and his immediate disciples and apostles, under his direction, established *his creed* of religion precisely in language, form, and substance as was desired by his wisdom; and it is so expressed as to effect, in the best possible way, the divine purposes intended by him. It is just plain enough and sufficiently mysterious, as it came to us from the pen of Inspiration. It was, therefore, and is, as I humbly conceive, nothing better than unmitigated irreverence, presumption, and impiety, on the part of any man, or body of men, to attempt any alteration of the Sacred Text whatever, and whether intended for better or worse, in any, *even the least particular,* and then to compel, in any way, others to believe, accept, or conform thereto, as a Christian creed. The Gospel creed, and as written therein, is the only one which should be recognized as the law under which heretics can safely be tried and punished; and it is the only true standard of Christian faith and practice.

It is not only right but eminently expedient, that Christians should often meet in council; and advise fully and freely together—as to matters relating to the spread of the Gospel, the general prosperity of the Church, and of questions concerning faith, practice, and discipline. For we are informed by the wise man, that, "Where no counsel is, the people fall; but in the multitude of counsellors, there is safety." All subsequent experience proves the truth of what he there says. But the difficulty has been, and yet is, that many ecclesiastical bodies have gone too far, and in the wrong direction.

If they had done no more than to consult, discuss, deliberate, and form their opinions, as best they could, on all such subjects, and on their return to their different flocks, informed them of all that had been done, giving the authorities and reasons, as fully and frequently as desired, for every conclusion arrived at, and then simply and affectionately have commended the same to the favorable consideration and observance of all, but attempting no *coercion* of the faith or Christian practice of any, on a question which is not clearly settled by the express Word of God, a vast amount of good and no probable injury would have been done.

The Evangelical Alliance is a step in the right direction; and, perhaps, has gone as far as was prudent to attempt at one move on the Christian chess-board. We have reason to believe that great good will be achieved through that instrumentality, by inaugurating a more perfect union, and that concert of action between the several great Protestant families who participate therein, which is indispensable to the meed of success which should, and would if fully united, attend their benevolent labors. That divine alliance may have progressed far enough already to justify a modest suggestion to the several pious Christian denominations, of which it is composed, as an efficient means of success in the godly enterprise on which they have entered, that we all learn to think and say less about our own peculiar views, on comparatively unimportant theological questions; on some of which we never have, and probably never will be able to agree, during our stay, as a race, in this lower world.

And should that august council go so far, when they again meet, as to extend a cordial and affectionate invitation to such of their Catholic brethren as may sympathize with their heaven-born desire to bring the whole Christian family together, in the holy bonds of perfect love, to meet in council with them, when and where they may resolve next to assemble, the happy consequences might exceed their fondest hopes. Such invitation, with assurances of fraternal welcome, and coming from such high authority, and from those also, whom the Mother Church has long looked upon as her enemies, might, under the favoring providence of God, be met in a manner, and accepted by a number, which would astonish with gladness those who gave it—make heaven rejoice—and an awe-stricken hell quake in despair!

Having taken the liberty to express myself so freely, and, as some may think, without sufficient necessity, against our present and long prevailing system of Church creeds and confessions, it may be no more than just to the reader, and all who disagree with me in regard to their worth, that I propose a remedy for the evil which I consider so disastrous in its consequences. This I proceed to do, and in as few words as practicable.

In the first place, I remark that I desire to see no new church or society of Christians formed, with a view to the correction of this *or any other evil*, whether real or imaginary, which may exist or be supposed to exist, in any branch of Christ's Church. But, to the contrary, let us all remain with the several congregations with whom we have been worshiping, if otherwise most desirable. Say but little about creeds, confessions, or those questions in relation to which Christians disagree, except on suitable occasions for commending the gospel creed as the only safe one, and suffer no fit occasion for doing so, in a Christian spirit to pass unimproved. Visit frequently churches of other denominations than your own. Encourage others to do likewise. Join in worship with all as cheerfully as if at home, unless something comes up in which you can not conscientiously participate. In such event, sit quietly by until that difficulty passes away; then fall in ranks again, and march on, as if no obstacle had been met on the way.

Propose no alteration of any creed, but permit your own to lie on the shelf and mold. We will, in that way, find more leisure to "search the Scriptures," and in them a far more wholesome food for the soul can always be found.

In a word, strive by all laudable means to reform the Church in this respect, not by forming others, but *inside* of her present organizations. And under no circumstances whatever, aid or encourage any discord within a Christian family, but labor, rather, to live in peace with each, and so to cause them all to glide gently into one, as so many rills, branches, and creeks quietly meet together, and each is swallowed up by the others, and all lose their identity in one great river.

If a church edifice is needed where there is none, as in a rural neighborhood, a newly settled village, or in a suburban locality, which is not sufficiently supplied with church facilities, encourage the building of but one, and let that be equally free to the use of all Christian denominations. By the joint and cheerful co-operation of all such persons as usually take an interest in church buildings, a large, comfortable, and creditable house could, in many instances, be erected, instead of half a dozen, more or less, cramped up, half finished little concerns, which do justice to nothing but the narrow prejudices and littleness of soul which prevail in the community around. This can easily be accomplished wherever a few resident and leading spirits of the different Christian names will put their hearts and heads together, and labor alone for the common weal of the great cause.

Draw up an agreement, securing the rights of Protestants, Catholics, and everybody else, who hope for salvation through the atoning blood of Jesus Christ, to worship there, and let that head your subscription list for a building fund. When your house is ready for use, let the Bible lie proudly and alone on the sacred desk. If two or more versions of that holy Book be desired, by as many ministers who officiate there, lay them side by side together; and let each use the one he prefers. The Books will not quarrel, while the preachers either agree, or agree to disagree in love. As many hymn books may be provided, and of such varieties, as may be necessary to enable every one worshiping there to have such as they desire.

Their priest can administer all the rites recognized by the Catholic church. The Baptist minister can serve his people; the Methodist his, and other Protestants theirs, clear through the chapter. These services can all be performed on such days, or different hours of the same day, as may easily be arranged by the congregation as one body or by the several officiating ministers; always pre-supposing that the love of Christ and his Church holds the highest seat in the affections of each shepherd and his flock.

In this way the congregation could be kept together, and the seats full, when the hour for worship arrives. The greatest trouble which would be likely to result from this manner of worship, would devolve on the shepherds themselves. By all feeding their sheep in the same fold, and allowing them to run in the same range, they would soon become so much attached to each other, and their taste, manners, and notions would get to be so much alike, that it might become very difficult for each of them to distinguish his own. They could learn to manage that matter in some way, however, as the *healing* process goes on. And it is not at all impossible that they might be affected *in the same way*, to such extent, as that each would care but little which flock he feeds.

But one Sabbath school should be constituted in such

churches. That should be strictly on the union plan, no sectarian books being used. And parents, teachers, and pupils should meet and work together as "a company of horses in Pharaoh's chariots." From a Christian community so organized and industriously at work, Satan would soon retire in disappointment and disgust. And then they could each and every one have things *their own way*; for the only *way* any of them would desire to know, would be that which leads from earth to heaven through faith in Jesus Christ.

That is "*the faith* which was once delivered unto the saints," and for which we "should earnestly contend." And this is *the way*, in which it is asked: "Can two walk together except they be agreed?" Nothing is more clear than that one who wishes to serve the Lord and get to heaven, and another who prefers the way of sin, which leads to hell, can not "*walk together*," for their roads lead in exactly opposite directions.

The *deceiver* has spouted storms of gas through the lungs of good men, by suggesting one or the other of the texts alluded to here, or some similar isolated one, to their inquiring minds; but in such distorted and wrested sense, as to suit his own disorganizing purposes.

Much may be done in the way of cultivating a more perfect union among the membership, by giving such ministers as direct their sermons more against Satan and sin, than against sister churches and their ministers, that encouragement which is due their faithfulness. And, above all others, those who have been called to preach *the Gospel* have the power to effect most in the divine work of restoring that long lost union to the Church of Christ, and in which alone there is strength. Are you not, dear brethren, as the shepherds whom he has sent to watch over, keep, and feed those of us who constitute his flock, under some *special* obligations to strive, in every proper way, to correct the evil of which complaint is here so justly made?

All ministers who really wish to lend a helping hand toward the restoration of the Christian Church to its primitive unity and purity, can do so without any sacrifice of individual opinion on any one of the controverted points.

This, all public speakers, of any worth, know as well as does the writer. "Where there is a *will*, there is a *way*."

These general remarks, it is hoped, will suffice as suggesting to the reader's mind ample ways and means by which all can do something to aid in healing the lacerated wounds from which our beloved Church has bled so long and so freely.

I fear to trespass further, at present, on the patience of the reader, even in advocacy of a reformation in which I feel so much interest. It involves one of the chief duties on the part of all who hope for salvation, through our blessed Redeemer, of this progressive age.

In the providences of him who presides over the destinies of men, I may, at some future time, find occasion to say something more of "CHURCH UNION."

Dear reader, the point is reached where we must part. Should we never, in person, meet, during our brief pilgrimage in this fickle world, where, as night follows day, so fear alternates with hope, failure with success, and sorrow with gladness—let us so live while we stay, that we may meet *again* in that heavenly home, where there will be no more night, fear, failure, or sorrow, but one eternal day. Then our fondest hopes will be more than realized, and all will be a regular round of success and rejoicing. There we can sing that "*new song*" before the throne, and which none can learn but they "*which were redeemed from the earth.*" And we may retire, at will, to the margin of the beautiful river which flows from the throne, and walk, stand, or sit, as we like best, on her velvet lawn of purest green, where grows the tree of life. There may we linger at our ease, fearing not the lapse of time, nor thirst nor hunger dread, for all eternity will be ours. Above our heads will hang, in clusters thick, of fragrance sweet, the rich ambrosial fruit of that life-giving tree; near by will roll the crystal stream of life-preserving water; so we may eat and drink at will, and there can live forever.

At leisure, then, may we recount, to other each, the thrilling scenes of our long night in prison—the brief, mysterious, and eventful life we each, on earth, have lived—the ups and downs we met with here—all we have seen, heard, read, or thought while in this darksome world; and, to be brief, all each has undergone for the false part we bore the more false chief of that ill-fated WAR IN HEAVEN.

END

www.ingramcontent.com/pod-product-compliance
Lightning Source LLC
LaVergne TN
LVHW020231110826
845151LV00003B/886

* 9 7 8 1 4 2 5 5 3 1 4 9 2 *